Performing Digital Activism

From the emergence of digital protest as part of the Zapatista rebellion, to the use of disturbance tactics against governments and commercial institutions, there is no doubt that digital technology and networks have become the standard features of 21st century social mobilisation. Yet, little is known about the historical and socio-cultural developments that have transformed the virtual sphere into a key site of political confrontation. This book provides a critical analysis of the developments of digital direct action since the 1990s. It examine the praxis of electronic protest by focussing on the discourses and narratives provided by the activists and artists involved. The study covers the work of activist groups, including Critical Art Ensemble, Electronic Disturbance Theater and the electrohippies, as well as Anonymous, and proposes a new analytical framework centred on the performative and aesthetic features of contemporary digital activism.

Fidèle A. Vlavo is Assistant Professor in Digital Communication at Universidad Iberoamerica, Mexico.

Routledge Studies in New Media and Cyberculture

For a full list of titles in this series, please visit www.routledge.com

28 **Digital Audiobooks**
New Media, Users, and Experiences
Iben Have and Birgitte Stougaard Pedersen

29 **Locating Emerging Media**
Edited by Germaine R. Halegoua and Ben Aslinger

30 **Girls' Feminist Blogging in a Postfeminist Age**
Jessalynn Keller

31 **Indigenous People and Mobile Technologies**
Edited by Laurel Evelyn Dyson, Stephen Grant, and Max Hendriks

32 **Citizen Participation and Political Communication in a Digital World**
Edited by Alex Frame and Gilles Brachotte

33 **Feminism, Labour and Digital Media**
The Digital Housewife
Kylie Jarrett

34 **The Politics of Ephemeral Digital Media**
Permanence and Obsolescence in Paratexts
Edited by Sara Pesce and Paolo Noto

35 **Studying Digital Media Audiences**
Perspectives from Australasia
Edited by Craig Hight and Ramaswami Harindranath

36 **Between the Public and Private in Mobile Communication**
Ana Serrano Tellería

37 **Performing Digital Activism**
New Aesthetics and Discourses of Resistance
Fidèle A. Vlavo

Performing Digital Activism

New Aesthetics and Discourses of Resistance

Fidèle A. Vlavo

Routledge
Taylor & Francis Group
NEW YORK AND LONDON

First published 2018
by Routledge
711 Third Avenue, New York, NY 10017

and by Routledge
2 Park Square, Milton Park, Abingdon, Oxon OX14 4RN

Routledge is an imprint of the Taylor & Francis Group, an informa business

Library of Congress Cataloging-in-Publication Data
CIP data has been applied for.

ISBN: 978-1-138-91124-6 (hbk)
ISBN: 978-1-315-69286-9 (ebk)

Typeset in Sabon
by codeMantra

MIX
Paper from responsible sources
FSC www.fsc.org FSC® C013604

Printed and bound by CPI Group (UK) Ltd, Croydon, CR0 4YY

A la mémoire de Hugues C. Vlavo

Contents

Acknowledgements ix

Introduction: Digital Performance 1

1 'I Come from Cyberspace': The New Stage of Resistance 15

2 'Little Electronic Shadow': The Virtual Body 39

3 'What CD once was, ECD is now': The Legacy of Contention 62

4 'Not Found on this Server': The Performance of Protest 86

5 'I Did It for the Lulz': The Humour of Disturbance 109

Conclusion: Tactical Performance 131

Bibliography 147

Index 159

Acknowledgements

I completed this book with the support and constant encouragement of many people and my thanks here can only partially express the extent of my gratitude. First, I would like to thank members of Critical Art Ensemble, Electronic Disturbance Theater and Anonymous, for agreeing to participate in this research, by giving their time and sharing their thoughts on their creative practice and their knowledge about digital activism. These encounters were personally enriching and essential to the realisation of this project.

I am grateful for the financial support I received from the British Academy, through its BA/Leverhulme Small Research Grants scheme (SG132964), in order to carry out part of my investigation. I also wish to thank the editorial staff at Routledge for giving me the support and the space to complete this book, as well as their assistance to publish the manuscript. In addition, I am thankful to the two anonymous reviewers whose expert and generous comments helped swerve the book towards its final direction.

Part of this monograph was based on my doctoral thesis and I would like to thank my supervision team, Hillegonda Rietveld and Suzy Kerr-Pertic, for their steady guidance and mentoring. Special thanks are also due to Andrew Dewdney who introduced me to the field of digital culture and media, and opened the path to an exciting research career.

For many years, Monday was the day to get the blues, fortunately I was surrounded by fantastic travelling fellows, thank you Maria Barrett, Edith Phaswana, Marcelo Batarce, and Diego Canciani, for the many uplifting and rewarding journeys.

The genesis of this book began during my time at the Department of Culture Media and Creative Industries, at King's College London, and I thank my former colleagues for their encouragement and advice in getting the project off the ground. Warm thanks to Melissa Nisbett, Bridget Conor, Christina Scharff, Btihaj Ajana and Hye-Kyung Lee. Special thanks also to Tim Jordan for his inspiring academic integrity and his kind mentorship.

Halfway through this project, I was fortunate enough to land a research position at the Universidad De Las Americas Puebla, Mexico.

This opportunity transformed my life in many ways. I would like to thank el grupo de investigación *Más allá del Texto Cultura Digital y Nuevas Epistemologías*, for welcoming me, and in particular, Alberto Lopez Cuenca, for overseeing my residency.

Part of this research would simply not have been possible without the kindness and generosity of many people. In particular, I would like to thank John Holloway for welcoming me into the world of Zapatistas and for leading me to Chiapas. John has the incredible ability to give hope when nothing seems to hold, and I certainly benefited from his brilliant advice and support. I am also lucky to have attended many sessions of the *Seminario de Subjetividad y Teoría Critica,* at the Benemérita Universidad Autónoma de Puebla, which opened my mind, through intellectual exchanges and cheerful conversations. I also wish to thank my travelling companions for the supportive environment created during the Zapatistas Seminario in San Cristóbal de Las Casas. Warm thanks go to the members of the Mesa Directiva of Acteal, Chiapas, who kindly opened their doors and guided me through the painful but necessary path of remembrance.

A book project can easily be started, but much more is required to bring it to conclusion. For this, many great thanks are due to my dear friends and colleagues who took the time to review and comment on various versions of the chapters. Thanks to Btihaj Ajana, Elefteria Lekakis, and Jesus- Mario Lozano. My dear Cholulteca friend, Stefania Charitou deserves a special mention and a huge thank you, for reading the entire script with great care, and providing valuable feedback. Your unwavering support has helped in the completion of this book. The other person whom I also owe a huge thank you to is my very dear, and very patient friend, Mario Lozano, whose encouragements and humour never failed to lift me up in the hardest moments of the writing. I am also thankful to my international Mexican family for making sure that I was in constant supply of food, shelter and laughter. Thank you to the chef Cristina Goletti, the spiritual guide Carolina Tabares, and the leader in cheers Lisa Kusanagi.

In Paris, London and Brighton, I would like to thank my close friends, Marie-Camille Bouchindomme, Eleftheria Lekakis, Carole Padonou-Loko, Antoine Rogers and Anja Boisten as well as the members of the Brixton bar closing crew.

Finally, my sincere and heartfelt thanks go to my family.

Je remercie Koffi Emmanuel et Bayivi Vlavo pour avoir toujours su m'encourager et me soutenir dans mes décisions, mes départs et mes retours. Vous êtes mes modèles et je suis fière de vous avoir pour parents. Merci à Pierrette Vlavo et à Victorine Vlavo, les meilleures amies d'une vie. En attendant que nos nouvelles aventures commencent, cet ouvrage est pour vous.

Acknowledgement of Sources

Sections of this work were originally published as follows: 'Framing Digital Activism: the Spectre of Cyberterrorism', *First Monday* (2015); 'Digital Hysterias: Decentralisation, Entrepreneurship and Open Community in Cyberspace', *Transformations, Journal of Media and Culture*, Issue 23 (2013); 'Click Here to Protest': Electronic Civil Disobedience and the Imaginaire of Virtual Activism. In: Mousoutzanis, A. & Breslow, H. (Eds). *Cybercultures: Mediations of Community, Culture, Politics.* Amsterdam, New York: Rodopi. pp. 125–148, (2012). I am grateful to the editors for granting me the permission to reproduce these texts here.

Introduction

Digital Performance

I'm going to tell you something very secret, but don't go spreading it around...or, go ahead, spread it around, it's up to you. ...

Okay, now I will tell you that back then, they began to say that the EZLN was the first guerilla group of the 21st century (yes, we who still used a digging stick to sow the land, things like teams of oxen – no offense intended – we had heard people talk about, and tractors we only knew from photographs); that Supmarcos was a cyber guerrilla who, from the Lacandón Jungle, would send into cyberspace the Zapatista communiqués that would circle the world; and who could count on satellite communications to coordinate the subversive actions that were taking place all over the world.

Yes, that's what they said, but ... compas, even on the eve of the uprising our "Zapatista cyber power" was one of those computers that used big floppy disks and had a DOS operating system version – 1.1. We learned how to use it from one of those tutorials, I don't know if they still exist, that told you which key to press and when you pressed the right one, a voice with a accent from Madrid said, "Very Good!" and if you did something wrong it would say "Very bad, you idiot, try again!" Besides using it to play Pacman, we used it to write the "First Declaration of the Lacandón Jungle," which we reproduced on one of those old dot matrix printers that made more noise than a machine gun. ...

Soon the Dialogues at the Cathedral followed. At that time, I had one of those light, portable computers (it weighed six kilos without the battery), made by HandMeDown Inc., with 128 ram, that is to say 128 kilobytes of ram, a hard disk with 10 megabites, so as you can imagine it could hold everything, and a processor that was so fast that you could turn it on, go make coffee, come back, and you could still reheat the coffee, 7 × 7 times, before you could start to write. What a fantastic machine. In the mountains, to get it to work, we used a converter attached to a car battery. Afterwards, our Zapatista advanced technology department designed a device that would let the computer run on D batteries, but the device weighed more than the computer and, I suspect had something to do with the PC expiring in a sudden flash, with a ton of smoke, which kept the mosquitos away for three days. What about the satellite telephone that the Sup used to communicate with "international terrorism?" It was a walkie-talkie with a reach of some 400 meters, max, on flat land (there are probably still photos floating around out there of the

> "cyber guerrilla" ha!). And you think we had internet? In February of 1995, when the federal government was pursuing us (and not exactly for an interview), the portable PC was thrown into the first stream that we crossed. After that we wrote our communiqués on a mechanical typewriter lent to us by the *ejidal* commissioner of one of the communities that took us in. This was the powerful and advanced technology that we had, the "cyber guerillas of the 21st century."
>
> I am really sorry if, in addition to my own already battered ego, this destroys some of the illusions that were created out there. But it was just like I am telling you now.
>
> Subcomandante Marcos

The lines above are extracted from a piece written by Subcomandante Marcos, one of the most prolific figures of the Zapatista liberation movement. Published almost 20 years after the 1994 uprising, the full essay, entitled *To look and communicate*, is a sample of the vast literary production of the *Ejército Zapatista de Liberación Nacional* (EZLN), commonly known as the Zapatistas. In this excerpt, Marcos directly addresses several of the exuberant comments that proliferated in the media, regarding the Zapatistas's access and use of digital technology.

Following the rapid spread of its political campaign via the internet, the Zapatistas experienced an unprecedented wave of international solidarity and support. This response to the uprising eventually led commentators to claim that the group had become 'the first informational guerrilla movement' (Castells, 1997: 79). Yet, as Subcomandante Marcos humoristically explained, and as will be discussed throughout this book, this vision was an idealised and inflated interpretation of a historical and complex mobilisation movement.

From the emergence of digital protest as part of the Zapatista rebellion, to the use of disturbance tactics against governments and commercial institutions, there is no doubt that digital technology and networks have become the standard features of 21st-century social mobilisation. Yet, little is known about the historical and socio-cultural developments that have transformed the virtual sphere into a key site of political confrontation. This is the purpose of this book. *Performing Digital Activism* provides a critical analysis of the developments of digital activism since the 1990s. The aim is to examine the praxis of electronic protest by focusing on the discourses and narratives provided by the activists and artists involved. The study covers the work of many activist groups, including Critical Art Ensemble, Electronic Disturbance Theater and the electrohippies, as well as Anonymous, the now (in)famous group of activists and hackers in operation since the 2000s.

Fuelled with discussions about the democratic potential of the internet, the study of digital technology and political activism has grown within both academic and activist circles. Many researchers have examined how digital technology can facilitate or hamper the organisation of protest. However, these actions have rarely been examined within historical and cultural contexts. More specifically, the creative and performative elements of digital protest have been neglected within digital scholarship. Considering this, my investigation explicitly replaces digital activism within the framework of cultural production. In doing so, I propose a new critical framework that considers performative and aesthetic features to further the contextualisation of current activist practices. To embark on this task, this introduction chapter will set the scene, presenting the plot, the actors, and the frameworks central to this investigation.

A Turn to Digital

The spin of our story begins in the early 1990s, with the collective of artists and activists working under the name Critical Art Ensemble (CAE). Originally formed in Tallahassee, Florida, the core of this collaboration consisted in Steve Kurtz and Steve Barnes, Hope Kurtz, Dorian Burr, Claudia Bucher and George Barker. Later, the group was joined by Ricardo Dominguez and Bev Schlee, for a brief period of time. In 1993, CAE published a short essay in which it proposed a new concept of socio-political activism. Based on the assumption that existing models of protest were now redundant, the collective formulated the theory of electronic resistance. In the course of three publications, *The Electronic Disturbance* (1994), *Electronic Civil Disobedience* (1996) and *Digital Resistance* (2001), the collective related the emergence of a virtual and nomadic power that ought to be defeated through radical direct action.

CAE first explained its rationale by describing the increasing failure of street demonstrations:

> Nothing of value to the power elite can be found on the streets, nor does this class need control of the streets to efficiently run and maintain state institutions. For CD [civil disobedience] to have any meaningful effect, the resisters must appropriate something of value to the state. Once they have an object of value, the resisters have a platform from which they may bargain for (or perhaps demand) change.
>
> (1996: 11)

This view was a direct echo to the perceived impotence of street protest in the United States during the 1990s. Speaking about protest movements, core CAE member Steve Kurtz recounts that

> There was great faith in confrontational street-level civil disobedience. Activists were thinking like this because of the victories in the late 1980s and early '90s, but unfortunately, by 1993, it was

> not really happening anymore. The police had figured out how to respond; they finally realized that it was best not to fight. When protestors congregated somewhere, police would set up the barricades and redirect traffic, with the belief that if they waited it out, the demonstrators would get tired and go home (a policing strategy that the Occupy movement later responded to). Then the police would take down the barricades and reopen traffic again. No one was arrested, and when the dust cleared, it was as if nothing had happened.
> (Vlavo, 2014)

McCarthy and McPhail (1998) examined this issue in their comparative study of street demonstrations. Using the example of Chicago in 1968 and 1996, the researchers noted a sharp contrast between the two periods, which illustrated 'the continuing institutionalization of protest that has occurred in the United States over the last three decades. Citizen protest has now become a normal part of political process' (ibid.: 84). The authors argue that over 30 years, the supervision of demonstrations has become highly standardised. As an example, they cite a lottery system, endorsed by the US District Court, used to allocate time slots for protests. In the past, protesters had to battle to obtain demonstration permits. Now, most activist groups receive full authorisations that also specify the areas designated for marches (McCarthy and McPhail, 1998: 84). The research also identified 'behavioral repertoires' between protesters and the police, which indicate that even demonstrators who actively provoke officers are unlikely to be arrested. As a result, the confrontation between people and the authorities has become 'routinized, predictable, and, perhaps as a result, of diminishing impact' (ibid.).

It is within this context that CAE made its famously controversial statement that 'as far as power is concerned, the streets are dead capital!' (1996: 11). The collective's core argument is that since strikes and street demonstrations are no longer effective, socio-political action needs to relocate into cyberspace. In other words, virtual oppression should be defeated through virtual resistance. This radical idea, which the collective labels 'electronic civil disobedience', has received enough attention, and various militant groups have embarked on the coordination of virtual protests since the 1990s. These actions entail the performance of blockades and sit-ins to disrupt corporations' and governments' websites, thus transforming cyberspace into the stage of political protest.

Since then, electronic civil disobedience has become the subject of academic inquiry. Located within a wide range of fields, including media, politics, sociology, cultural studies and cyberculture, most early studies have examined digital action as a new form of socio-political activism. Research by Meikle (2002, 2008) has provided several useful distinctions between electronic civil disobedience and other forms of actions, such as online sabotage, hacktivism or netwar. His analysis focused on the technical aspects and the legal implications of digital action. Klang's (2005) work has also made a useful contribution, providing philosophical definitions of online and offline protests. His analysis predicted some of the legal and societal challenges faced by digital activists. Similarly, Jordan and Taylor's (2004) critical discussion of electronic civil disobedience as 'hacktivism' has identified some of the contradictions of digital action that will be further explored in this book.

Generally, those considering digital activism as the merge of socio-political activism and digital technology have two main research approaches available to them. One route is to examine how technology is reshaping traditional forms of activism, and the other route is to investigate the relation between digital media and activism. McCaughey and Ayers's (2003) early collection of studies about cyberactivism provides many examples of these works that consider the internet as a tool, but more recent studies have also followed on or extended this trend. Lievrouw's (2011) research, which links traditional activism to digital practices, establishes the use of digital media as an alternative practice that opens up new possibilities for social change. Earl and Kimport (2013) focus on the use of e-petitions, e-mobilization and e-tactics to evaluate their efficacy for political engagement. A variant of this approach is Hands's (2011) research, based on technological theories, which provides a philosophical analysis of digital activism and its impact on society. Many of these studies often conclude that digital technology, and more specifically the internet, either facilitates or hampers social mobilisation.

The work that perhaps has influenced many subsequent studies is Joyce's (2010) edited volume, *Digital Activism Decoded*, in which she explicitly advocates the use of the term 'digital activism'. Joyce explains that this term is the most appropriate as it is 'both exhaustive and exclusive. Exhaustive in that it encompasses all social and political campaigning practices that use digital network infrastructure; exclusive in that it excludes practices that are not examples of this type of practice' (2010: viii). Joyce therefore dismisses the use of terms such as 'cyberactivism', 'online activism', and 'e-advocacy', on the basis that these words are too narrow. Yet, one could question the lasting value of a study that aims to tackle such a broad term. By bringing together diverse types of digital activism, discussions are bound to miss out on the uniqueness of certain projects. Karatzogianni's (2015) recent work suffers from this ambitious stance. While her research provides a useful chronology of the development of digital activism over two decades, the decision to include all possible forms counters the main benefit of a historical perspective, that is, an overview of the developments within and between practices.

In the same way, studies that tend to consider digital technology as a tool for social mobilisation will find it difficult to notice that technology *itself* has become the object of contention. What is overlooked is the signal that digital technology is not a mere instrument for organising protest. The social and political engagement developing in the digital space is as much about the technology, as it is about other issues, and this point has always been central to the practice.

Digital activism cannot therefore simply be understood as a merge between technology and activism. The obvious sign is the current digital activist movement that is questioning the management and control of the internet. One of the purposes of this book is to demonstrate that, counter to many assumptions, early theories of digital action already focused on challenging the power dynamics developing within the digital space. This study is therefore not about digital activism in its broadest sense, quite the opposite. *Performing Digital Activism* focuses on the type of activism developed to take place *within* digital networks. It does not address the use of digital technology for traditional campaigning, or campaigning involving social media. Nor is it concerned with the ways in which the internet is used by politics to mobilise people. All of these practices have their own values and are worthy of examination, but they are not the present subject. As a result, and despite its ambivalence, the term 'digital activism' is used in this book to refer to social and political actions that are exclusive to the internet.

Some critics have argued that digital activism scholarship suffers from a lack of data, and that too much research has focused on isolated case studies (Joyce, 2010). Yet, this position betrays a narrow view of what constitutes data. Certainly, the characteristics of digital direct action do not facilitate preservation and archiving, but there exists a vast amount of accessible resources that have been created and disseminated by activists themselves. Many original discourses and rationales have been neglected. For instance, researchers easily retraced electronic civil disobedience to CAE, but no extended study has examined the group's original publications, or considered the creative context of their production. This explains why the artistic and performative features of digital action have remained unexplored. It also explains the title and frameworks of this book. The aim is to contribute to a brand new perspective of digital action, by paying due attention to its aesthetic qualities. Hence, and along with a turn to the digital, this project requires a turn to the study of performance.

A Turn to Performance

For decades now, the use of performance as a theoretical and methodological framework has shuffled many established academic disciplines. Erupting from the boundaries of theatre, the concept of performance has expanded to integrate new social practices. Seminal works have emerged from this shift, transforming the field of social research. Sociologist Goffman (1982 [1967]) first initiated a dramaturgical analysis of face-to-face interaction. Anthropologists Geertz (1973) and Turner (1982) considered rituals such as religious practices and play as everyday performances. More recently, critical ethnographer Conquergood (2002) examined the theatricality of capital punishment. Even 'jihad/terrorism' has been addressed within the framework of performance studies (Schechner, 2006).

This new performance paradigm, or 'turn to performance', is commonly traced to the work of Austin (1975) who introduced the concept of 'performative utterances' in his text *How to do things with words*. Austin's proposition is that words and expressions do not merely describe the social world – they actually perform specific actions, as in the case of declarations such as 'I do' or 'I pronounce you husband and wife'. Thus, Austin suggests that 'to *say* something is to *do* something' (1975: 94, original emphasis). Speech, and the act of speaking, can therefore be considered as performance. Many fields of studies have been influenced by this philosophical and linguistics stance, including Derrida's (1982) account of performative text and Butler's (1990) theory of performativity, which will both be referred to in this investigation.

As suggested by literary critic Elin Diamond, 'performance' has been used outside of its original theatre context to refer to various social practices, including 'popular entertainments, speech acts, folklore, political demonstrations, conference behavior, rituals, medical and religious healing, and aspects of everyday life' (1996: 2). Furthermore, and for performance scholar Janelle Reinelt, this turn is 'an attempt to relate more traditional forms of performance to a wide variety of cultural practices that together constitute "culture" and form the sites of legitimation and contestation of social and political power' (2002: 210). The rationale for examining digital direct action through the lens of performance derives precisely from this turn, and the term 'performance' is used in this study to refer to digital actions. In addition, locating these uniquely situated powers by (re)placing digital activism within a cultural context is the purpose of this book.

Along with others in the field, performance theorist Carlson (1996) clearly acknowledges the unworkable task of producing a complete survey of the various theoretical and practical uses of the term 'performance'. Nevertheless, Carlson isolates three clusters that, he argues, relate to different types of performance practices. As he describes, one type is the display of specific, and often, creative skills, as in the practice of singing or acting. Another type relates to the performance of specific cultural behaviours and social rituals such as in weddings, funerals or graduation ceremonies. The third type is linked to the measurement of the efficiency or progress of social actors, such as a team of professionals, but also the performance of a machinery, for example, a car engine. Considering this diversity, Carlson highlights the 'futility of seeking some overarching semantic field to cover such seemingly disparate usages' (1996: 5). This means that scholars engaging in the study of performance have the complex task of selecting, or creating, frameworks that can sustain their investigation.

This task is further complicated by the fact that over time 'performance' has extended into concepts of 'performative' and 'performativity', and that these terms come with their own definitions and frameworks. Although fascinating, these issues can only be outlined very briefly, as further discussion would distract from the primary focus of this book. The overview that follows is therefore mainly to contextualise the use of the words 'performance', 'performative' and 'performativity', in the context of this study and in relation to digital action.

In her own study of performance, Reinelt (2002) provides a succinct, yet very useful account of the three terms, suggesting that although they share a basis and are often used without discrimination, they have distinctive theoretical trajectories. In many ways, the term 'performance', as applied to the social and cultural world, developed at the distance from its origins in theatre studies. Initially, performance referred to the practice of art that evolved outside of conventional theatre. Reinelt relates it to early avant-garde and experimental theatre, which promoted the idea that performance did not have to exclusively take place on stage. This realisation, that social practices outside of artistic contexts can be considered as 'being performed', means that the notion of performance can be stretched to include everyday practices. The equal status this gives to various types of performance allows for a new political critique whereby 'distinctions between high and low culture, primitive and mature, elite and popular seem to disappear' (Reinelt, 2002: 202). Hence, the relevance of these newly framed performances resides in their social and political dynamics, 'as they become *performative*' (ibid.: 203, my emphasis).

Considering this, and as Austin (1975) argues, if we do things by saying them, it could equally be stated that we say things by doing, or *performing* them. Examining the performative features of an event or practice, be it a marriage ceremony or a digital protest, can therefore tell us about the specific norms and values held by the actors, or on a wider scale, by society. In this study, I assume that a performance, including a speech act, does more than describing; it actually produces what it performs. It is thus *performative*. In relation to digital direct action, the performative element refers to the process through which resistance actually occurs – in other words, *what* and *how* the performance is performing. This may imply that actions are assessed for their effectiveness; however, the analysis here is much more concerned with the type of resistance created; whether, for instance, the resistance is symbolic or actual, threatening or playful, ironic or poetic. Based on the assumption that all performances are performative, the analysis focuses on processes rather than successes.

While I use 'performative' to refer to the ability of a performance to produce meaning, I resort to 'performativity' to interpret the consequences of these meanings, which Reinelt describes as 'the power of performance as a performative action and as the site for the emergence of novelty in representation' (2002: 205). Philosopher Judith Butler is associated with the theory of performativity. Building on existing analyses of performative utterances, Butler proposes a radical interpretation of gender, suggesting that gender is not a natural and permanent attribute but something that we do, or that we perform. As she explains, 'there is no gender identity behind the expressions of gender; that identity is performatively constituted by the very "expressions" that are said to be its results' (1990: 25). Gender is therefore performative. Based on this performative function, as well as the necessity for these performances to be perpetually re-enacted, Butler not only explains that the power of performativity is confining and oppressive, but she also suggests that the same process can be resisted or subverted.

From this premise, performativity can be seen as the process of being performative. It is also the domain of performance that social actors may control the least. As new meanings are created through the development of radical performances, performativity becomes the realm where relations of power and control become visible. For example, following the early digital direct action staged in 1998, the US government briefly considered classifying virtual disturbance as a terrorist act, a decision that influenced many shifts in the rationales for the developments of digital protest. At the same time, the developments of creative and playful aesthetics within the practice of digital direct action may have helped activists circumvent these same accusations of terrorism (a key argument developed in this book). These are the unintended consequences of the performativity of digital action, which underline oppressive, but also subversive potentials. It is also a reminder that 'power can neither be withdrawn nor refused, but only redeployed' (Butler, 1990: 124).

While theories of performance, performative and performativity have become part of social and media research, so far, no significant work has brought them together with theories of digital activism. This book is a first attempt, and it aims to provide a new framework of analysis. At the same time, this multidisciplinary stand is not idiosyncratic. The cases of digital action examined in this study clearly feature creative and performative elements. What is more, activists have made extensive use of theatre and performance references to describe their political project. To be sure, CAE's production of *Electronic Civil Disobedience* was initially part of a window installation for the 1994 New York City *Anti-Work Show*, an art exhibition calling for the rethinking of social and political activism. This book therefore brings these existing aspects to the forefront of the debates. While performance theory has tended to distance itself from theatrical and artistic contexts, the analysis here will specifically display these connections. The point is that the analytical framework conceived is not imposed but emerges from the material, and a close examination of these elements can contribute to a deeper understanding of digital direct action.

A Turn to Discourse

Throughout this book, many stories about technology and digital action will be explored. As mentioned before, one of the aims is to understand how the virtual space has been constructed as a legitimate sphere for political activism. The analysis focuses on the discourses that have shaped current debates and practices. In particular, it retraces the historical and ideological foundations of digital action which directly relate to the development of technology. This approach not only echoes the performative framework described previously, but it also draws from discourse analysis.

Similar to performance theory, the study of discourse assumes that language use is a social practice that participates in the construction of the social and cultural world. As a methodological approach, discourse analysis owes much to the work of Michel Foucault who, moving away from a Saussurean interpretation of language, proposed to study discourse as a system of representation. Foucault (1990) argues that, as a collection of statements representative of a particular subject, discourse produces knowledge and power relations over the said subject. For him, 'it is in discourse that power and knowledge are joined together' (1990: 100).

So far, studies that have investigated digital activism have steered away from the critical analysis of its discourse, and yet, using this approach can help in recognising the dominant narratives that have shaped our contemporary understanding of technology and promoted the development of digital protest. Far from revolutionary, digital action is connected to previous activist practices, and a critical examination of current and historical discourses will clarify these relations. As explained by critical discourse analysis (CDA) scholar Norman Fairclough,

> Critical approaches differ from non-critical approaches in not just describing discursive practices, but also showing how discourse is shaped by relations of power and ideologies, and the constructive effects discourse has upon social identities, social relations and systems of knowledge and belief, neither of which is normally apparent to discourse participants.
>
> (1992: 12)

The other important aspect of CDA is that while it provides a framework that enables the study of discursive constructions, it also positions researchers at the centre of the analytical process. As Margaret Wetherell best explains,

> The analyst is in no sense a bystander or dilettante but someone who chooses to work on pressing social and political problems rather than on issues which can be easily funded or are good for careers.

> The aim is to feedback the knowledge gained into the political process in a way that is most likely to bring about the desired changes.
> (2001: 384)

As a consequence, the discussion in this book does not merely aim to retrace historical events and stories; I offer an interpretation of the ways in which dominant discourses come into existence, how they circulate, and why they are re-appropriated (Foucault, 1992). For instance, this approach allows me to establish that the metaphor of cyberspace can be associated with the theory of the Western frontier, and that the emergence of digital activist bodies can be retraced to the Civil Rights movements. I am also able to link early counterculture activists with digital technology geeks. In the process, the use of discourse analysis helps in identifying many of the contradictions and limitations of digital direct action, but also its potential.

As mentioned previously, the basis for this investigation includes the narratives and rationales formulated by the activists and artists involved in digital action. The study relies on a wide range of textual material, digital archives and interviews, including original writings from Electronic Disturbance Theater, the electrohippies and the more recent production of Anonymous. These are supported by in-depth interviews with activists from CAE and Electronic Disturbance Theater, as part of a reflective process that covers more than two decades of digital activist practice.

One important source that will be examined at length is the work of CAE. CAE's writings on electronic disturbance constitute the first substantial theorisation of digital direct action, and this study is their first extensive analysis in relation to performance theory. At first, the literary genres of *The Electronic Disturbance*, *Electronic Civil Disobedience* and *Digital Resistance* are not easy to recognise. Indeed, they could all be read as political statements, cyberculture essays or artistic manifestos. This complexity means that the pamphlets should not be approached with a single theoretical frame in mind. Instead, critical readers should become aware that the texts regularly shift between different literary genres, according to their internal argumentation.

For instance, a political statement will adopt the genre of political speech, as illustrated here:

> At least one factor responsible is the continued presence of the remnants of the 60s New Left within the ranks of activist groups. Preoccupied as they are with the means used to achieve past victories (primarily the contribution that the New Left made to the withdrawal of American troops from Viet Nam), members of these groups see no need to invent new approaches.
> (Critical Art Ensemble, 1996: 10)

Yet, the writing also switches to a more metaphorical genre when the argument relates to more abstract concepts, as in the following case:

> Treading water in the pool of liquid power need not be an image of acquiescence and complicity. In spite of their awkward situation, the political activist and the cultural activist (anachronistically known as the artist) can still produce disturbances, Although such action may more closely resemble the gestures of a drowning person, and it is uncertain just what is being disturbed, in this situation the post-modern roll of dice favors the act of disturbance.
>
> (Critical Art Ensemble, 1994: 12)

These discursive patterns become even more apparent when placed under the lens of a semantic reading. However, for the purpose of remaining focused, the analysis here will not extensively dwell in these elements. What is important is to realise that the effectiveness of the pamphlets is based on the exploitation of various literary genres, and this further justifies the combination of discourse and performance as an analytical framework.

Along with the analysis of CAE's writings, the study brings into conversation many other accounts of digital technology and socio-political activism. These stories often provide parallel narratives that support or hamper dominant discourses. Some of them are well rehearsed within cyberculture studies, such as the role of science-fiction literature in the representation of cyberspace, or the seemingly decentralised structure of the internet. This study examines some of the texts that have shaped our vision and understanding of digital technology. Although many of these narratives are considered to be outdated, my contention is that they still provide the central *imaginaires* that help validate digital direct action.

One limitation is that this book may give the impression that digital protest mainly happens in the United States and Europe. Clearly, this is not the case. As any other type of activism, digital direct action takes place worldwide. Yang's (2011) recent analysis of online activism in China is an illustration, and his critical study helps in understanding how political contexts shape specific forms of digital activism and how global variations operate. Another example is the transnational formation of digital activists that emerged as part of the African and Arab Spring in the 2010s. There is no doubt that an analysis of the performativity of digital action in these national contexts would greatly benefit the field. Considering the discursive and linguistics aspects of this type of research, however, a command of multiple native languages would be beneficial. This is why the study here remains centred on Anglo-Saxon and Hispanic cases and material.

Chapter Overview

In many ways, *Performing Digital Activism* provides a narrative of the events that have formed the wider history of digital direct action. While it follows a loose chronological trail (mostly that of CAE's publications), its chapters should be read as snapshots of these events, in the ongoing development of digital protest. To begin this process, the discussion in Chapter 1 examines the narratives that have established cyberspace as the new stage of social and political actions. Using the concept of *cyber-imaginaires* (a term borrowed from Patrice Flichy), I explain the discursive influence of seminal texts such as Barlow's *Declaration of Independence of Cyberspace* and CAE's *The Electronic Disturbance*. My argument is that many of these *cyber-imaginaires*, which were prompted by the emergence of personal computers and early internet communities, have provided the early rationales for the development of digital action. As such, the idea of performative utterances also applies to textual material, and this chapter explores these works as primary examples of speeches that create what they describe, often with unintended consequences.

Chapter 2 explores in more detail CAE's initial rationale for the relocation of political dissent. In particular, the analysis retraces the formulation of digital sovereignty and identifies this as a way to reposition the body in protest. The chapter also dwells on the original descriptions of digital resistance. It is in these fictional stories that digital action fully adopts its performative and theatrical features. Far from considering this as a novelty, however, I suggest that the theatricality and performativity of resistant bodies is part of the historical legacy of social mobilisation. What CAE does achieve is to expose new dynamics between power and digital technology, and the analysis here clearly recognises the potency of this new *imaginaire*.

The discussion in Chapter 3 centres on one of the most persuasive accounts of digital direct action: the formulation of electronic civil disobedience. This new framework, initially proposed by CAE, has been the privileged trope of many activist groups, such as Electronic Disturbance Theater, the electrohippies and even Anonymous. As the logical succession of civil disobedience, electronic civil disobedience is meant to renew social mobilisation by transferring protest in the digital sphere. To support this, CAE suggests a new tactic in the form of information blockade. In the process, technology is given a new status, along with those who can control it, such as computer hackers. Despite its immediate appeal, this new framework contains crucial shortcomings. The discussion in this chapter therefore begins to assess some of the theoretical tensions that will eventually come to affect digital activists.

The notorious case of the SWARM protest, staged against the Mexican government in 1998, is the focus of Chapter 4. While this event has featured in most discussions of digital activism, its remarkable performative and theatrical aesthetics have been mostly overlooked. Electronic Disturbance Theater's first attempt at digital direct action exposes some of the challenges and contradictions of the practice. The analysis unfolds these tensions, between original conceptions and practical applications, and I argue that the project raises many questions about the globalisation of social movements. Further issues relate to the simulation of electronic civil disobedience and its legal implications. Despite all these complications, however, the reassertion of the theatricality of digital protest is compelling, and the SWARM project offers a most powerful and poetic gesture of resistance and remembrance.

Chapter 5 considers the activist practice of Anonymous as a new, technology-driven movement. The discussion centres on the ways in which Anonymous activism represents a radical shift towards a politics of information. In a social context where access and use of digital technology have turned into an open conflict between governments, corporations and citizens, digital direct action leaves the sphere of simulation to generate radical and controversial disturbance. Emerging from a hacker milieu, Anonymous has succeeded in globalising the *cyber-imaginaire* of a free digital space, becoming in the process the number one defender of free information. At the same time, and as with earlier practices, the aesthetics and performative features of Anonymous are conspicuous. Specifically, the analysis examines how the use of humour and playfulness extend the theatricality and performativity of digital protest. The chapter reflects on all of these elements and assesses the opportunities and challenges brought by this new stage of digital direct action.

Finally, the conclusion chapter revisits the main themes examined in the course of the book, in light of recent developments in social protest, such as the waves of occupation movements that rose at the beginning of the century. As will become evident throughout this work, the reading of social protest as performance is not new. Yet within more recent social mobilisation, performance has taken on a new role that is entwined with pre-figurative politics. Performance protest does not simply happen, it is carefully crafted and relies on citationality to function; in other words, performance becomes tactical.

Perhaps one of the challenges of this book, and most studies using performance as a theoretical framework, is the assumption that all social activities can be considered as performative. Indeed, could there be a part of social life that cannot be examined as 'performance'? The many definitions of the term would suggest that there is not. This is why the task of the research is not to distinguish performance from non-performance (assuming that these exist). Instead, it is to examine *what*, *how* and for what *purpose*, performances *perform*. By doing so, *Performing Digital Activism* offers an original insight, and a brand new narrative, regarding the developments of contemporary social and political activism.

1 'I Come from Cyberspace'
The New Stage of Resistance

> Governments of the Industrial World, you weary giants of flesh and steel, I come from Cyberspace, the new home of Mind. On behalf of the future, I ask you of the past to leave us alone. You are not welcome among us. You have no sovereignty where we gather.
>
> —John Perry Barlow

In February 1996, John Perry Barlow, lyricist of the rock band Grateful Dead, wrote the *Declaration of Independence of Cyberspace*. In a flaming email directed to the US government, Barlow condemned the new Telecommunications Act which sanctioned the circulation of indecent and obscene material on the internet. This act infuriated many users who denunciated an infringement to the First Amendment.[1] For Barlow, who also co-founded the Electronic Frontier Foundation, an organisation dedicated to the protection of free speech online, this latest governmental interference was insufferable. Thus, taking matters into his hands, he declared the independence of cyberspace:

> I declare the global social space we are building to be naturally independent of the tyrannies you seek to impose on us. You have no moral right to rule us nor do you possess any methods of enforcement we have true reason to fear.
>
> (Barlow, 1996: para. 2)

Barlow's text is a grandiloquent statement which proclaims cyberspace as the new territory that will provide social and economic prosperity to all. Most importantly though, this digital land is, and should remain, outside of governmental control:

> This bill was enacted upon us by people who haven't the slightest idea who we are or where our conversation is being conducted. … Well fuck them. Or more to the point, let us now take our leave of them. They have declared war on cyberspace. Let us show them how cunning, baffling and powerful we can be in our own defense.
>
> (Barlow, 1996: preface)

The declaration of independence is a seminal piece not only for its discursive construction of cyberspace as a free and self-governed environment, but also for its underlying threat of radical action to protect the space. It is a fascinating example of the type of narratives that have popularised the vision of cyberspace as a brand new world.

Needless to say, the piece received virulent responses when it was first published, partially because of the pompous style that Barlow adopted, but mainly because of his elliptic account of the development of digital technology. The idea that perhaps the internet was never free, or autonomous, is alien to Barlow. On this account, it is very tempting to consider the *Declaration of Independence of Cyberspace* as an idiosyncratic text and many critics have been keen to dismiss it. Yet, Barlow's piece epitomises the libertarian discourse that underpins the very idea of digital direct action, that is, the assumption that cyberspace is open and democratic, and that it should stay outside of state control.

In one way or another, this conception of the virtual space runs through most of the rationales supporting the development of digital activism. This first chapter thus explores the discourses that construct cyberspace as the new stage of social and political action. The discussion begins with the analysis of specific narratives, or *cyber-imaginaires*, that posit digital technology as the central engine of social progress. Embedded in these stories is the belief that technology can address the deficiencies of our world. As will become clear from the discussion, many of these narratives are rooted in the history of American culture and society. These *cyber-imaginaires* require close examination as they embody the core interpretations that have shaped our understanding of digital technology. The chapter therefore focuses on several key texts, including Barlow's *Declaration of Independence of Cyberspace* and CAE's *The Electronic Disturbance*, and examines their performative ability to lay the grounds of digital direct action.

Imaginaires of Cyberspace

In *The Internet Imaginaire*, Flichy (2007) introduces the concept of digital *imaginaire*, explaining that many stories about technology emerged from scientific discoveries, before becoming trendy topics for literature, counterculture movements and mass media publications. Flichy identifies two dominant *imaginaires* related to cyberspace. The first one comes from the stories created by politicians, industrialists, computer scientists and hackers alike. This *imaginaire* is embedded in key scientific developments and innovations, such as the internet and mobile technologies. It centres on the possibilities offered by the digital and encourages the production and consumption of electronic commodities. As with many grand narratives about technology, this *cyber-imaginaire* is linked to the dominant American culture and supported by the excessive enthusiasm generated by public access to computers, and the emergence of online communities.

An account of this trend can be found in the early stories created by the group of American technophiles and business entrepreneurs, known as the digerati. In 1996, Brockman published *Digerati: Encounters with the Cyber Elite*, an early version of a "who's who" book about the internet. The term 'digerati' was coined by combining 'digital' and 'literati' (intellectuals), and referred to a specific circle of elite internet users that Brockman introduced in 36 interviews. At the time, he suggested that although not exhaustive, the list still represented the most influential network of individuals in the internet industry. Brockman referred to them as the cyber elite:

> A critical mass of the doers, thinkers and writers connected in ways they may not even appreciate, who have tremendous influence on the emerging communication revolution surrounding the growth of the internet and the World Wide Web. Although they all happen to be Americans, their activities have a worldwide impact.
>
> (1996: xxvi)

A close reading of these interviews brings to attention the contradictory discourses that shaped early interpretations of cyberspace. Consider for example, the case of Stewart Alsop, business entrepreneur and former Editor-in-chief of *InfoWorld*, who is introduced as 'The Pragmatist': 'He likes doing business. He likes making money. He likes things that people are willing to pay for' (ibid.: 1).[2] Alsop is said to believe that 'if the web is going to change our lives substantially, there are going to be plenty of ways to make money, and some will be the ways we already make money' (ibid.: 2).

Another example is David Bunnell, a cyberelite and founder of the *PC Magazine* and *PC World* publications, who explains that to make money online, 'you need multiple revenue streams. You need advertising revenue, transaction revenue and subscription revenue' (*cited in* Brockman, ibid.: 32). Yet, in the same interview, Bunnell, also known as 'The Seer', provides another argument, typical of the cyberelite paradoxical approach to digital technologies:

> We need a free, unfettered Internet. You can't trust commercial online services to respect your rights. They are too susceptible to commercial pressures, too likely to cave in when their profits are on the line. The Internet is different, and it should stay that way. The future of our democracy depends upon this, because the Internet has the potential to give individuals much more say in government affairs. (Maybe this, not dirty pictures is what the government is really afraid of?)
>
> (ibid.: 35)

The last comment is a clear reference to the 1996 *Communications Act* with which the US government attempted to censor the internet (the same one that prompted Barlow's *Declaration of Independence of Cyberspace*).

Turner (2006) offers a fascinating account of another context where early ideas of digital technologies fermented. In his book, *From Counterculture to Cyberculture*, Turner recounts the story of Steward Brand, the personage behind the creation of the most popular early online community. Brand was the central figure of The Whole Earth Lectronic Link, commonly known as The Well, an online community project related to the American counterculture magazine, *Whole Earth Catalog*. Started in the mid-1980s, The Well was an online bulletin board conceived to facilitate meetings, publications and networking amongst its members. It included well-known contributors such as John Perry Barlow, Howard Rheingold, Kevin Kelly and Esther Dyson, all part of Brockman's list of digital elite (in *Digerati*, Stewart Brand's is known as 'The Scout').

The discussions taking place online covered various topics, including counterculture movements, homesteading ecology and mainstream consumption culture, but also, science and computing. Turner (2006) suggests that The Well reflected the entrepreneurial spirit of the Californian Bay Area in the late 1970s, and soon became a space for professional and social networking. The discussions of the board also influenced on the conceptualisation of computer technology and the virtual space:

> Over time, the network's members and forums helped redefine the microcomputer as a "personal" machine, computer communication networks a "virtual communities" and cyberspace itself as the digital equivalent of the western landscape into which so many communards set forth in the late 1960s, the "electronic frontier".
>
> (Turner, 2006: 6)

Steward Brand successfully brought together separate social groups that began to promote social transformation through digital technologies. These people were elite technophiles as well as dominant players in the industry of computing and software design. Their approach of digital technology therefore readily mixed utopian hippie counterculture with business entrepreneurship. As Brand declared in the first edition of the Whole Earth Catalog: 'We are as gods and might as well get good at it' (1968).

Barbrook and Cameron (1995) coined this paradoxical tendency the 'Californian Ideology'. The two critics retraced the emergence of early digital utopias to the radical transformations of the 1960s, arguing that the new breed of activists and artists emerging from the Bay Area came to view communication technologies as a way to achieve more freedom, but also to fulfil their economic ambitions. This combination of social engagement and libertarian capitalism characterises the Californian Ideology:

> This new faith has emerged from a bizarre fusion of the cultural bohemianism of San Francisco with the high-tech industries of Silicon Valley. Promoted in magazines, books, TV programs, websites, newsgroups, and Net conferences, the Californian ideology promiscuously combines the free-wheeling spirit of the hippies and the entrepreneurial zeal of the yuppies.
>
> (Barbrook and Cameron, 1995: para. 2)

The Californian Ideology is central to the *imaginaire* of cyberspace as a new world of possibilities. In particular, the 'bizarre fusion' transpires from most early accounts by influential internet users, and as will be discussed in the next sections, these cyberelites have conveniently ignored any narratives or events that could challenge their new technological aspirations.

While today The Well could be considered one of the first successful online communities, it must be stated that the digerati constructed their virtual global village at a time when access to the internet was still very limited. In its early days, the project operated on a teleconferencing system and subscribers had to dial up a central computer line to post messages. Participation in the project was therefore unequal. Conversations and debates were often dominated by the same few people. According to Flichy (2007: 74), 1% of the participants (around 70 people), produced half of the messages. Flichy explains that 'the community was not linked to a geographic territory, very few people expressed themselves and the vast majority simply observed the debate (read messages) as in most online communities' (ibid.).

Flichy also suggests that the virtual community did not operate as globally as anticipated, since 'in BBS [bulletin board services] writing was the only form of interaction between individuals, and that interaction was possible only if members shared a common vocabulary, form of speech, and, more generally, culture' (ibid.: 85). In addition, those who participated were more inclined to reproduce the dominant discourse of virtual community promoted by the founders. In the end, The Well was not the digital public sphere it claimed to be, and the digerati's *imaginaire* of a virtual open community, responsible for its own politics, economy and ecology, seems to reflect a desire to assert ownership of the internet.

At the time of her interview with Brockman, *New York Times* columnist, Denise Caruso, rightly brought attention to the fact that most internet users were predominantly white privileged males. She therefore called for increased awareness about access, and for governmental support in the development of public infrastructure (1996: 53). The alias Brockman had for Caruso was 'The Idealist', a rather ironic choice, considering the role of many members of the digerati and The Well who circulated idealistic tropes about the transformative power of technology and virtual communities, with little introspection about their own positions.

Along with the primary *imaginaire*, Flichy identifies a second *imaginaire* which is not associated with specific technological innovations or directed to a particular audience. This other *imaginaire* assumes that digital technology is the foundation of social progress and the transformation of the human condition. Flichy describes it as 'a complete imaginary construction encompassing all aspects of the new digital society: individual life, relations between body and mind, micro and macro social management of society, and production and distribution of wealth' (2007: 107).

A key element is that this *imaginaire* tends to be shared by distinct social groups that would otherwise have little in common. Lister *et al* explain the phenomenon, suggesting that 'some tendencies that may have been originally posited (in psychoanalytical theory) as belonging to individuals are also observed to be present at the level of social groups and collectivities' (2003: 60). For instance, the idea that digital technologies could have a redeeming function is a belief shared by many people outside of the technological field. These beliefs in the transformative power of technology are usually spread through idealistic narratives that promise the emergence of new social order, fair economic growth and democratic systems. The internet is a core example of a technology that has prompted the resurgence of ideals of democracy. In this internet *imaginaire*, cyberspace is perceived as a digital miracle, a 'new' virtual world, which supersedes geographical frontiers and revives the collective dream of global social change.

For Flichy, these utopian constructions come from early writings on digital technology, such as the work of Howard Rheingold on virtual reality and community. These texts transpose complex scientific developments into the sphere of 'ordinary sociability' (2007: 90), through which they become part of everyday's accounts and understanding of technology. Flichy further explains that as the first generation of personal computer users became dissatisfied with the limited and slow development of technology, utopian projections and digital dreams functioned as imaginary substitutions.

This is when science-fiction literature takes on a central role. From novels depicting the merging of humans and machines, to stories about the triumph of artificial intelligence; from the writings of H.G. Wells and Isaac Asimov to those of Bruce Sterling and Neal Stephenson, science-fiction has contributed to the ways in which human and computer interaction is conceived and experienced. The most famous book in this genre is certainly *Neuromancer* by Canadian author William Gibson. This novel is regularly cited as the preeminent work of cyberpunk literature, a science-fiction genre which emerged in North America during the early 1980s. Written in 1984, as part of the *Sprawl* trilogy, *Neuromancer* recounts the story of Henry Case, a prodigious cyberspace hacker and drug addict, who is given a second chance to enter the virtual world and complete a perilous mission. The novel contains the first definition of 'cyberspace', presenting it as an environment made out of data spaces that users access by connecting their brains directly to computers.

Neuromancer won many science fiction awards and it is now a well-rehearsed reference within digital and cyberculture theory. The work is often subject to grandiloquent praises that far exceed sensible interpretations. Mike Davis's early review is one example out of many:

> The opening section of *Neuromancer*, with its introduction of cyberspace, is the kind of revelation—of a possible but previously unimagined future—that occurs perhaps once a generation. Charles Babbage's and Ada Lovelace's anticipation of a programmable computer in the 1820s, Friedrich Engles' [*sic*] 1880s prophecy of a mechanized world war, and H. G. Well's prevision of the atomic bomb in 1900 are comparable examples.
>
> (1993: 10)

More surprising however is the interest that academic fields have developed for science-fiction literature and the cyberpunk movement. For instance, social scientist Tomas (1991) undertook an in-depth anthropological study of cyberspace based on Gibson's novel. In his work, Tomas argues that the metaphor of cyberspace facilitates understandings of technology, particularly in its relation with bodies, and with virtual spaces. Following his analysis of *Neuromancer*, Tomas concludes that cyberspace has become a new social sphere, and that 'Gibson's description and contemporary work on virtual worlds technologies does indeed hold the promise of new spatial configurations and related post organic life forms' (ibid.: 33). This illustrates that cyberpunk has not only shaped visions of cyberspace, the science-fiction genre has built a technological *imaginaire*.

In contrast to this position, Jordan (1999: 20) contends that the focus of cyberpunk is not to predict the future but to 'analyse current society and technology by making them appear fictional and strange'. Jordan explains that most of these literary works have been read outside of their science-fictional context and this tendency produces anachronistic interpretations. For him: 'such a mistaken reading of the actuality of the virtual lands from the fiction of Gibson, and others, is all the more seductive because this genre of science fiction has been read as social and cultural theory' (ibid.: 22). Jordan convincingly argues that these interpretations of cyberspace (such as the one by Davis included above) function as '"prefigurative social theory" that is an already existing theory of a yet to exist society' (ibid.).

A similar line of argument has emerged from more recent research. Bukatman (2007) also defends that cyberspace is a representation of the present. For him, the digital space 'does have its precursors. The notion of a dark and crowded space broken by neon forms and corporate structures is surely not unfamiliar' (ibid.: 82). Bukatman suggests that Gibson's cyberspace is a re-contextualisation of the 1980s expansion of urban spaces such as Time Square, and cities such as Las Vegas or Tokyo. Cyberspace is therefore not a radically new space: it is an abstract version of our contemporary world.

Nonetheless, the fictional perceptions of cyberpunk literature cannot be ignored as many computer users have worked towards their realisation (Jordan, 1999). It is no coincidence that the one word selected to signify digital networks originates from science fiction literature. As Bukatman concludes 'cyberpunk's techno-surreal images and narrative strategies have added at least one new word to the lexicon (*cyberspace*) and have significantly altered the representation of electronic narrative' (2007: 89).

Other media critics such as Chesher (1994) maintain that the dominant interpretations of science-fiction literature raise many issues. Chesher explains that although cyberpunk has often been described as a highly pessimistic and dystopian genre, this is rarely acknowledged in early discussions of computer technology:

> Gibson's vision of cyberspace was broken up and reassembled in a different context. (...) the VR [virtual reality] industry accepted imaginative suggestions, while ignoring the ironic and critical context. The elements which were excessively critical or unacceptable were stripped off, reinterpreted or ignored. The ideas are repackaged, their critical challenges neutralised, and attached to more comfortable discourses.
>
> (1994: 7)

While some of the concepts borrowed from science-fiction have helped understanding human-computer interaction, the extent to which they have been manipulated and exploited is clearly problematic. Gibson himself talks about the misconception of his novel and explains that for him, the production of *Neuromancer* was 'a way of trying to come to terms with the awe and terror inspired in me by the world in which we live' (Gibson *cited in* Chesher, ibid.: 6).

The claims made by Chesher resonate strongly with the argument developed here, in particular, the references made to acts of ignorance, reinterpretation and neutralisation. Most of these practices act for the wider benefit of *cyber-imaginaires* and the belief in the redemptive function of technology. Yet, to understand this process, we need to further explore the narratives that proclaim the emergence of a new virtual world and a new social order.

Performances of Cyberspace

The *Declaration of Independence of Cyberspace* is an acclamation of the most powerful *imaginaire* created about digital technology. The text epitomises the many contradictions that technologists and cyber-enthusiasts have dispersed since the emergence of the internet. As mentioned before, it is tempting to dismiss it as an idiosyncratic piece, however, this would conceal the central role that Barlow's narrative plays in the discursive construction of cyberspace. The *Declaration* is a performative manifesto which produces the independence it declares. Derrida (2002) discusses this performative function in his short analysis of the *United States Declaration of Independence*, and describes how the *Declaration of Independence* creates the American State, and the American people, as independent entities at the same time that it is being written. Thus, the argument is that the United States of America (or any other state for that matter) does not exist before the text that declares them. What is more, there is no other way to create an independent state than to declare it as such, and this what Barlow attempts with his very own declaration of independence.

In a previous essay, *Across the Electronic Frontier*, Barlow describes his vision of the virtual as follows:

> Cyberspace, in its present condition, has a lot in common with the 19th century West. ... Large institutions already claim to own the place, but most of the actual natives are solitary and independent, sometimes to the point of sociopathy. It is, of course, a perfect breeding ground for both outlaws and new ideas about liberty.
>
> (1990: para. 8)

While this passage depicts cyberspace as a new territory where brave digital settlers can gain independence and prosperity, it is worth remembering that in the early 1990s, most users experienced the internet through text-based interface and interaction. Barlow's own experience was through his interactions with The Well virtual community. His spatial description of cyberspace as a digital Wild West is therefore highly metaphorical. The representation of this environment as a free land inhabited with lonesome calamity computer users is a science-fiction construct, or a *cyber-imaginaire*. Similarly, when Barlow refers to the 19th-century West he is using a metaphor that has dominated the American psyche and culture for centuries, that is, the metaphor of the frontier.

Many metaphors have been used to describe digital technologies such as, superhighway, shopping mall, cardiovascular system, global copying machine, and even, 'the ocean' (Yen, 2002: 3). Yet, the one metaphor that has persisted is the 'electronic frontier'. According to Alfred Yen, it is 'a version of the Western Frontier, a historical phenomenon that glorifies individuality and the benefits of minimal government' (ibid.: 5). Since metaphors are often selected for the context and meaning they convey, it is worth questioning how, and why, the pervasive and colonial metaphor of the frontier has come to shape early interpretations of digital technology and the internet.

The frontier metaphor can be traced as far back as 1921, in a thesis by Frederick Jackson Turner, entitled *The Significance of the Frontier in American History.* In his paper presented before the American Society of Historians, Turner explains the separation between the Eastern part of the United States and the American West, and argues that the absence of authoritative structures and the limitation of governmental interference provided the grounds for the rapid development of the country. As a symbol of freedom and economic prosperity, the frontier allows for 'the promotion of democracy here and in Europe' and it is 'productive of individualism' (1921: 30). Turner also contends that the American intellectual and social qualities were born to the frontier:

> That coarseness and strength combined with acuteness and inquisitiveness; that practical, inventive turn of mind, quick to find expedients; that masterful grasp of material things, lacking in the artistic but powerful to effect great ends; that restless, nervous energy; that dominant individualism, working for good and for evil, and withal that buoyancy and exuberance which comes with freedom – these are traits of the frontier, or traits called out elsewhere because of the existence of the frontier.
>
> (ibid.: 37)

Over time, this *imaginaire* of the 'Western frontier' became a powerful metaphor and, according to Yen (2002), it has remained a central reference from which Americans build their identity.

This idealised vision of America's history has been heavily criticised, however. As William Cronon states, '[Turner's] reputation has been subjected to a devastating series of attacks which have left little of his argument intact' (1987: 158). Of primary concern is the argument that the thesis does not address the brutal and destructive conquest of the continent prior to the arrival of the first settlers. The fact that the Western territories were not 'wild' or 'virgin' spaces but were actually inhabited by native populations is of little relevance to him. For Turner, 'the frontier is the outer edge of the wave – the meeting point between savagery and civilization' (1921: 3). The other illustration of his contentious narrative is his comment on slavery which contends that 'when American history comes to be rightly viewed it will be seen that the slavery question is an incident' (ibid.: 24).

As with most *imaginaires*, Turner articulates his thesis through a selective dismissal of events that are likely to challenge his romantic historisation of America. His argument is that conquest is imperative to the subsistence of the country and its citizens: 'America has been another name for opportunity, and the people of the United States have taken their tone from the incessant expansion' (ibid.: 37). Hence to deny the frontier thesis implies the rejection of America's legitimate quest for freedom and economic growth. What is more, the closure of the frontier and the limitation of the conquest would lead to the decline of the country. To avoid this scenario, Turner advocates that America perpetually seized new frontiers and territories. This is the power of the frontier metaphor, and the reason why 'popular culture capitalizes on the loss of the Western Frontier to create American nostalgia for the frontier's return' (Yen, 2002: 16).

Indeed, the frontier metaphor returns at various important periods of American history. For example, in the late 1970s, the American physicist Gerard O'Neill (1977) published *The High Frontier: Human Colonies in Space*, his scientific project about space colonisation. In the book, O'Neill contends that the technology to allow large human communities to subsist in space is available. As he explains in his introduction:

> We now have the technological ability to set up large human communities in space: communities in which manufacturing, farming, an all other human activities could be carried out. Substantial benefit, both immediate and long term, can accrue to us from a program of expansion into that new frontier.
>
> (1977: 19)

O'Neill's projection is based on the US developments of Space research and the Apollo missions of the 1950s and 1960s, but his account also includes speculative descriptions of space settlement that have, so far, only materialized in science-fiction literature and animation.

What is relevant is the extent to which this vision of space colony resonates with Turner's thesis of the Western frontier. For O'Neill, Space colonisation promises freedom, progress and prosperity. It is 'the opportunity for increased human options and diversity of development' (ibid.).

This conception of Space as a new frontier clearly responds to Turner's picture of 'incessant expansion' and, as suggested by the semantic, the project also promises mass colonisation and destruction.

The same link between the frontier metaphor and cyberspace can be found in Barlow's writing which makes direct references to the 19th-century American West. Cyberspace is the electronic frontier, a revival of the Western frontier. This new metaphor works as a powerful imagery for digital technology, as illustrated by the popular magazine *Mondo 2000* which titled its summer 1990 edition: 'The Rush Is On! Colonizing Cyberspace' (Mondo 2000, 1990).

The fact that the metaphor remains dominant should not be viewed as arbitrary. Particularly if one considers the strong criticism formulated against the thesis of the Western frontier. As mentioned before, many images have been used to describe cyberspace; however, the frontier is the only metaphor that revives America's conquering past. Turner (1999: para. 2) argues that the important consequence of the frontier metaphor is that 'in the face of such hyperbole, it is hard to remember that "cyberspace" is not a place at all, let alone a futuristic mirror of the American past'. For him, this construction of cyberspace can be linked to a particular group of people:

> This rhetoric has emerged less from the mists of literary history than from the deliberate efforts of a particular community of computer manufacturers, software developers, corporate consultants and academics. (...) they've done so partly in order to gain social and economic advantages for their class.
>
> (1999: para. 2)

Other critics have drawn attention to the problematic connotations of the electronic frontier. Miller (1995) criticises the use of a metaphor that replicates gender divisions and implies the necessity of protecting women and children from the potential hostility of cyberspace. As she states, 'the Western narrative connects pleasurably with the American romance of individualistic masculinity; [it is] small wonder that the predominantly male founders of the Net's culture found it so appealing' (1995: 22). Similarly, Wilbur (2000: 46–47) points to the problematic re-appropriation of the metaphor, 'the notion of an electronic frontier has gained considerable currency on-line, even among computer users who might otherwise have reservations about a metaphor so steeped in traditions of imperialism, rough justice and the sometimes violent opposition of any others'.

The argument here is that the discourses produced by members of elite groups, such as the digerati or the 'virtual class' (Kroker and Weinstein, 1994) are central to the dissemination of the electronic frontier metaphor. In the same way that the original concept of the Western frontier disregards incompatible narratives, the concept of the electronic frontier fails to engage with some of the core characteristics of digital technology. This failing is what contributes to problematic interpretations of the virtual space.

In the *Declaration of Independence*, Barlow presents cyberspace as a place within which virtual and egalitarian communities are emerging. Although governments are attempting to control it, cyberspace remains open to exploration and conquest. As a world in its own right, it encompasses 'ethics', 'unwritten codes' and 'social contract' (1996: para. 4). In addition, it has a viable economic system with not only 'marketplaces' and 'transactions' but also reproduction and distribution systems at 'no cost' (ibid.). Barlow consistently describes this collective ownership of cyberspace using the words 'our', 'us', 'we', and the expressions: 'You do not know us, nor do you know our world'. 'Our world is different' (ibid.: para. 3). Yet, it is never clear who Barlow is referring to with these terms. While he mentions the 'citizens' of cyberspace, these remain mostly unidentified:

> We are creating a world that all may enter without privilege or prejudice accorded by race, economic power, military force, or station of birth. We are creating a world where anyone, anywhere may express his or her beliefs, no matter how singular, without fear of being coerced into silence or conformity.
>
> (1996: para. 7–8)

By contrast, the invader of cyberspace is clearly identified. The US government's attempt to control the internet through legislation is a threat to democracy, a plot to 'ward off the virus of liberty by erecting guard posts at the frontiers of Cyberspace' (ibid.: para. 13). For Barlow, social, legal and economic freedom has been achieved independently from governments. Thus, the declaration of independence is aimed at those who 'have not engaged in our great and gathering conversation', and did not 'create the wealth of our marketplaces' (1996: para. 4).

This description of cyberspace as self-contained and self-sufficient, which ignores the role of national governments in building internet infrastructures, has prompted virulent responses. At the time, media critic Bennahum (1996: 41) contended that he could not 'fathom how internet users like Barlow can dismiss the importance or role of government in shaping this medium and claim that it can have no positive influence from now on'.

By the 1990s, the origin of the internet as a US military defence project was already common knowledge. Most historical accounts retraced the internet to ARPA, the Advanced Research Projects Agency, part of the Department of Defense and directly funded by the US government. The ARPA project was created during the Cold War in reaction to the

Soviet Union's early Space programme, but even after the opening of the internet in the late 1980s, funding remains mostly governmental. Issues regarding the management and infrastructures emerged after increased governmental investment. In their compelling book *Who Controls the Internet?*, Goldsmith and Wu (2006) recount the extended conflict that opposed a group of engineers considered as the 'fathers of the internet' to the US government in the 1990s. The dispute related to the control of the root authority system that enables computers to communicate. For over a decade, the US government had remained distant from the administration of the internet, leaving most decisions to national agencies and, later on, corporate companies. Yet, with the increasing commercialisation of the network, and the threat of a monopolistic control of the domain name registrations, the original contributors and administrators voiced their concerns, condemning the collapse of an initially altruistic project.

The conflict escalated in January 1998, when Jon Postel chose to redirect all of the internet server names to his own computer.[3] The attempt was successful and, for a few days, all of the computers connected to the internet identified Postel's workstation as the main computer. After this incident, the administrative control of the internet root function was resolved at once. The US government reclaimed authority and declared the unauthorised modification of root file as a criminal offence (Goldsmith and Wu, 2006: 46). The initial detachment of the US state could explain why the internet and cyberspace came to be viewed as independent and self-governed. Until the mid-1990s, the government had relinquished the administration of the internet to subsidised agencies and universities. These bodies were not primarily seeking profit. Instead, they worked towards the harmonisation of a rapidly growing information and communication system.

The sudden change in administration was perceived as a serious threat by early internet users. On one side, they invoked the not-for-profit character of the internet and claimed the right to freedom and independence from the state. On the other side, the US government invoked another fundamental right. As clearly stated by Ira Magaziner, Bill Clinton's Science Policy Adviser at the time, 'the United States paid for the Internet, the Net was created under its auspices. And most importantly everything Jon [Postel] and Network Solutions did were pursuant to government contracts' (Magaziner *cited in* Goldsmith and Wu, 2006: 41). From this stand, it is difficult to sustain the view that the internet was ever a free and independent structure without tacitly dismissing its historical and technological developments.

For Flichy, this situation corresponds to the shared desire from privileged users to claim ownership of the internet and establish a form of independence:

> At the very beginnings of the Internet, government funding seemed to be one of the conditions for the development of the computer republic...

> However, with the massification of the Internet and the arrival of commercial enterprises on the network, state intervention became less necessary and even futile, and the libertarian position triumphed. The California Ideology consequently forgot its debt to the state.
>
> (2007: 169)

Yet, the digerati did more than forget its debt to governments. It insisted on promoting the *imaginaire* of an electronic community responsible for its own politics and economy, through a discourse that neutralised and romanticised digital technologies. In the case of Barlow, the conflict rests on a contradiction between an ideal of social equality and neoliberal demands.

The boldness of his declaration is to actually invoke the US *Declaration of Independence* to protest against governmental interference:

> In the United States, you have today created a law, the Telecommunications Reform Act, which repudiates your own Constitution and insults the dreams of Jefferson, Washington, Mill, Madison, DeToqueville, and Brandeis. These dreams must now be born anew in us.
>
> (1996: para. 11)

Barlow's *Declaration* produces an unpredictable shift. By arguing that cyberspace and its so-called 'citizens' are being denied the right to self-governance, he re-appropriates the narrative of oppressed populations struggling against domineering governments. Barlow appeals to the electronic frontier metaphor to imply a separation between two worlds and qualify the regulation of online activities as governmental 'tyrannies', 'impositions', and 'physical coercion' (ibid.: para. 2–10). In this process, the positions along the electronic frontier radically change. The internet users that are initially presented as new cyberspace settlers have acquired the unlikely position of oppressed native populations. As Barlow argues 'these increasingly hostile and colonial measures place us in the same position as those previous lovers of freedom and self-determination who had to reject the authorities of distant, uninformed powers' (ibid.: para. 15).

Yet, the 'inhabitants' of Barlow's new virtual world are most likely members of the digerati, or cyberelites, and his discourse should be related to what Lockard (2000) identifies as 'Internet nationalism'. Lockard considers the *Declaration of Independence of Cyberspace* as an attempt to claim cultural sovereignty for a specific group of privileged internet users. For him, Barlow's recuperation of the US *Declaration of Independence* is ignorant of the partiality and discrimination of the original text. He explains that 'in both declarations, a privileged minority parades as an auto-liberating majority' (2000: 181). Indeed, many analyses of the text fail to question the identity and rationale of those claiming the autonomy of cyberspace.

Barbrook and Cameron (1995) also challenge Barlow's references to the original *Declaration of Independence*. They argue that 'by championing this seemingly admirable ideal, these techno-boosters are at the same time reproducing some of the most atavistic features of American society, especially those derived from the bitter legacy of slavery' (ibid.: para. 3). The authors of the *Californian Ideology* remind us of the antithetical relationship between slavery and America's independence. They rightly point out that the dream of freedom and economic entrepreneurship championed by one part of the population was grounded in the systematic exploitation of the other part of the population:

> Thomas Jefferson was the man who wrote the inspiring call for democracy and liberty in the American Declaration of Independence and – at the same time – owned nearly 200 human beings as slaves. ... in "Jeffersonian democracy", freedom for white folks was based on slavery for black.
>
> (ibid.: para. 24)

The *Declaration of Independence of Cyberspace* has, of course, no legal status. Cyberspace is nowhere considered to be independent, and as such, the text could be considered as a failed, or parasitic, speech act (Austin, 1975). However, the questions raised by Derrida (2002: 53) about the process of declaring independence are still relevant, that is, 'how is a state made or founded, how does a state make or found itself?'. This is the performativity of Barlow's declaration, the unpredictable effects of its enunciation. With no political validity, it succeeded in cementing the idea that cyberspace *is* an autonomous sphere that *should* be free and accessible.

Barlow's use of the electronic frontier metaphor has captured the minds of those waiting for the revival of the American dream. His vision has become a powerful and pervasive representation which has shaped early understandings of cyberspace. Very few critical commentators would make explicit references to his text, yet many discussions are based on similar propositions. The *imaginaire* has made its way into the mass media and is referenced within academic debates (see Bell, 2001; Jordan, 1999, for a definition of 'Barlovian cyberspace'). This same *imaginaire* also underlays discussions about free speech, right to privacy and resistance to mass surveillance. The *Declaration* thus provided a vision of the virtual space that has persisted and, to a large extent, it is the view that has framed cyberspace as a sphere for direct action.

Powers in Cyberspace

In contrast to Barlow's providential cyberspace, which depicts a new free world, the vision presented by Critical Art Ensemble is a more negative and alarming *imaginaire*. In the introductory chapter of *The Electronic Disturbance*, CAE describes a world where virtuality has become the dominant mode of existence and where society is ruled by a new form of abstract power. As the group declares solemnly:

> The rules of cultural and political resistance have dramatically changed. The revolution in technology brought about by the rapid development of the computer and video has created a new geography of power relations in the first world that could only be imagined as little as 20 years ago: people are reduced to data, surveillance occurs on a global scale, minds are melded to screenal reality, and an authoritarian power emerges that thrives on absence. The new geography is a virtual geography, and the core of political and cultural resistance must assert itself in this electronic space.
>
> (1994: 3)

This introduction to 'The Virtual Condition', as CAE aptly terms it, is in sharp contrast with the utopian interpretations of the digital world. Whilst cyber-enthusiasts such as Barlow argue against state control, CAE rejects the *imaginaire* of an open and autonomous electronic space, to pronounce instead, the failure of digital systems. In many ways, this depiction of the digital world adheres more closely to the type of dystopian narratives developed in cyberpunk literature. Comments about the complete loss of human control and the over-reliance on computerised information seem to bring science-fictional content closer to everyday life. Many of William Gibson's novels feature worlds where people have become socially, economically and sometimes physically, dependent on electronic systems and machines. Often, these digital entities are controlled by powerful and untraceable mega-corporations. In the *Sprawl* fiction trilogy, which includes *Neuromancer*, people have built destructive and inescapable relations with technology, as they spend most of their lives in a virtual reality produced by a digital matrix, which feeds from their addictive tendencies. The matrix is also the super global computer that virtually holds all information ever produced in the history of humanity, while nobody can trace its ownership or control (a theme explored by Hollywood in *The Matrix* movies).

CAE's rationale for portraying the virtual condition as a devastating phenomenon is hinted at in the last sentence of its account, *the core of political and cultural resistance must assert itself in this electronic space*. In one paragraph, the collective lays down its purpose, which is to call for the development of digital direct action. At this stage, one could expect a lengthy discussion of the reasons why resistance should be developed in the digital sphere, but instead, CAE offers another, contradictory statement about this same virtual condition. They suggest that 'The West has been preparing for this moment for 2,500 years' (1994: 3). The explanation is given in the form of short poetry-style narratives that describe the apparent origins of the virtual world. This history however does not date back to the development of digital technologies.

According to CAE, it all began in ancient times:

> I
> 385 B.C.
>
> This artisan is able to make not only all kinds of furniture but also all plants that grow from the earth, all animals including himself and, besides, the earth and the heavens and the gods, all things in heaven and all things in Hades below the earth.
>
> This program is able to make not only all kinds of furniture but also all plants that grow from the earth, all animals, itself, and, besides, the earth and the heavens and the gods, all things in heaven and all things in Hades below the earth.
>
> II
> 60 B.C.
>
> There is no visible object that consists of atoms of one kind only. Everything is composed of a mixture of elements. The more qualities and powers a thing possesses, the greater variety it attests in the forms of its component atoms.
>
> There is no visible object that consists of pixels of one kind only. Everything is a recombinant mixture of representation. The more qualities and powers an image possesses, the greater variety it attests in the forms of its component pixels.

These poetic and playful descriptions go on chronologically, until 1321, making regular references to virtuality and digitality. Although this literary style is a direct reminder of CAE's creative roots, it is also important to grasp the discursive effects of this peculiar interpretation of virtuality.

The 2,500-years timeframe relates approximately to 500 B.C., the European Iron Age that saw the development of iron and steel artisanal crafts and the emergence of new social practices. By establishing a direct relation with this era, CAE effectively retraces the virtual condition to pre-historical times. This clearly echoes the early writings of media critic Howard Rheingold who published, back in the early 1990s, the highly influential book *Virtual Reality.* Amongst other things, Rheingold explained that early crafts and tool-making led to computer technologies. Formulating the startling idea that pre-historical tools and creative cave rituals paved the way to virtuality, Rheingold defends that 'these primitive and effective cyberspaces may have been instrumental in sitting us on the road to computerised world-building in the first place. Tool making was the beginning of the road that led to the opening of cyberspace' (1991: 379).

The main problem with these accounts is that they have promoted a linear reading and understanding of the history of technology. They imply for instance that digital media is the last link in a chronological chain of communication that started with handwriting. The term 'teleology' is used to qualify this type of historical account that considers the development of new media as a direct consequence of past innovations. As Lister *et al* explain:

> In such historical schemas there is often an underlying assumption or implication – which may or may not be openly stated – that new media represent a stage of development that was already present as a potential in other, earlier media forms.
>
> (2003: 46)

Many critics have challenged these narratives, denouncing a deterministic historisation that inevitably requires the dismissal of cases where technological developments have failed (Winston, 1998; Flichy, 1999). In addition, Brian Winston argues that the processes through which certain technologies are accepted or rejected do not respond to a logical or predictable pattern. An important role is played by what he calls 'supervening social necessities' (1998: 6). In other words, society, and people, play a leading part in the recognition or dismissal of technological developments.

In contrast, teleological interpretations tend to bestow some kind of autonomous agency to technology. They assume that technology is always progressing and improving, independently of any social, cultural or political settings. By relating the virtual condition to pre-historic and ancient eras, even if only metaphorically, CAE also infuses the idea that this condition is somehow self-determined and inevitable. As the collective suggests:

> There has always been an idea of the virtual, whether it was grounded in mysticism, abstract analytical thinking, or romantic fantasy. … What has made contemporary concepts and ideologies of the virtual possible is that these preexisting systems of thought have expanded out of the imagination, and manifested themselves in the development and understanding of technology.
>
> (1994: 3)

What emerges from this narrative, is a paradoxical *imaginaire* in which virtuality is the default, inescapable condition, one that *The West has been preparing for*, but also, a condition that is sentencing people to electronic control and oppression. This state of virtuality thus becomes both the cure and the cause. The idea, however, that the virtual environment has always existed, dating back to the beginning of time, makes it difficult to acknowledge the politics of technology. This equates to

Barlow's misconception of cyberspace as a free and autonomous sphere which functions outside of existing power dynamics. As mentioned before, CAE's has a clear reason to assert the supremacy of the virtual space, but this particular *imaginaire* already displays some of the contradictions that will challenge the development of digital direct action.

Alongside the conception of original virtuality, CAE also embraces the representation of cyberspace as a decentralised space. In this sense, its construction resembles the cyberworld Barlow describes in the *Declaration of Independence.* As evidence, the cover of 'Nomadic Power and Cultural Resistance', the second chapter of *The Electronic Disturbance*, welcomes readers to a 'world without borders' (1994: 10), echoing the metaphor of the electronic frontier and the rhizomatic vision of cyberspace. Yet, this version of cyberspace is not free. In comparison to Barlow's attempt to keep authorities out of the digital space, CAE argues that power structures have already relocated and taken control. As they explain, 'The location of power—and the site of resistance—rest in an ambiguous zone without borders. How could it be otherwise, when the traces of power flow in transition between nomadic dynamics and sedentary structures—between hyperspeed and hyperinertia?' (ibid.: 11).

At this point, the group introduces one of its most powerful arguments which exposes the core reason why resistance needs to take place in cyberspace. According to CAE, power has become nomadic and relocated in cyberspace. This concept of 'nomadic power' is borrowed from Deleuze and Guattari's 'Treatise on Nomadology', one of the chapters of *A Thousand Plateaus* (1987). In this book, Deleuze and Guattari describe how early tribes of Scythians adopted a nomadic lifestyle to escape control from the state. By regularly changing their physical location, their nomadism became a means of resistance and opposition to imperial authority. It formed a defensive system that Deleuze and Guattari refer to as 'the war machine' (ibid.: 380). CAE re-appropriates this narrative but reverses it to argue that power elites have redeployed the tactics of nomadic societies to control cyberspace:

> [The] archaic model of power distribution and predatory strategy has been reinvented by the power elite of late capitalism for much the same ends. Its reinvention is predicated upon the technological opening of cyberspace, where speed/absence and inertia/presence collide in hyperreality. The archaic model of nomadic power, once a means to an unstable empire, has evolved into a sustainable means of domination. (1994: 15)

For CAE, this relocation of power in cyberspace requires the development of a new form of resistance within that same space. Yet, a closer reading of Deleuze and Guattari highlights a more nuanced vision of nomadicity, one that foresees the potential limitation of a nomadic resistance:

> One of the fundamental tasks of the State is to striate the space over which it reigns... It is a vital concern of every State not only to vanquish nomadism but to control migrations ... If it can help it, the State does not dissociate itself from a process of capture of flows of all kinds, populations, commodities or commerce, money or capital, etc. (1987: 385–386)

This implies that if the authoritarian powers have indeed relocated in cyberspace, resistance may not be straightforward or undisputed.

The nomadicity of power that CAE identifies relates to the imaginary of cyberspace as a decentralised space. While its representation as an auspicious uncharted territory is based on the metaphor of the electronic frontier, the decentralisation of cyberspace is related to the metaphor of the rhizome. Borrowed again from Deleuze and Guattari, the rhizome represents a system that is 'non-linear; anarchic; nomadic; smooth and deterritorialised' (ibid.: 7–9). Its structure is opposed to that of a tree which is considered to be 'linear; hierarchic; sedentary; striated; and territorialized' (ibid.). One of the main characteristics of the rhizome is its 'a signifying rupture' which implies that it 'may be broken, shattered at a given spot, but it will start up again on one of its old lines or on new lines' (ibid.: 9). It is this particular property that is seen relevant to the internet. In one essay, digital activist and writer, Stephan Wray, affirms that the term 'rhizome' became popular around the same time that Gibson published *Neuromancer*, and that Deleuze and Guattari's theory may have served as 'an important marker in the history of ideas about the rhizomatic nature of cyberspace' (1998a: para. 4). Clearly, the myth of the decentralised network of the internet and its representation as an infinite and indestructible system has remained persistent.[4]

As a case in point, we could consider the internal rhetoric of a short text produced by an enthusiastic critic. Comparing Deleuze and Guattari's rhizomatic model to the internet, Robin Hamman (1996) established that whilst a stand-alone computer could not be considered part of a rhizome, it could become so, once connected to a network of networked computers. Hamman explains that:

> Typically, an Internet user will only have one Internet access account, and thus one entryway on to the Internet. To resolve this problem, I move to a theoretical level. In theory, anyone can set up a computer or server on the Internet which would allow them to create their own access point or node as it [is] called by computer networking professionals. Similarly, anyone can sign up for Internet access with any of the companies that provide such a service. In theory, this resolves the problem of multiple access points, however things do not always work out in the same way that things on a theoretical level would make usbelieve. (Hamman, 1996: para. 14)

Hamman concluded his analysis by stating that the internet does not function as a rhizome for all users, but only for a select few.

Clearly, Deleuze and Guattari's model of the rhizome does not readily fit in with the internet. Hamman's naïve decision to 'move to a theoretical level' illustrates a common eagerness to posit the internet as a decentralised environment. However, this position remains problematic. As hypertext theorist George Landow warns:

> We must take care not to push the similarity too far and assume that [Deleuze and Guattari's] descriptions of rhizome, plateau and nomadic thought map one to one onto hypertext, since many of their descriptions of the rhizome and rhizomatic thought appear impossible to fulfil in any information technology that uses words, images, or limits in any sort. ... The rhizome is essentially a counter paradigm, not something realizable in any time or culture.
>
> (2006: 61–62)

The concept of the rhizome may be a counterparadigm, but like the frontier metaphor, it is a powerful one, which upholds the *imaginaire* of a nomadic and deterritorialised virtual space.

CAE uses this power of representation to describe nomadic power as a 'pool of liquid' which 'thrives on absence' (1994: 13). Unlike sedentary power, nomadic power is never clearly identifiable and at no point in its writing does CAE clarifies the nature of 'power', or its beholders. As the collective defends, 'knowing what to subvert assumes that forces of oppression are stable and can be identified and separated – an assumption that is just too fantastic in an age of dialectics in ruins' (idid.: 12).

Yet for the collective, this challenge should not be considered as a motive for compliance. The point is that socio-political protest needs to be relocated to the virtual space, whether or not power elites can be identified. Since nomadic power has reached global status, the consequence of refusing this relocation will lead to the development of resistance strategies that focus on symbolic and localised representations. For CAE, this is exemplified by the staging of street demonstrations that are 'caught in a historical tape loop of resisting the monuments of dead capital' (ibid.). It is with this argument that the collective thus begins its quest to establish cyberspace as the only possible sphere of political resistance.

In his seminal work, *The Production of Space*, Henri Lefebvre proposes the radical theory that '*(social) space is a (social) product*' (1991: 26, original emphasis). Lefebvre argues that our conception and understanding of space is not restricted to natural science and physics. Instead, space can be understood as a social and cultural production. If we consider cyberspace to be such a production, then its creation is no doubt related to CAE and John Perry Barlow's interpretations, amongst others. The performativity of their literary productions is proven by their lasting influence. Despite many inconsistencies, Barlow's declaration of independence *does* establish cyberspace as a new independent world, and CAE's account of virtuality and nomadic power *does* justify the development of digital direct action, even though, these *imaginaires* are built up on selective and often idealized accounts of technology.

As discussed in the Introduction, however, this performativity is not always planned. As Lefebvre points out, the production of space can easily go unnoticed:

> If it is true that (social) space is a (social) product, how is this fact concealed? The answer is: by a double illusion, each side of which refers back to the other, reinforces the other, and hides behind the other. The two aspects are the illusion of transparency on the one hand and the illusion of opacity, or 'realistic' illusion, on the other. (1991: 27)

With the dominant use of the cyberspace metaphor, it is indeed easy to forget that the virtual world is a discursive construction. In particular, the general acceptance of fictional descriptions assures that cyberspace is not *something*, but is *somewhere*. Turned into a 'place', cyberspace thus becomes intelligible, and can be described as 'free' and 'open'. The produced illusion of transparency constitutes the first element of the 'double illusion' which conceals that cyberspace does not exist *per se*. Instead, it is performed, cited and reiterated through a series of specific science-fictional and technological accounts.

The illusion of opacity which is, paradoxically, 'the illusion of natural simplicity' (ibid.: 29) is the process through which the social space appears natural and instinctive, to the point that its constructedness is not easily conceivable. As Lefebvre explains: 'the illusion of substantiality, naturalness and spatial opacity nurtures its own mythology' (ibid.: 30). This is, again, the performative ability of the many accounts that describe cyberspace as a new frontier or as a dematerialised space. The representation of cyberspace as an infinite, decentralised and deterritorialised place works to consistently conceal its condition as a social product.

As any social product, cyberspace is produced according to specific ideological pursuits. Hence, a close reading of the dominant discourses brings to the forefront the politics and power dynamics embedded in digital technologies. Many of these accounts explain how the virtual space has come to represent a new socio-political sphere, and they also shed light on the many possible outcomes of the conflicts rising between individuals, societies and states.

Conclusion

This chapter has examined the narratives that construct cyberspace as the new stage of social and political action. It focused on the various *cyber-imaginaires* that place digital technology at the centre of society.

Many of these *imaginaires* have been prompted by the development of personal computers and the early virtual communities that formed during the 1970s and 1980s. Encouraged by the potential of open communication and free information, these early groups of internet users conceived a new imaginary. In their vision, digital technology extends their knowledge, social network and new entrepreneurial ideals, but also, improves society as a whole.

The most eloquent example of these utopian *imaginaires* is certainly Barlow's *Declaration of the Independence of Cyberspace*. While it is easy to dismiss this text, its performative functions have been established here. What must be retained is that the dominance of these *cyber-imaginaires* is not arbitrary. It corresponds to a shared desire to construct cyberspace as a new ideal world. The metaphor of the electronic frontier, in particular, has persisted against other interpretations because of the many possibilities it projects onto digital technology. These stories also ignore and reinterpret many contradictions. The electronic frontier rejects the materiality of digital technology and the role played by national governments in the management of infrastructures. The nomadic and rhizomatic metaphors ignore the hierarchisation of communication networks in an attempt to construct a new public sphere. Deconstructing these narratives allows for a better understanding of our relations with technology and our persistent desire for it to address our social deficiencies.

Building on these *cyber-imaginaires*, CAE offers its own interpretation of virtuality, power and resistance. Through a unique account of the virtual condition, the collective describes cyberspace as an environment controlled by an invisible and nomadic power. With this departure from more utopian accounts, CAE establishes the basis for its radical model of virtual resistance, later known as electronic civil disobedience. As with most *imaginaires*, the proposal implies the ignorance, reinterpretation and neutralisation of specific stories about technology, but it also produces a poetical and compelling account of a revolutionary and transformative potential. This ideal will be rapidly taken up by artists and activists alike, but not before the collective further develops its rationale for digital direct action, by bringing the body into resistance.

Notes

1 The US Supreme Court eventually overruled the *Communication Decency Act* on the ground that it violated the First Amendment.

2 In the book, Brockman assigns an alias to each of his respondents. Alsop is 'The Pragmatist'; Barlow is 'The Coyote'; Rheingold 'The Citizen'; Kelly 'The Saint'; Turkle 'The Cyberanalyst' and so on.

3 Jon Postel is sometimes referred to as the 'God of the internet'. From the late 1970s he was the main authority for the design, administration and control of internet protocol numbers.

4 See Jordan (1999: 35) for an account of the erroneous claim that the internet was initially built to survive nuclear attacks.

2 'Little Electronic Shadow'
The Virtual Body

> It's like this little electronic shadow on each and everyone of us, just begging for someone to screw with.
>
> —Angela Bennett

In the 1995 Hollywood movie, *The Net*, the main character Angela Bennett, played by Sandra Bullock, is a computer programmer who uncovers a major security breach during one of her debugging sessions. Having realised that the hack is part of a criminal scheme, Bennett becomes the prey of a mysterious and powerful organisation that is determined to silence her. After failing to murder her, the agency adopts a different approach. They proceed to electronically erase her existence, and Bennett returns from a set-up holiday to find that she no longer exists. Her documents and personal belongings are missing, and she no longer has her car, her house or her bank account. Even her medical records have been deleted and she is now identified as Ruth Marx, a drug addict wanted for murder. Conveniently for the script, Bennett is portrayed as a loner who works exclusively on the internet, from her house, and has no opportunity to make friends. In addition, her only family is a mother who suffers from Alzheimer's and cannot confirm the identity of her daughter. Needless to say, Bennett eventually overturns the situation and recovers her real life and her real identity.

While this movie is a perfect example of the type of techno-paranoia that emerged during the early years of the public internet, it is very far from the usual representations of technological anxiety. In classic dystopian stories, 'imperfect' humans use their resources to build 'perfect' machines that end up taking over the world. This is a very popular theme in science fiction, as exemplified by movies such as *Metropolis*, *The War of the Worlds*, *The Terminator*, *The Matrix*, *I Robot*, and many more. In these apocalyptic productions, humans finally lose control of their electronic creations and become victims of the revengeful machines they themselves created.

By contrast, the type of threat that emerges with the internet is linked to information and communication. The premise is that control is not lost because of robots, but because of the intractable accumulation of digital data. When Ruth Marx, aka Angela Bennett, is arrested for her alleged crimes, she tries to explain to her sceptical lawyer that all of the information they have about her is false:

> Just think about it. Our whole world is sitting there on a computer. It's in the computer, everything: your DMV records, your, social security, your credit cards, your medical records. It's all right there. Everyone is stored in there. It's like this little electronic shadow on each and everyone of us, just begging for someone to screw with, and you know what? They've done it to me, and you know what? They're gonna do it to you.
>
> (*The Net*, 1995)

Bennett has become an early victim of the virtual body, that is, the body made out of electronic data that cannot be controlled but still dictates every aspect of our lives. According to CAE, this is a body which needs to be reclaimed as part of our digital sovereignty: we need to take control of the ways in which our personal information is created, collected and utilised.

This chapter explores the *imaginaire* of this new body as a core justification for digital resistance. While the previous chapter introduced nomadic power as the force behind virtual domination, the focus here is on the concept of the 'body without organs'. Borrowing still from Deleuze and Guattari, CAE presents the data body as the virtual counterpart of accumulated information. The argument is that 'bodies without organs' have taken precedence over us. To counter this new domination, the collective proposes the development of a radical practice named 'recombinant theatre', which can be understood as a recombination of different theatric situations. This new type of theatre related to digital technology effectively reformulates digital direct action as a theatrical practice.

The discussion in this chapter thus provides an analysis of the fictional stories that can be read as initial plays, or scripts, for digital direct action practice. These accounts conceptualise electronic resistance as theatrical performance, and while they suggest a radical shift in the practice of resistance, their focus on the digital body echoes a long tradition of embodied protest, from civil rights movements to contemporary data performances. By introducing the data body, CAE highlights the intrinsic relationship between digital technology and power, and effectively provides a new justification for the development of digital direct action.

Body of Sovereignty

One of the reasons why Angela Bennett consistently fails to prove her identity is because the electronic information available about her has taken precedence. Whether it is at the bank, the embassy, the hospital or the police station, Bennett is faced with the same comments regarding her non-existence: 'it's not on the computer here'; 'according to the computer'; 'the computer shows', 'the computer records'. Despite her objections, nothing she says about herself can override the forged data, and she has no direct means to challenge this new digital identity.

When *The Net* was released, many critics sarcastically focused on the fact that Bennett could order a pizza online, rather than on the issue of data storage and manipulation. Yet, if the story seemed farfetched back then, there are now many instances where digital data has been retrieved and used with little or no supervision.

In 2013, a US local newspaper reported that someone had spent over 2 years trying to rectify a series of false information collected about them. The fictitious data was discovered after the person was denied a bank loan. For years, the credit rating company had accumulated incorrect details about their identity, spending and repayment history. Despite many attempts, none of the data could be accessed or rectified – that is, until the case was brought to court. During the trial, the attorneys argued that the errors were a breach of privacy and had caused their client damage to reputation and a lost opportunity to obtain credit (Gunderson, 2013: para. 4). While the outcome of this particular case was unprecedented (the US court of Oregon awarded USD$18 million in compensatory damages to the plaintiff), the newspaper concluded that thousands of people faced similar situations on a daily basis.

CAE had predicted this use of electronic information for technological control. In *The Electronic Disturbance*, the group introduced the body without organs to describe a digital system that transforms people into 'credit histories, consumer types, patterns and tendencies' (1994: 16). The body without organs, a concept borrowed from Deleuze and Guattari (who themselves borrowed it from Antonin Artaud), is designed to take control over us. It is the virtual counterpart of accumulated information, about our identity, health, education, profession and much more, that is produced, stored and commodified, reducing our existence to electronic data.

The collective illustrates this process through a remarkably playful story about P, a person who is denied a bank loan due to poor credit history:

> Consider the following scenario: A person (P) walks into a bank with the idea of securing a loan. According to the dramaturgical structure of this situation, the person is required to present h/erself as a responsible and trustworthy loan applicant. Being a good performer, and comfortable with this situation, P has costumed h/erself well by wearing clothing and jewelry that indicate economic comfort. P follows the application procedures well, and uses good

> blocking techniques with appropriate handshakes, standing and sitting as socially expected, and so on. In addition, P has prepared and memorized a well-written script that fully explains h/er need for the loan, as well as h/er ability to repay it. As careful as P is to conform to the codes of the situation, it quickly becomes apparent that h/er performance in itself is not sufficient to secure the loan. All that P has accomplished by the performance is to successfully convince the loan officer to interview h/er electronic double. The loan officer calls up h/er credit history on the computer. It is this body, a body of data, that now controls the stage. It is, in fact, the only body which interests the loan officer. P's electronic double reveals that s/he has been late on credit payments in the past, and that she [*sic*] has been in a credit dispute with another bank. The loan is denied; end of performance.
>
> (CAE, 1994: 59)

With this short story, CAE confirms that electronic bodies have taken precedent.

Confronted with the information revealed by the electronic double, the bank officer has no choice but to reject the loan request. Here the collective offers a theatrical account of a very mundane situation. The playfulness of the narration is in the use of a performative terminology, which includes distinct theatrical directions and cues. This suggests that the story could be staged as a play.[1] The performativity also derives from the mundanity of the scenario. Indeed, it would be difficult to deny that such events regularly take place in financial institutions. Nowadays, a bad credit score *will* prevent most people from obtaining bank loans, regardless of how honest or reliable they may appear to be in person. The power of CAE's narrative thus resides in its playful rhetoric. Whether it is read as a theatrical performance or not, the story of P is hard to dismiss.

In his fascinating book, *The Digital Person*, privacy law expert Solove (2004) suggests that while George Orwell's figure of Big Brother is often used in discussions about information and privacy, it is not the most pertinent metaphor. For him, a more accurate comparison can be found in Franz Kafka's novel, *The Trial*. Solove suggests that the aggregation of personal data, also described by CAE, can be considered as a 'digital dossier'. He explains that 'dossiers are used in European courts to assemble information about a person in order to reach a judgment. Today, through the use of computers, dossiers are being constructed about all of us' (ibid.: 1–2). For Solove, however, the notion that these dossiers are created and used to survey and control people in an Orwellian fashion is misguided. This is because the collection of data is not centralised or organised. Instead, each institution, whether private, public or governmental, carries out its own data collection with little transparency and little accountability.

This is why for Solove, Joseph K.'s story is a much more appropriate metaphor to understand the phenomenon:

> In the context of computer databases, Kafka's *The Trial* is the better focal point for the discourse than Big Brother. Kafka depicts an indifferent bureaucracy, where individuals are pawns, not knowing what is happening, having no say or ability to exercise meaningful control over the process. This lack of control allows the trial to completely take over Joseph K.'s life. *The Trial* captures the sense of helplessness, frustration, and vulnerability one experiences when a large bureaucratic organization has control over a vast dossier of details about one's life. At any time, something could happen to Joseph K.; decisions are made based on his data, and Joseph K. has no say, no knowledge, and no ability to fight back. He is completely at the mercy of the bureaucratic process.
>
> (2004: 38)

There is indeed a paradox between our reliance on electronic information and the limited control that we exercise over these digital dossiers.

What is pertinent in Solove's analysis is the interrelation between the many agencies controlling the information. He identifies these as different 'information flows' (ibid.: 3). One flow circulates between large databases that are owned by private companies, another flow comes from governmental public records and a third flow is the combination of the previous two. This last flow redirects information to law enforcement agencies. The more information is accumulated, the less people can access and control it. Yet, more information also implies more power to control and surveil.

Solove makes a salient case regarding public records, suggesting that this source alone provides a considerable amount of personal data, including, addresses, phone numbers, ages, names of family members, legal records, political affiliations, voting patterns and financial information (ibid.: 4). Most of this data is made accessible to the public, especially through the internet. It is accessible to private companies that retrieve it in order to capitalise on it. The aberration is that individuals who request access to this information are often required to pay. What is more, the task of those who dare to question the data, data which in many cases was collected without their consent or even knowledge, resembles the senseless quest of Joseph K.

CAE's vision of the body without organs, a body made out of data, signals this new form of control. This vast accumulation of information is only made possible through computers. For the collective, this new paradigm is having a radical impact on society. It indicates the loss of authority and sovereignty. The idea that people have become submissive to their electronic counterparts confirms that the virtual condition has become authoritarian. The digital revolution that was meant to empower us is actually generating a deep sense of insecurity and powerlessness.

The discourse can sound alarmist and exploitative of a technological anxiety, but it also draws attention to the dominant tropes used to surveil people. As CAE argues:

> According to the political right, the individual must surrender h/er sovereignty to state power. From the point of view of the left, the individual must submit to enriched repression. In each case, the individual loss of sovereignty is crucial. The authoritarians regard this loss as positive—the beneficent state provides the individual with security and order in exchange for h/er obedience...the differences between the two stem from their opposite interpretations of this act of surrender.
>
> (1994: 129–130)

Unwittingly or not, many governments have used the *imaginaire* of the digital identity to enforce new legislations. For example, in the early 2000s the so-called practice of identity theft was turned into a growing social and economic concern. In 2006, an estimate from the UK Home Office stated that the cost of identity fraud had reached £1.7 billion ($3.4 billion) (Home Office UK, 2010). Governments reacted by providing information about this new type of crime, and legal actions were taken against digital thefts. Meanwhile, financial institutions were setting up premium insurance schemes that offered customers protection against possible fraud. In addition, the UK Home Office created a dedicated website, identity-theft.org.uk, which contained information about the diversity of identity crimes and the means to protect oneself.

On the website, visitors were informed that their 'identity is valuable' and that they should 'not become a victim'. Yet, a closer look at the 'identity theft' narrative shows that the concept has been ill-defined. Many of these official definitions describe the practice as the misuse of personal data and information, including names, birth dates and home addresses. While identity is not a straightforward term to define, it would be reasonable to state that attributes such as gender, age, birthplace or occupation do not alone determine identity. Thus, the stealing here is not of someone's identity but of someone's personal data. Yet, as currently articulated, the notion of identity theft tends to produce a greater sense of personal threat by conflating personal data with identity. In this confusion, the solution is to diligently follow official instructions or pay for protection.

It is worth mentioning that by now, the official use of the term 'identity theft' has been discarded, and the UK website no longer exists. Similarly, most financial institutions have discontinued their protection schemes. Yet, our reliance on electronic information increases as fast as, if not faster than, our knowledge and control over the systems.

In a moment of great despair, Angela Bennett questions the reasons behind her ordeal and why her private life had been so deeply infiltrated:

> I just don't understand. Why me? I am nobody. I am nothing. But they knew everything about me. They knew what I ate, what I drank, what movies I watched. They knew where I was from. They knew what cigarettes I used to smoke. And everything they did, they must have watched it on the internet.
>
> (*The Net*, 1995)

Two decades ago, the story would have been considered as a classic case of paranoia. Today, it has become common practice and the internet is indeed the primary source of data collection.

CAE foresaw the effects of this uncontrollable accumulation of data, and in this regard, their prediction is difficult to challenge:

> Information on spending patterns, political associations, credit histories, bank records, education, lifestyles, and so on is collected and cross-referenced by political-economic institutions, to control our own destinies, desires, and needs. This information cannot be accessed, nor can we really know which institutions have it, nor can we be sure how it is being used.
>
> (1994: 131)

The point is not only that we are being reduced to data, we also cannot easily access or control this data. We have consequently lost our digital sovereignty, that is, our ability to have a say about the ways in which our personal data is accumulated and used. Our right to privacy should protect us from the production of these electronic doubles but this right is mostly circumvented. This is why, for CAE, 'extraction of power from the individual by the state is to be resisted. Resistance itself is the action which recovers or expands individual sovereignty, or conversely, it is those actions which weaken the state' (1994: 130). Thus, the only solution is to recover authority over these virtual bodies, by controlling and monitoring the process of their creation.

The decision to reclaim sovereignty echoes Barlow's call for self-governance. There is a distinct alignment between the *imaginaire* of a virtual state and the *imaginaire* of virtual sovereignty, but it also presents similar limitations. CAE does not elaborate on the context within which the electronic bodies emerge. In their account, the digital double stands alone, as if autonomous and self-motivated. Yet, it is important to remember that electronic machines are used by some people to have authority on other people. Going back to the case of performer P, it should be clear that the virtual body which takes precedence does not appear from nowhere. These data bodies are created by the banks in order to control and regulate the way people access funds. In many ways, it seems more appropriate to directly confront those in charge and challenge this use of data.

However, the main objective of CAE is elsewhere. The conception of the body without organs works as an effective justification for relocating direct action in cyberspace. For the group, a direct confrontation with economic and political institutions is not a viable strategy. Since domination is virtual, resistance should also be virtual. This discourse certainly capitalises on some form of technological anxiety but as a rationale for radical direct action it functions as an appealing proposal.

Body of Performance

Since electronic bodies have taken precedent over people, the only solution is to regain control over them. The tactic proposed by CAE is to hack into electronic databases. The project is described in detail in 'The Recombinant Theater and the Performative Matrix', the fourth chapter of *The Electronic Disturbance*. Similar to the story of performer P, the hack is presented as a hypothetical scenario that promises entertaining chaos and confusion:

> Consider the following scenario: A hacker is placed on stage with a computer and a modem. Working under no fixed time limit, the hacker breaks into data bases, calls up h/er files, and proceeds to erase or manipulate them in accordance with h/ er own desires. The performance ends when the computer is shutdown.
>
> (CAE, 1994: 62)

Again here, CAE frames the resistance as a theatrical performance which, 'albeit oversimplified, signifies the heart of electronic disturbance' (ibid.).

In a sequel story, the performer operates a gender modification as part of the hack. CAE explains that: 'the hacker is also a female to male cross-dresser. In the performance she accesses h/er identification files, and changes the gender data to "male." S/he leaves the stage, and begins a performance of gender selection on the street' (ibid.: 63). The hacker now wanders the streets topless and when s/he is stopped by the police, an identity check confirms that the performer is male. As a result, s/he cannot be arrested since 'it is not illegal for a man to go shirtless' (ibid.: 64). The concepts of virtual resistance and digital sovereignty are clearly articulated within a performative and theatrical discourse. This corresponds to CAE's concept of a recombinant theatre. This radical theatre can be understood as the abstract and performative stage that operates between three different spaces. The first is the 'traditional theatre', that is the type of theatre that refers to the performance of a scripted play. The second is the 'theatre of everyday life' which may refer to any daily activity or practice inscribed in social life. The third one is the 'virtual theatre', which is more directly connected to digital technology. Recombinant theatre functions as a combination of these three theatres.

To have a better understanding of how this works, we can reconsider the bank loan scenario. In the script, performer P uses formal attires and behaviours to apply for a loan but these attributes have no impact on the outcome of the request. This is determined by the credit history retrieved from electronic data. The three types of theatre are embedded in this performance. The interaction between P and the bank clerk functions as part of a traditional theatre. Two performers are placed on a stage and enact the scenario of a bank loan request. This play can be seen as the performance of a common activity, which is considered part of the theatre of everyday life. The third theatre emerges when one of the performers, the bank clerk, conducts an electronic credit check. At this point the story becomes a virtual theatre, one where P and the bank clerk no longer have command.

While they may have reasonable control over the first two theatres, the virtual theatre gives them no power. Neither of them can control or contest the outcome of the electronic request. It is this absence of control that signals the loss of sovereignty. For CAE, this space can only be reclaimed through computer hacking, or a 'postmodern theater of resistance' which utilises 'interlocking recombinant stages that oscillate between virtual life and everyday life' (ibid.: 65).

This account of a resistant theatre is even more fascinating if we consider the link between virtuality and theatre that was first made by French playwright Antonin Artaud. There is no doubt that Artaud's manifesto for a radically new theatre directly influenced CAE's recombinant theatre. In his seminal text, *Theatre and its Double*, Artaud repudiates traditional theatre and calls for the development of plays that generate a new type of 'theatre that wakes us up: nerves and heart' (1958: 84). The term he uses for this is 'theatre of cruelty', a theatre that should present immediate and violent action (ibid.). Artaud also makes the first reference to virtuality, as the condition through which radical theatre can create what is not, and what is impossible:

> The theater also takes gestures and pushes them as far as they will go…it reforges the chain between what is and what is not, between the virtuality of the possible and what already exists in materialized nature…. The theatre restores us as our dormant conflicts and all their powers, and gives these powers names we hail as symbols: and behold! before our eyes is fought a battle of symbols, one charging against another in an impossible melee; for there can be theatre only from the moment when the impossible really begins and when the poetry which occurs on the stage sustains and superheats the realized symbols.
> (1958: 27–28)

While this description is evidently far from any of our technological representations of virtuality, its reference to symbols and symbolic practice that produce a new type of reality is striking. For the playwright, this virtuality, which takes place in the midst of both internal conflicts as well as external power struggles, cannot be devoid of creative and poetic gestures. This is effectively CAE's recombinant theatre. As suggested here, it is the theatre that will wake us up:

> It is time to develop strategies that strike at virtual authority. As yet, there are none. Performers have been too mired in the traditional theater and the theater of everyday life to even realize how the virtual world acts as the theater of final judgment ... New theaters should tell the viewer how to resist authority, regardless of its source along the political continuum. If we seek liberation through the control of our images, performance should illustrate resistant processes and explicitly show how to achieve autonomy, however temporary it might be.
> (CAE, 1994: 64–66)

The process of liberation is the recovery of digital sovereignty. Through virtual performance, people should have access to the theatre which controls their virtual body: 'greater freedom in the theatre of everyday life can be obtained, once the virtual theatre is infiltrated' (ibid.: 63). The virtual theatre is therefore the sphere of resistance, whilst the body is the stake of digital direct action.

It is not surprising that the body turns out to be the focus of electronic resistance. After all, the notion of body sovereignty has been the raison d'être of most social movements for at least two centuries. Whether humanist, feminist, civil, or environmentalist, many activist movements have emerged to claim freedom from social oppression, but also, to assert people's right to control their own body and their existence. This is still a primary concern across the world as resistance and protest do not happen in the absence of bodies. As feminist theorist Margaret McClaren rightly declares:

> What besides bodies can resist? It is my body that marches in demonstrations, my body that goes to the polls, my body that attends rallies, my body that boycotts, my body that strikes, my body that participates in work slowdowns, my body that engages in civil disobedience. Individual bodies are requisite for collective political action. Whether engaging in the macropolitics of collective struggle, or in the micropolitics of individual resistance, it is bodies that resist.
> (2002: 116)

This question has drawn attention to the role of bodies and body tactics in social and political activism, and more and more studies are examining the performativity of the body in resistance.

Unlike many studies suggesting a distinction between social actions where the body is the main focus and actions where the body is a tool for protest,[2] the intrinsic relationship between bodies and resistance unravels when considering the question of performativity. Choreographer and dance scholar Susan Leigh Foster provides an original reading of historical protests in relation to the physicality of resistant bodies. In *Choreography of Protest*, Foster (2003) challenges the distinction often made, in social movement studies, between symbolic action and physical intervention. She argues for an interpretation of the body as being capable of 'both persuasion and obstinate recalcitrance' (2003: 395). Using the case of the lunch-counter sit-ins during the 1960s US Civil Rights movements, Foster establishes how bodies performed non-cooperation through a series of rehearsed procedures, developing into what she terms 'recalcitrant physicality' – that is, a physicality which 'refuses to comply with the bodies of those in positions of authority (ibid.: 396).

One of the most documented lunch-counter protests was the Greensboro sit-ins that took place in Greensboro, North Carolina, in 1960. In February, four black students sat at the 'white only' lunch counter of the Woolworth store waiting to be served. Although they were asked to leave and were never attended to, the men remained seated until closing time, only to return the next day to perform another sit-in. The Greensboro protest was not the first of this kind, but its resonance and media coverage rapidly provoked other lunch-counter protests throughout the Southern United States.

What is relevant is that these protest events were carefully orchestrated. Protesters received advice on how to stage the sit-ins and many undertook special training. Foster explains that protocols were developed to limit potential violence but also to help activists control their own behaviour. In order to engage in lunch-counter protests, participants strived to 'sit upright and never talk back or laugh at those around them ... above all, they aspired to meet all threats and acts of violence toward them with a stoic, non-compliant non-action' (ibid.: 399). Many had been encouraged to attend workshops where they could practice role-play as protesters and aggressors.

During these training sessions, they would learn to protect themselves and others from beating, using their own bodies, and they would also practice how not to strike back. Hence, these bodies that seemed to passively engage in everyday life activities, such as ordering drinks at a lunch counter, were in fact involved in careful, but nevertheless dangerous, performances of resistance.

In his detailed analysis of role-play training directed to Black protesters, Hohle (2009) describes how activists were taught to become 'good citizens' by controlling their bodies and emotions. He argues that the black Civil Rights movement 'deracialized ideas of good American citizenship by disassociating black stereotypes from black citizenship (2009: 284).

This took place 'through shaping bodily postures and embodied affective responses while engaged in civic performances' (ibid.). According to Hohle, the deracialisation of citizenship disconnected ideas of whiteness from good citizenship and allowed the embodiment of the 'good black citizen', a process that was central to the passage of the Civil Rights Acts and the Voting Rights Act (ibid.).

In the citizenship school training offered by groups such as the Committee on Racial Equality (CORE) or the Southern Christian Leadership Conference (SCLC), the taught techniques focused on the control of bodily postures and the management of emotions. The idea was that by displaying good manners, black activists could challenge the stereotypes that associated them with irrationality, violence and danger. For Hohle, 'the social movements learn to stylize bodily gestures, postures, grammar, and physical appearances to construct and project idealized citizenship' (ibid.: 287). By doing this, the movements 'attempt to overcome the limits imposed on the body by using and manipulating civic norms' (ibid.: 286).

These training sessions often involved the use of manuals and workbooks, such as the SCLC *Citizenship Workbook*, or Oppenheimer and Lackey's *Manual for Direct Action*. These documents provided detailed explanations on the postures and behaviour to adopt in direct protest. As Hohle explains:

> The manual emphasized: (1) bodily postures; and (2) training the body on the best way to absorb physical punishment. First, when marching or picketing, participants must appear neat and orderly at all times by exhibiting the proper postures when picketing. "Expect participants to walk erectly and not slouch, call out, laugh loudly, or use profanity; smoking may be ruled out in some situations" (Oppenheimer and Lackey, 1965: 75). The embodied performance of picketing linked the demonstration with good citizenship. While picketing, bad bodily postures like slouching, improper language, and volume of speaking should be limited because it represented the disorganized, sloppy, and uncommitted bad citizen.
>
> (ibid.: 294)

The fact that protesters were following rehearsed scenarios of resistance that involved learnt bodily postures means that the body was not used as a *tool* for protest, it was the protest itself. In the case of the lunch-counter sit-ins, resistance occurred not because of the action of requesting a service but because of the bodies that were making the requests. The four black students were engaging in actions that were forbidden only to them, and only through a bodily performance that rejected prejudices could they challenge the ban.

Trying to establish the theatricality of these practices could result in an excessive decontextualisation, and yet the performative elements are difficult to dismiss, first, because this type of social movements challenges the typical representation of protest as an impulsive and chaotic gathering of mobs, and second, because these events closely followed a script-like organisation which resulted in staged resistance. In many ways, CAE's theatricalisation of digital resistance is inscribed in this legacy of performative protest, albeit in a more self-referential and playful mode.

One way to further grasp this theatricality is perhaps through the work of Guevara (2008), which analyses environmental protest in Nicaragua. In 2005, thousands of plantation workers demonstrated in the streets of the Nicaraguan capital, Managua, to alert public opinion of the fatal consequences of farming chemicals. Most protesters were survivors or family members of the victims of the deadly pesticide Nemagón. This substance which was banned in the United States in the 1970s was still being used by multinational companies in many developing countries, causing farmers illness and death.

In his article entitled 'Pesticide, Performance, Protest: Theatricality of Flesh', Guevara explores the interrelation between bodies, social violence and theatricality. The author describes the series of protests which took place in Nicaragua, and consisted in slow marches of hundred-plus kilometres where victims displayed their distressed and damaged bodies:

> Afflicted by excessive weight loss, loss of fingernails and hair, they carry their pain vociferously and prominently. These haematoma-covered bodies are affected by nemagón ... Covered in dust and tired they narrate with their bodies a continuous theatricality of flesh. They penetrate the city space and the unconscious space of its citizens. What do they want? Who are they?
>
> (Guevara, 2008: 2–6)

Guevara considers the theatricality of these protests as a way of representing a social issue. For him, the protesters 'wield their suffering flesh as theatrical weapons' (ibid.: 1), with the intention of activating audiences's reaction and action. In this context, theatricality can be understood as a form of non-verbal spectacle where bodies are experienced as political, and in this case, tragic performances.

Not unlike the lunch-counter protesters, the victims of Nemagón rejected the dominant social norms and civic practices around bodily presence. They placed themselves in proscribed bodily states, within unwelcoming spaces. Faced with rejection and indifference they proceeded to display their suffering, using ownership of their bodies as a last demonstration of power. Yet, they did not subvert their bodies in order to resist; theirs were the subversive body. Similar to the black students, their bodies were the protest itself. The explicit exposure of the inflicted physical, social and political violence is what makes the theatricality of the protest palpable.

If the theatricalisation of protest still needs to be demonstrated, then the work of the activist movement that emerged during the 1980s and 1990s global health crisis is exemplary. At the centre of the social upheaval was ACT UP, a US advocacy group created to raise awareness of the AIDS crisis. Formed in 1987, The AIDS Coalition to Unleash Power (ACT UP) dedicated itself to challenging the slow response of medical and governmental bodies to the AIDS pandemic. In particular, they aimed to confront the dominant discourse that amalgamated the disease with the gay community. Central to ACT UP's activism was the development of radical action and theatrical performances. In her early analysis, Alisa Solomon (1998) explains that the campaign actually started on stage, with the first actions taking place as part of the theatrical productions of playwrights William Hoffman and Larry Kramer. The theatre community was severely hit with many of its members dying of AIDS, leading Larry Kramer to form ACT UP.

Initially starting with street blockades and demonstrations, ACT UP went on to stage highly rehearsed theatre performances, with the aim of drawing public and media attention. Solomon describes one of these actions, known as 'die-ins', which became the organisation's trademark form of protest:

> Every 32 minutes – the rate at which an American dies of AIDS – one group of demonstrators cuts through the incessant chanting with shrill air-raid whistles and falls 'dead' to the pavement. Another affinity group made up of people with AIDS collapses to the ground beneath cardboard tombstones reading, 'I needed aerosol pentamadine' (a drug that treats pneumocystis pneumonia, an opportunistic disease common to people with AIDS). 'AZT wasn't enough', another tombstone explains. 'Buried by the System', adds yet one more. Of more than 1000 protesters, nearly 180 are arrested. They go limp and are dragged off, just as they rehearsed it.
>
> (1998: 45)

Kramer confirms that the actions were akin to enormous production shows, 'we're divided into committees doing banners, logistics, media, just like a producer would hire people for scenery, costumes, publicity' (*cited in* Solomon, ibid.).

Alongside the strategic performances, ACT UP activists also performed provocative actions which aimed to confront heterosexual norms. One was known as 'kiss-ins', an action that involves activist couples engaging in same-sex kissing in public spaces, including shopping malls and government buildings. Christiansen and Hanson (1996) explain in their discussion of the tragic and comic frames of ACT UP's activism, that most performances made it clear that many protesters were gay. The kiss-ins, however, were part of a strategy that specifically challenged the 'powerful social norms that all evidence of homosexuality must be kept hidden and that homosexuals do not have the same privileges as heterosexuals to express publicly their love for one another' (ibid: 166).

In the direct legacy of the civil rights movements, activists positioned themselves in forbidden spaces, and undertook forbidden activities. Yet, these actions were forbidden only to them. The activists attracted attention by performing the banal action of kissing in a public space, but their homosexual bodies and beings changed these actions into moral and social transgressions. Hence, resistance happened through the mere visibility of these people that had been excluded from public view. As Solomon deduces, 'for the large percentage of ACT UP members who are gay, simply saying so aloud in this homophobic culture is a political act (1998: 47). This realisation will lead, later on, to the formulation of the now famous chanting slogan of Queer Nation, 'We're here, we're queer, get used to it!'.

All of these examples illustrate that the body rarely functions as an instrument for socio-political dissent. To rephrase a famous statement, the body is not the medium, it is the message. Under the lens of a performative reading, claims that bodies can be involved in protest that are 'not about bodies' become harder to sustain. Indeed, when can it be declared that a protest is not about bodies or body issues? Yet, the question takes on a new meaning when resistant bodies are not made of flesh and organs, but of bits of electronic data.

Body of Resistance

The idea that bodies of accumulated data could be controlling our life still sounds fictional. While virtuality is gradually taking precedence, the electronic body remains mostly invisible in this process. The reason for this is because our *imaginaire* of the human-machine interaction is based on the belief in a biological and organic relationship with technology.

In his seminal paper *Man-Computer Symbiosis,* written in 1960, psychologist and computer scientist JCR Licklider presented his project for human and computers. His hope was that:

> In not too many years, human brains and computing machine will be coupled together very tightly, and that the resulting partnership will think as no human brain has ever thought and process data in a way not approached by the information–handling machine we know today.
> (1960: para. 2)

With its unique interpretation of the future relations between humans and machines, the essay became central to the study of cybernetics. Licklider describes how machines should be constructed to facilitate a corporal fusion with humans. Predicting that computers would eventually perform intellectual tasks more effectively than humans, he advocates for a symbiotic approach to tackle the challenges. As he explains, 'a symbiotic cooperation, if successful in integrating the positive characteristics of men and computers, would be of great value' (ibid.: para. 17). The only trial that Licklider identifies in his grand scheme is the differences in speed and language between humans and machines, differences that would need to be addressed if the fusion were to be successful.

While this post-war prediction is still awaited for, the *imaginaire* of the physical fusion between humans and machines has become popular. The best representation of this concept is the cyborg: the organism constituted of both biological and artificial components.[3] As always, science-fiction has helped laying the grounds of this new entity. Many of the fictional characters that could be considered as cyborgs all resorted to the symbiotic fusion with machines as a means to survive. For example, in the famous TV series *The Six Million Dollar Man*, former astronaut Steve Austin was rescued from a certain death by having his body combined with electronic components. The same thing goes for professional tennis player Jaime Sommers from *The Bionic Woman,* police officer Alexander James Murphy from the motion picture *Robocop*, or police detective Del Spooner in *I, Robot.* These early cyborgs were all victims of serious accidents that necessitated the introduction of electronic devices into their bodies. Unlike Licklider's conception, the symbiosis fusion was initially justified for medical treatments.

The aesthetical decision to introduce artificial elements in human organisms becomes more recurrent in dystopian novels. For instance, many characters of Gibson's novels, *Neuromancer*, *Comte Zero,* or *Idoru,* have come to implant electronic machines into their bodies to enhance their physical appearance or physiological abilities. This is how they also become cyborgs. In these stories, the use of electronic devices is not so much for medical reasons as it is to address the inherent limitations of a decaying body. When it is conceptualised in opposition to the mind, the body quickly becomes an impediment. While the mind is perceived as having infinite functions and capacities, the body of flesh is the constant reminder, and ultimate vessel, of death. This preoccupation is at core of the science-fictional concept of uploaded consciousness. Mind transfer, or the uploading of consciousness, is the theory that human brains can be relocated onto computer devices that can reproduce the activity of the brain. The belief is that we can continue to live through computers without the need of our organic bodies. In *Neuromancer*, Case's final mission is completed with the help of a former hacker, Dixie Flatline, whose brain was retrieved post-mortem and transferred into an electronic console.

The same principle is explored in the renewed version of television series *Battlestar Galactica*. Although technically not humans, the Cylons have developed the technology to endlessly download their consciousness whenever their physical body is destroyed. The uploading of consciousness thus renders the physical body replaceable, or altogether obsolete. This separation between mind and body is embedded in the conception of a virtual world. As a reminder, Barlow's *Declaration of Independence* refers to cyberspace as 'the new home of mind', a world where 'there is no matter', and where 'identities have no bodies' (1996: para. 1–10). Of course, Barlow's conception of an immaterial and bodiless cyberspace is part of his attempt to reject governments, by disconnecting virtual and material worlds. Here again, digital technology is perceived as the solution to human deficiency, and in this case, to mortality. Like a religious discourse that promises eternal life to devoted followers, the *imaginaire* of uploaded consciousness feeds into the perpetual quest for immortality.

With this dominant *imaginaire*, it seems difficult to conceive that the threat of technological domination can come from the endless production of digital data. Yet, this is the point raised by CAE:

> The body without organs is the perfect body—forever reproducible. No reduction to biology now. (...) the body without organs is free to drift in the electronic rhizome. (...) The electronic body, free of the flesh, free of the economy of desire, has escaped the pain of becoming.
>
> (1994: 72–73)

By suggesting that data bodies are ruling, the collective implies that our physical selves have become redundant and that our value resides in the digital information created about us.

In 2010, media artist Dave Kemp presented his piece *Data Collection* as part of an exhibition entitled *Sorting Daemons: Art, Surveillance Regimes and Social Control*. For the project, Kemp collected the personal information of about 100 people in the form of identification cards. These included driving licences, staff cards, student cards, store cards and credit cards. For each person participating in the project, the artist photographed the IDs into a single image which was later enlarged and displayed on the walls of the gallery space. The enlargements were done so that the information on the cards was readable to the viewers, including full names, date of birth, addresses and credit card numbers. Kemp (2009) explains that his goal was to challenge the common notion of privacy and draw attention to data collection and databases related to identification cards. The artist refers to Solove's concept of the digital person to explore people's awareness of data aggregation, but also their power to control these processes.

As part of the project, participants were required to sign a consent form and could decide to remove any identification cards they did not want to see displayed in public. These missing cards were represented by a black placeholder card with the word 'withheld' written on it. Kemp stated that this approach was a way for people to remain in control of their personal information, with the power to release and retrieve data. The project clearly attempted to show the effects of having one's personal data publicly available. The photographs openly suggest the end of individual privacy. While the participants gave their consent for the information to be displayed, there is a realisation that this transparency does not happen in everyday life. The ID cards represent the visible practice of data collection and accumulation, but they also raised awareness of other, invisible, data collection processes.

At the end, Kemp's approach conforms with CAE's vision. Since data gathering cannot be stopped, the only solution is to gain control over the process. What is missing from this creative project is perhaps a sense that unmonitored data collection actually poses a bigger problem, in particular, the risk of using bodies of data to control and discipline people. The assumption is that if we clearly understood the extent of these data collection practices we would not so readily disregard them, or worse, consent to them.

In his theorisation of power and control, Foucault (1977) identifies the body as a central element in the exercise of surveillance and discipline. His argumentation begins with the acknowledgement of the gradual disappearance of corporate punishment within the 18th-century criminal justice system. However, he soon describes how modern systems have re-appropriated the body to create new techniques of subjugation. This new modality of control is based on the production of docile bodies. As an illustration, Foucault refers to the 17th-century soldier easily recognisable from his so-called natural strength, courage and pride. The same soldier could also be identified from his unique bodily posture and presence, described as 'a lively, alert manner, an erect head, a taut stomach, broad shoulders, long arms, strong fingers, a small belly, thick thighs, slender legs and dry feet' (Louis de Montgomery *cited in* Foucault, ibid.: 135). Yet, by the end of the 18th century, the soldier was no longer a predetermined figure. Instead, he could be made out of any individual, through subjugation, transformation and improvement, turning into a docile body (ibid.: 136).

Foucault further explains that this production of docile bodies takes place through the development of various disciplinary practices. These techniques, or 'disciplines', are meant to control and monitor movements of the body. The aim is to maximise the economic and labour potential of the individual, through a mixture of control and coercion. As he clarifies 'the body becomes a useful force only if it is both a productive body and a subjected body' (ibid.: 26). Examples of these disciplinary systems are varied but they include authoritative institutions such as the army, the school, the hospital or the prison. Another aspect is that the instruments of discipline do not need to be complex. They include hierarchical observation, normalising judgement and systematic examination. Accordingly, the process requires:

> A mechanism that coerces by means of observation; an apparatus in which the techniques that make it possible to see induce effects of power, and in which, conversely, the means of coercion make those on whom they are applied clearly visible.
>
> (Foucault, 1977: 171)

By introducing the data body, CAE isolates a new form of disciplinary practice. Alongside the prison, the hospital or the school, the virtual space brings its own reformulation of docile bodies. Considering the scenario of the bank loan once more, we can see how the electronic body functions as an instrument of control in a Foucauldian sense. The aggregation of personal details, attributes and patterns is the result of a hierarchical and systematic observation. There is also a process of normalisation whereby people are aware that they have to meet specific criteria, or provide specific information to access services. The electronic double therefore operates as a disciplinary tool. It clearly signals that rewards will be based on the performance of the digital body. Those who fail to comply will be rejected from the system as in the case of performer P. This process of psychological coercion may be internalised, but the practice is as powerful as it is visible. All good citizens, or in this case good clients, are aware that their digital counterparts will need to demonstrate appropriate behaviour within controlled environments.

As discussed previously, opposition takes place when individuals or social groups reject the disciplinary methods that would want to keep them docile. Resistance often comes from those who suffer the most from the coercion, as the black students of Greensboro's lunch-counter sit-in, who put their bodies in forbidden spaces, or the Nicaraguan victims of industrial poisoning, who displayed their unsightly wounds to reluctant spectators. Similarly tactics that aim to resist the dominance of the digital body have emerged.

In 2002, Bangladesh-American media artist Hasan Elahi was detained by the FBI while travelling back to the United States. The story goes that US authorities had mistakenly put his name on a terrorist watch list, following the attacks of September 11. After hours of interrogation, Elahi was allowed to complete his journey, but from this point, he decided to inform the FBI of all his travelling plans. This lasted for six months, until Elahi decided that since the agency was monitoring his life, he could facilitate their task by providing detailed information about his daily activities. What initially started as close surveillance became an art project. The artist began to track himself and meticulously register all of his moves by taking pictures. At first, he would send the information to the

FBI agents that were monitoring him. He later built a website, Tracking-Transience.net, dedicated to the archiving of his life.

In one interview, Elahi explains his idea of countering the FBI surveillance programme by providing the information himself. For him, 'the best way to protect privacy is to give it away' (Thompson, 2007: para. 5). He therefore photographed every aspects of his life: the places he visited, the food he ate, the things he bought, the dishes he cooked, and even the public toilets he used. Over the years, the image gallery expanded to reach almost 70,000 images. In addition, Elahi placed a GPS device on himself and, to this day, visitors to his website can see his geographical location live, using Google Maps.

According to the artist, the server logs of his website show that several governmental institutions have accessed the site, including the FBI, the CIA, and the Pentagon (Elahi, 2014). Yet, he contends that his art project simultaneously reveals everything and nothing about his life. The artwork is a tactic to counter-surveillance; it is a strategy of information overflow that could become more effective, if everyone engaged in it.

This is far from CAE's radical proposal of hacking performances, and yet, Hasan Elahi's project does fit into the concept of a virtual theatre of resistance. By displaying detailed accounts of his every movement, the artist offers the perfect docile body. Making this virtual body available to all, including the government, also allows him to turn tables; Elahi is able to surveil his surveillance. A power shift occurs as the artist carefully chooses the information he releases. It may seem that every moment of his life is on display but the data provided is not random.

Instead, the images represent the theatrical staging of his life. As Elahi himself explains:

> While I'm perfectly fine opening up every aspect of my personal life to the public, I'm still aware that I'm only telling one part of the story… Most of the images here are of empty, desolate, and at times outright depressing surroundings. That is not to say that I am never around any people or that I don't spend any time in festive situations. What the viewer doesn't see is what's going on the other side of the camera—and that's a very deliberate decision on my part.
> (2014: para. 3–4)

This type of digital activism is clearly appealing, especially because of its playful renegotiation of surveillance practices. One advantage of Elahi's performance is that it does not raise immediate ethical or legal questions. The information released is his own, none of the images features other people, nor do they contain confidential details. In addition, the project is easily replicable. To this extent, it could be argued that our current use of social media platforms and applications encourages similar, but perhaps apolitical, practices of self-exhibition and self-surveillance.

On the one hand, self-exhibition takes place through a constant distribution and circulation of data that could at first be considered as private, such as personal details, addresses, relationships, images, posts and so on. On the other hand, self-monitoring, and group surveillance, occur through the public viewing of this circulation of data, as well as the sanctioning of this data through peer recognition and approval.

Yet, processes of control and surveillance become most problematic when undertaken by external entities. In one almost science-fictional story, journalists recently recounted how a US insurance company had used electronic data from 'satellites, social media and even cigarette sales at gas stations to help identify risks and build up customer profiles' (Gould, 2014: para. 1). The financial company based its decision on the assumption that 'smokers typically buy only one pack of cigarettes at a time, very often from petrol stations' (ibid.) As one insurance officer defended:

> If you know from your technology that somebody goes to the gas station once a day, including the weekends, it might be right that (that person) is a smoker. Unless someone is driving 360 miles (579 kilometres) a day to their job, there is no reason to stop for petrol every day, so it might be a reason to enquire further.
>
> (ibid.: para. 14–15)

In this instance, the electronic body, created from an unsuspected collection of digital data, fulfilled its duty, providing information on each and every movement and life events. The story reminds of the practice of credit check companies, but also of the tribulations of Joseph K, or anyone becoming victim of these conflations. Without transparency, the consequences of these misappropriations can only be imagined, since cases are rarely made public.

Unfortunately, this case is not isolated, quite the contrary. The spectacular revelations in 2013 of the global surveillance programme set up by the US National Security Agency are an edifying confirmation of the wrongful use of data collection and information processing. CAE predicted these derelictions two decades ago, by identifying a loss of control and the need to claim digital sovereignty. This process effectively requires that people have a say over the regulation and use of digital information, including freedom of expression, as well as the right to privacy. Yet, most digital activists would argue that none of these rights are currently protected. Moreover, governments and corporations are keen to enforce further digital surveillance and data mining practices, which suggests that unless strong objections are voiced, these rights will escape us even further.

Like the unfortunate character of *The Net*, Angela Bennett, we have become submissive to the demands of our digital counterpart. Unlike

Bennett, however, we have currently no direct means to regain authority over these virtual bodies. Resistance projects of artists such as Hasan Elahi and David Kemp certainly prove that we cannot minimise the extent to which data affect our daily life, and perhaps even our very existence. Digital sovereignty is our right to have authority over our digital information. Thus, a digital activist practice that draws attention to the relationship between technology, body and power is no doubt necessary. CAE's re-formulation of the body without organs, or data body, isolates the new form of control that needs to be challenged and signals how agency can be recovered. As with the long historical tradition of social resistance, it indicates that bodies are never mere tools and can never be bypassed.

At the same, the collective's grand performative project of data control brings up many issues related to computer hacking that are not directly addressed. In particular, the dominant role of hackers in the performance of digital direct action already points to important limitations, which will be discussed in the following chapter. Nonetheless, the *imaginaire* of the virtual body successfully positions digital sovereignty at the core of electronic resistance and it further establishes the rationale for direct action.

Conclusion

With the data body, a new *imaginaire* emerges which threatens to shatter social life. Our reliance on electronic information to administrate every aspects of society is only matched by our general lack of control over these procedures. CAE associates this condition with a loss of sovereignty and argues for the retrieval of the body without organs. This chapter has examined the formulation of virtual resistance through the discursive analysis of several fictional performances. It has established how digital direct action has been conceived as a new form of radical practice, named 'recombinant theatre', which focuses on the recovery of digital sovereignty. This approach is also a way to further justify the relocation of socio-political dissent in the digital space – the argument being that since the domination is virtual, so should the resistance be.

Of particular relevance here is CAE's distinctive interpretation of the relationship between technology, virtuality and the body. The argument that the dominance of machines occurs through the formation of virtual bodies effectively (re)positions the body at the core of digital resistance. This stand leads to the identification of new disciplinary practices that aim to control people and society. Meanwhile, electronic protest is inscribed into a historical tradition of embodied resistance. Similar to many past, and current social movements, regaining sovereignty over one's body becomes a core rationale for protest.

The other original aspect of this framing is its theatricality. The playful construction of the virtual theatre as the unique sphere of direct action is fascinating. The use of distinct theatrical directions and cues as part of the narration clearly illustrates the performativity of the project. At the same time, it leaves many questions unanswered. CAE does not elaborate on this potentially new and powerful theatre. While they may be captivating, the descriptions of the hacking performances contain no technical details. Yet, legitimate questions arise from the examination of the project. For example, how does one access protected data? What skills are required to alter the files? Does one need to be, or become a hacker? Is the strategy based on a single performance or does it require periodical actions? Little information is provided for the staging of these protest performances.

Under close scrutiny, many of these shortcomings become problematic, but for now the collective provided a convincing and motivating activist project against the collection of data and against surveillance. This is why the abandoning of this trail in the next publication, *Electronic Civil Disobedience* comes as a surprise. One of the reasons may be related to the increasing ethical and legal issues raised by computer hacking. It may also explain why CAE's reframes its activist project around new conceptions of disobedience and power-values.

Notes

1 In its early days, members of the artist-activist group Electronic Disturbance Theater would go into banks to perform this same scenario.

2 For examples of this theoretical division see Deluca's (1999) work on body rhetoric in Earth First! and Sasson-Levy and Rapoport's (2003) work on body knowledge in protest movements.

3 The subject of virtual bodies, cyborgs and electronic embodiment has been widely explored by critical theorists such as Donna Haraway, Katherine Hayles and Allucquere Stone. The mention here relates more directly to the idea of symbiosis in relation to Deleuze and Guattari's concept of 'body without organs', and its subsequent redefinition by Critical Art Ensemble as the data body.

3 'What CD once was, ECD is now'
The Legacy of Contention

ECD is CD reinvigorated. What CD once was, ECD is now.

—Critical Art Ensemble

In 1849, Henry David Thoreau published his seminal text, *Resistance to Civil Government*. In the essay, Thoreau explained his public opposition to the American slave trade and the Mexican war, presenting in the process his conception of civil disobedience. For Thoreau, the American government was failing as a civil institution because it did not keep the country free, settle the West, or educate its people (1888: 124). Thoreau further argued that 'the character inherent in the American people has done all that has been accomplished; and it would have done somewhat more, if the government had not sometimes got in its way' (ibid.). For this reason, Thoreau believed that '"government is best which governs least"'; but also that '"government is best which governs not at all"; and when men are prepared for it, that will be the kind of government which they will have' (ibid.: 123).

Despite his grand declarations, Thoreau was not against government. His call was not for the suppression of government but for the establishment of a better one; one that would be based on the logic of conscience rather than on the logic of legislation. The way in which Thoreau called for resistance to civil government was to refuse to pay his taxes. His point was to disobey laws that he strongly believed were unfair. As he questioned, 'unjust laws exist; shall we be content to obey them, or shall we endeavor to amend them, and obey them until we have succeeded, or shall we transgress them at once?' (ibid.: 133). Thoreau's own answer was unequivocal. Referring to the corrupted government as 'the machine', he declared 'if [the injustice] requires you to be agent of injustice to another, then, I say, break the law. Let your life be a counter friction to stop the machine' (ibid.: 134). For his act of disobedience, Thoreau was jailed for a day, and later defended his action by writing one of the most influential essays in American history.

Over time, the praxis of civil disobedience has developed to become a key element in political mobilisation. Acts of civil disobedience were performed as part of most social movements of the last two centuries, including the independence movements of former colonies, Women's

Rights, and the Civil Rights movements. What Thoreau could have never predicted, however, is that his philosophy would also serve as a rationale for the development of digital direct action. And yet, civil disobedience has been a central theme in the justification of digital resistance.

The discussion beginning in this chapter examines the construction of digital direct action as electronic civil disobedience. The analysis proposes a reading of Critical Art Ensemble's second pamphlet, *Electronic Civil Disobedience*, as a reformulation of digital protest within the legacy of civil disobedience. From this point onwards, Critical Art Ensemble abandons its initial argument for the re-appropriation of virtual bodies, and the claim for individual sovereignty is no longer part of the rationale. Instead, electronic disturbance is redefined as a new strategy that confronts nomadic power, what Thoreau would have most likely considered as part of 'the machine'.

This new position offers an insightful account of the new dynamics of control and resistance generated by digital technology. In the process, the collective proposes a new form of digital direct action that is compelling but also comes with its own limitations. One consequence of this re-positioning is that electronic civil disobedience is no longer associated with performance and recombinant theatre. As will be discussed in the last part of the chapter, this loss of theatricality, in favour of computer hacking and hackers, betrays a disregard for the historical role of art, artists and creativity within social mobilisation, which, in turn, limits the conceptualisation of electronic civil disobedience.

Strategies of Contention

Two years after the publication of *The Electronic Disturbance*, Critical Art Ensemble presented its second pamphlet *Electronic Civil Disobedience*. In the introduction, the collective self-reflected on the rationale of its project, promising that it would address the many criticisms related to the practice of electronic disturbance. Yet, an important discursive shift takes place in the book that the group does not explicitly address. In *Electronic Civil Disobedience,* electronic disturbance is discussed within the framework and conceptual legacy of civil disobedience. As a result, the concepts of digital sovereignty and the reclaiming of digital bodies are no longer part of the discussion. Instead, CAE formulates the concept of electronic civil disobedience (ECD). ECD is presented as the new model of activism that can respond to the relocation of power into the virtual space.

In accordance to its declaration about the declining effectiveness of mass demonstrations, CAE argues for the progressive forsaking of traditional civil disobedience strategies:

> Blocking the entrances to a building, or some other resistant action in physical space, can prevent reoccupation (the follow of personnel),

> but this is of little consequence so long as information-capital continues to flow. These outdated methods of resistance must be refined, and new methods of disruption invented that attack power (non) centers on the electronic level.
>
> (1996: 9)

The main point is that electronic civil disobedience is the renewal of civil disobedience in the digital era, and as such, the transition between the two practices should be seamless:

> The strategy and tactics of ECD should not be a mystery to any activists. They are the same as traditional CD. ECD is a nonviolent activity by its very nature, since the oppositional forces never physically confront one another. As in CD, the primary tactics in ECD are trespass and blockage. Exits, entrances, conduits, and other key spaces must be occupied by the contestational force in order to bring pressure on legitimized institutions engaged in unethical or criminal actions. Blocking information conduits is analogous to blocking physical locations; however, electronic blockage can cause financial stress that physical blockage cannot, and it can be used beyond the local level. ECD is CD reinvigorated.
>
> (1996: 18)

Although electronic civil disobedience is presented as the logical succession of civil disobedience, CAE does not provide any further details about these links. For instance, the history of civil disobedience contains important debates and challenges that have remained salient today, and many of these do not disappear through digital transposition. On the contrary, and as will be examined here, the theoretical debates of civil disobedience also become critical to the development of electronic civil disobedience.

When Thoreau wrote his proposition for disobedience, his essay considered several ethical and legal issues. One of the first points was to establish the very status of the legal system. Thoreau made it clear that his aim was to reform, rather than abrogate, legal principles. Still, many conflicting interpretations have emerged, mostly because Thoreau's essay does not provide a clear definition of the term 'civil disobedience'.[1]

Several theorists have suggested that the term 'civil' implies the existence of a formal legal structure which allows for 'disobedience' (King, 1963; Rawls, 1971). In this logic, legal theorist Jeffrie Murphy argues that:

> An act *A* is properly called an act of civil disobedience only if there is some law *L* according to which *A* is illegal, *L* is believed by the agent to be immoral, unconstitutional, irreligious, or ideologically

> objectionable, and this belief about *L* motivates or explains the performance of *A*.
>
> (1971: 1)

An act of civil disobedience thus consists in the infringement of a law found to be unfair or immoral, but it also implies general obedience to the rule of law and its representatives. This is how civil disobedience distinguishes itself from anarchism, revolution or criminality. Above all, there is the belief that civil disobedience is a moral act, even though the question of morality is also prone to its own definitions and debates. The moral right to disobey can be influenced by factors such as religious beliefs or social status.

In his address to white American clergymen, Civil Rights activist, Martin Luther King Jr., reiterated this stance on the moral of law breaking. Following his arrest during the 1963 protests in Birmingham, Alabama, and writing from jail, King defended:

> One may want to ask: "How can you advocate breaking some laws and obeying others?" The answer lies in the fact that there are two types of laws: just and unjust. I would be the first to advocate obeying just laws. One has not only a legal but a moral responsibility to obey just laws. Conversely, one has a moral responsibility to disobey unjust laws. I would agree with St. Augustine that "an unjust law is no law at all".
>
> (1963: para. 12)

Along with the duty to disobey unjust law, many disobedient activists, including King himself, strongly advocate for the practice of public announcement. The argument is that making public an intention to disobey reaffirms one's engagement and shows a willingness to bear the consequences of the breach. This approach often goes hand in hand with the practice of non-violent resistance. As civil disobedience aims to target unjust laws, disobedience activists should not engage in acts of violence that would likely breach other laws. This results in the acceptance of punishment, through fines or imprisonment, and this acceptance is often considered as evidence of the activist's respect for the general rule of law. Yet, these principles presuppose a legal system that is mostly fair, and in which only certain laws become subject to contention. In this context, the concept of civil disobedience does not comfortably fit in with social movements that aim to challenge entire justice systems or states that have been identified as untrustworthy. For these actions, the discourse of revolution or radicalism is often deployed.

Many historical examples, such as the non-violent opposition to British ruling that led India to its independence, or the marches and demonstrations of the US Civil Rights movements, and later on the anti–Vietnam

War protests, have been brandished as successful practices of civil disobedience. However, the prolonged effectiveness of peaceful actions has also been questioned, and recent socio-political activists have had to rethink their practice in the face of recurrent failure.

In her analysis of civil resistance and the anti-globalisation movement, Conway (2003) elected the case of the Seattle protests to examine what has prompted activists to consider tactics beyond lobbying and mass demonstration. In November 1999, Seattle witnessed one of its largest protest movements surrounding the World Trade Organisation (WTO) conference meeting. As one of the largest inter-governmental institutions, the World Trade Organisation is the body in charge of regulating commercial exchange between member states, including trade agreements and disputes. The conference planned in Seattle was meant to initiate a series of international negotiations that many considered to be promoting neo-liberal politics and global inequality. The protests organised against the meeting were some of the largest ever seen in the city (Seattle Municipal Archives, n.d.), and according to some reports over 40,000 people descended in the streets within a month, causing the Washington governor to declare a state of emergency (ibid.).

Conway recounts the many internal conflicts between protesters that insisted on remaining non-violent and those who defended radical action, in the form, for example, of property damage and vandalism. On the one side, those who advocated non-violence argued that media's focus on sensational stories would result in negative representations of the protest, and in the loss of public support. Those on the other side of the debate criticised the unproductive dichotomy created between violence and non-violence, as well as the 'highly ritualized forms of civil disobedience that had evolved during the peace movement, where protesters passively handed themselves over to the police' (Conway, 2003: 511). The division grew to the extent that some protest leaders chose to denunciate to the police those who were taking part in property damage (ibid.: 514–515).

The escalation of the protest within the protest eventually led some activists to propose a diversity of tactics. As Conway describes it:

> The decisive feature of respect for diversity of tactics is an ethic of respect for, and acceptance of, the tactical choices of other activists. This tolerance of pluralism involves an explicit agreement not to publicly denounce the tactics of other activists-most controversially, rock-throwing, window-breaking, garbage can burning, and vandalism.
>
> (2003: 511)

Yet, this account seems to suggest a distinction between civil disobedience and direct action, whereby the former is considered non-violent, while the latter assumes the use of violence.

Graeber (2009) discusses at length this contention surrounding direct action, and particularly the position that activists take before representatives of the state. Graeber explains that:

> In its essence direct action is the insistence, when faced with structures of unjust authority, on acting as if one is already free. One does not solicit the state. One does not even necessarily make a grand gesture of defiance. Insofar as one is capable, one proceeds as if the state does not exist.
>
> (2009: 203)

This position, which clearly draws from anarchist principles, underscores the limitations of the practice of civil disobedience in its acceptance of the general rule of law. As mentioned before, civil disobedience does not account for instances where whole legal systems, not only single laws, are unjust. In comparison, Graeber's description of direct action implies a refusal to recognise the authority of governments. It also considers the possibility of engaging in direct confrontation with the authorities. As Graeber concludes, direct action encompasses 'any form of political resistance that is overt, militant, and confrontational, but falls short of outright military insurrection' (ibid.: 204). This does not imply that direct action is inevitably violent, however to engage in it, activists would technically need to do more than marching down the streets.

These theoretical issues clearly indicate that civil disobedience and direct action are conflicting strategies of resistance, and that any attempt at re-appropriation would require substantial consideration. Yet, far from addressing these complexities, CAE opts for a rather smooth recuperation.

The most significant discussion on the validity of electronic civil disobedience is provided by the electrohippies. During the Seattle protests, this collective of activists and artists attempted to transpose social protest into cyberspace by directing a virtual sit-in against the World Trade Organisation (WTO) website, while thousands of alter-globalisations demonstrators were marching down the streets. Similar to the radical actions promoted by CAE, the strikes aimed to disrupt the flow of information, by blocking access to the WTO website. These virtual sit-ins were conceived as an alternative for those who found themselves enable to take part in the demonstrations. According to the activists, the event 'provided an opportunity for around 450,000 people (over 5 days) across the globe to express their dissatisfaction with the WTO—and without the risk of being gassed by Seattle's "robocops"' (electrohippies collective et al., 2001: 272).

Lead member of the group, Paul Mobbs, defends the conception of ECD and the decision to use denial-of-service (DoS) to disrupt websites, as a protest tactic. His argument is based on the now familiar vision of cyberspace as a free and open environment. Mobbs describes the internet as a structure originally created for public interaction, which has been re-appropriated by major corporations. The group justifies digital direct action as a legitimate means to protect the 'public space' of cyberspace. As they argue, 'there is no practical difference between cyberspace and the street in terms of how people use the Net' (ibid.: 269). The activists suggest that mass participation to the virtual strike demonstrated a shared concern for social change, '*our method has built within it the guarantee of democratic accountability. If people don't vote with their modems (rather than voting with their feet) the action would be an abject failure*' (ibid.: 270, original emphasis). The electrohippies thus considered their digital protest as having similar value and purpose as a street demonstration, albeit in the form of electronic disruption, since it allowed protesters who could not be in Seattle to have their voices heard. At the same time, by promoting the mass participation of digital activists, the electrohippies fuelled the *cyber-imaginaire* of a burgeoning public sphere.

This assumption that militant citizens can resort to the internet to take action against government and corporate institutions is not only rooted in the *imaginaire* of a free digital space, it also relates to the idea of a virtual public sphere. It implies a re-consideration of Habermas's concept of the public sphere within digital communication. In *The Structural Transformation of the Public Sphere*, Jürgen Habermas (1991) offers an historical and sociological account of the public sphere as a critical space for civil debate. Habermas associates the bourgeois public sphere with the emergence of the new capitalist order. For him, capitalist politics and economies enabled the rise of the public sphere as a place for the free expression of ideas. As he defines:

> The bourgeois public sphere may be conceived above all as the sphere of private people come together as a public; they soon claimed the public sphere regulated from above against the public authorities themselves, to engage them in a debate over the general rules governing relations in the basically privatized but publicly relevant sphere of commodity exchange and social labor.
>
> (1991: 27)

The spreading of social sites such as coffeehouses and salons, as well as independent press, were also important factors, as they were considered public, autonomous and opened to everyone.

This somehow resonates with the early interpretations of cyberspace and the emergence of virtual communities. It echoes the conversations taking place within virtual environments such as The Well, and the narratives presented by digerati such as Brand Steward, Howard Rheingold or John Perry Barlow. In many ways, they nourish the *imaginaire* of the virtual public sphere where freedom and democracy prevail. For these first internet users, the internet offered an immunisation against authoritarian power. Political scientist Hubertus Buchstein (1997: 250) refers to them as the 'Optimists', a group of people that imagine a critical public sphere where interactions 'subvert traditional power structures by enhancing citizens independence from government agencies and big business'. Yet for Buchstein, far from constituting the adequate domain for a new public sphere, the internet can distort the very concept of citizenship.

Indeed, Habermas's original model of the public sphere has raised many criticisms that the virtual environment has not begun to address. As James Finlayson explains:

> In practice, the participation in the public sphere that existed in the coffee houses, salons, and the literary journals of 18th century Europe was always restricted to a small group of educated men of means. Property and education were the two unspoken condition of participation. In reality, the majority of poor and uneducated people, and almost all women, were excluded.
>
> (2005: 12)

These points have led critics to suggest that Habermas's portrayal of the public sphere was neither public nor democratic, as the alleged democratic conversations developed, most likely, within parameters that prevented undesired people from fully participating.

Political theorist Jodi Dean extends the critique to suggest the non-existence of the public sphere. For her, the internet cannot be considered as a new public sphere, not merely because of the technology, but because of the very idea of public sphere. As she declares, 'the territorialization of cyberia as the public sphere tries to prevent the collapse of an outmoded concept by installing new technology', and as such, 'there is no public sphere' (1997: 266). As most critics of the *imaginaire* of the virtual public sphere, Dean brings attention to the idealisation of the technology but also the highly controlled environment that is cyberspace. Clearly, this is not a space inherently open to democratic social and political exchanges. Yet, technological enthusiasts, including early digital activists, have been keen to spread the idea. The main issue is that the discourse of a virtual public sphere rarely engages with the critiques and limitations of the public sphere itself. The transposition of Habermas's model into cyberspace does not resolve its shortcomings, and these do not disappear into virtuality.

This point is illustrated by the electrohippies's approach to digital direct action which stands unaware of the dynamics of digital communication. Paradoxically, questions of authority and control are never clearly addressed, although, the collective declares a strong engagement towards accountability and openness. The primary focus is on the justification of electronic civil disobedience, and mainly consists in the commitment to non-encrypted communication and to the full disclosure of all digital activities.

To this aim, the electrohippies prepared a Do-It-Yourself kit for digital protests which provided instructions and software for the staging of virtual sits-ins. The kit was accompanied by a list of set requirements for the practice of denial-of-services. For example, digital activists were instructed to formally identify themselves prior to the protest (with a name and/or a website) and to provide full details of their actions and motivations. Ideally, the strikes ought to be part of a street event or mobilisation movement. In addition, no anonymous denial-of-service action ought to be authorised, and all target institutions ought to be notified of the strikes beforehand. The rationale for this was that law enforcement authorities could 'track us down in a few hours' (ibid.: 272).

In the tradition of civil disobedience, Mobbs also argues that activist groups should use mass participation and public announcement to validate their digital actions:

> If the 'Net is to be used as a valid tool for protest and dissent then we must develop it in a manner that makes it hard for the State and law enforcement authorities to challenge the validity of the tactics.
> (ibid.: 273)

This approach is not without contradiction, however. If target institutions were informed of a forthcoming strike against their websites, it seems likely that they would prepare for it, in order to keep disruption to a minimum. These digital protests would unlikely generate the type of disturbance that could lead to negotiations. In this context, the rationale for ECD could be questioned. Why indeed develop a practice that appears inefficient and symbolic, when the technology enables the production of actual disruption?

The answer to this question is related to rising concerns about the legal implications of digital protest. One of the central pending issues of electronic civil disobedience is its position in relation to the law. CAE's decision to redefine digital action was unclear up to this point, however, it becomes apparent that by connecting digital resistance to an established mode of dissidence, such as civil disobedience, the project can be recognised as a valid form of social engagement, which may in turn define its legal treatment.

Spaces of Contention

To understand CAE's forecasting of the legal treatment of electronic civil disobedience, it is essential to examine the key story introduced in the first chapter of *Electronic Civil Disobedience*. In November 1990, three computer hackers were sentenced to jail for accessing the network of a private company. Robert Riggs, also known as 'The Prophet', Frank Darden, as 'The Urvile' and Adam Grant as 'The Leftist', all pleaded guilty to several charges of hacking and unauthorised access to BellSouth computer system (Goldstein, 1990). Along with prison sentences between 14 and 21 months, the offenders, nicknamed the Atlanta Three, were also required to pay restitution fines that amounted to $233,000 USD (ibid.). This was not the first time that hackers had been arrested and charged. Since the implementation of the US Computer Fraud and Abuse Act in 1986, many hackers have been tracked down and jailed for unauthorised access to electronic devices (Sterling, 1993).

Yet, the case of the Atlanta Three, named after the city of their court jurisdiction, was rather unique. The lawsuit revolved around the unauthorised access and distribution of an electronic file (the E911 document) retrieved by Robert Riggs from the BellSouth server, which led to the charges of 'computer fraud', 'access device fraud', and 'interstate transportation of stolen property' (Sterling, 1993: 270). At the same time, in the state of Illinois, a fourth hacker, Craig Neidorf, known as 'Knight Lightning', was also on trial for the same offence. During Neidorf's court hearings, it emerged that the allegedly stolen electronic document was in fact available to members of the public for a small fee. Based on this information, all charges against Neidorf were dropped and his court case was dismissed. Having already pleaded guilty to all charges, however, Riggs, Darden and Grant saw their sentences confirmed a year later in Atlanta.

Many critics questioned the outcome of the trials and challenged the treatment of the hackers as criminals. In particular, the court cases presented two major issues. First was the legal interpretation of the allegations. As mentioned previously, Riggs, Darden and Grant pleaded guilty to several charges including the stealing of property, that is, BellSouth's electronic file. The problem is that as a digital file the document was not taken away from BellSouth. The company still had the E911 document in its possession. If anything, the file had been 'copied', as opposed to 'stolen', by the hackers. Bruce Sterling clearly explains this in his account of the event[2]:

> No one noticed that Prophet had done this. He had 'stolen' the E911 Document in some sense, but notions of property in cyberspace can be tricky. BellSouth noticed nothing wrong, because BellSouth still had their original copy. They had not been "robbed" of the document itself. Many people were supposed to copy this document—specifically, people who worked for the 19 BellSouth 'special services and major account centers', scattered throughout the Southeastern United States. That was what it was for, why it was present on a

> computer network in the first place: so that it could be copied and read—by telco employees. But now the data had been copied by someone who wasn't supposed to look at it.
>
> (1993: 112–113)

And yet, the judgment was issued as if the hackers had committed a burglary and BellSouth had been defrauded of its belongings.

Considering the startling lengths of the prison terms, it becomes clear that the hackers were not condemned on the ground of retributive punishment, as this would have required the judgment to be proportional to the crimes committed. Instead, their sentence was utilitarian; a punishment clearly designed to become exemplary.

The second problem also relates to the sentencing of the hackers. One factor which influenced the judgment was that as part of the prosecution, BellSouth had declared that the document E911 had a value of almost $80,000; a sum that 'offered a good legal pretext for stern punishment of the thieves' (Sterling, 1993: 128). Clearly, this information had an impact on the Atlanta Three court hearings. For the fourth hacker, Craig Neidorf, things took a different turn. During his trial, Neidorf's lawyers got hold of a catalogue of publications from one of BellSouth's branches. The booklet contained a copy of the E911 document that had been declared stolen. In addition, the same document was available for anyone to order, at the cost of $13 USD. The lawyers thus successfully argued that BellSouth's financial claim was inconsistent and inadmissible. From there, the judge concluded on a mistrial and dismissed the case.

The important part of the story is that Neidorf was not technically cleared of the charges of 'computer fraud' and 'interstate transportation of stolen property'. The court case was not dismissed because he was found 'not guilty'. The trial was terminated because his defence had argued that the document central to the prosecution was financially worthless. In other words, the lawsuit was not about the breach of BellSouth computer system, but rather, about the alleged, and in this case, highly inflated, financial loss to the company.

Thus, the sanction against the three hackers should be read as an exercise of power which followed a capitalistic logic. The judicial court redeployed intellectual property and copyright law to sentence the hackers. Despite clear legal contradictions, the intrusion into BellSouth servers was established as a breach of property, and the sharing of the files as an infringement of copyright (Godwin, 1994). For CAE, who also emphasised the highly disproportionate character of the prison sentences, the outcome of the trial signalled the increasing value given to digital information. As they argue in their discussion of the case, 'with only the charge of trespassing against them, jailing these individuals seems a little extreme; however, when considering the value of order and private property in cyberspace, extreme punishment for the smallest of crimes should be expected' (CAE, 1996: 15).

These legal contradictions may seem obvious but they are often blurred by the misconception and detrimental view of computer hackers. Despite their many attempts to challenge stereotypes, hackers are often perceived as criminals. The term, 'hacker' first appeared in the field of computer sciences to designate those who had developed advanced skills in computer programming (Levy, 1984). A hacker is someone with expertise in computing but also with high creative abilities. Hackers developed the languages and programmes that transformed personal computers. Yet, over time, with the increasing commercialisation of information technology, their contributions began to be seen as counter to the capitalist model. Hackers were more and more perceived as malicious individuals working against the IT industry. They began to be associated with trespassing, computer damaging and criminality.

This situation forced some hackers and experts to establish a distinction between practices. In 1991, *The New Hacker's Dictionary* provided the following definition of a *hacker*:

> Hacker: n. [originally, someone who makes furniture with an axe] (1) A person who enjoys exploring the details of programmable systems and how to stretch their capabilities, as opposed to most users, who prefer to learn only the minimum necessary. (2) One who programs enthusiastically (even obsessively) or who enjoys programming rather than just theorizing about programming. ... (6) An expert or enthusiast of any kind. One might be an astronomy hacker, for example. (7) One who enjoys the intellectual challenge of creatively overcoming or circumventing limitations. (8) [deprecated] A malicious meddler who tries to discover sensitive information by poking around. Hence password hacker, network hacker.
>
> (Raymond, 1991: 191)

This lengthy description is meant to separate hacking from cracking; a 'cracker' being someone who breaks the security of a computer system with criminal intentions. The term was coined by hackers as a 'defense against journalistic misuse of the term hacker' (ibid.: 110). These terminologies have been mildly effective however, and debates about hacking are still fierce. While most hackers defend their drive to acquire skills and to develop the technology, popular media discussions and representations have remained antagonistic. This explains why the case of the Atlanta Three did not raise further polemic or attention in the media.

Still, the application of utilitarian sanctions against specific digital practices rapidly extended, along with the re-interpretation of laws. For instance, in 2000, a famous lawsuit was filed against music file sharing service Napster, an early peer-to-peer file sharing service that allowed users to exchange music online. The service had remained exempt from legal scrutiny, until several music companies began to declare that peer-to-peer downloading was to be blamed for the decline of music sales. In an attempt to halt the distribution of copyrighted material, the industry initiated a number of lawsuits against digital services, but also individuals. However, Napster did not immediately cease all exchange of copyright materials. The company referred to the principle of 'fair use' to explain that consumers had the right to reproduce music material for private use. File sharing could therefore not be considered illegal (Ante, 2000).

All the same, the case prompted the tightening of copyright legislation in favour of music and media corporations. Since then, new legislations have been implemented that incorporate digital technology. Many more site owners and users are now facing jail sentences and hefty fines for circulating copyrighted material. This time the offenders were not just hackers, but everyday people engaging in everyday digital practices. In 2007, one user was condemned to pay $222,000 USD for downloading and sharing copyright songs. Another user faced a fine of $675,000 USD for a similar offence (Kravets, 2012).

Far from reaching any resolution, these issues are currently epitomised by the ongoing conflict that opposes another popular file-sharing service, The Pirate Bay, against several international media companies. Created in 2003 by a Swedish organisation, The Pirate Bay was set up with an explicit political agenda. Since its inception, the owners have expressed a clear opposition to copyright and intellectual property laws. This ethos is based on the belief in the free circulation of information. The Pirate Bay offers indexes of file-sharing protocols (bittorents) which facilitate file transfer, although it does not host any actual material, copyrighted or not (The Pirate Bay, n.d.). In many ways the service can be considered as a form of digital activism against copyright laws, which could further explain why media companies have been keen to dismantle the site.

Six years after its creation, a Swedish court condemned to prison sentences and millions of dollars of compensation those responsible for The Pirate Bay (Manner et al., 2009: 197). Among the plaintiffs were several media companies, including Sony Music Entertainment, Warner Bros, EMI and Columbia Pictures. The Pirate Bay was found guilty of contributing to copyright infringement and the defendants were asked to pay for the alleged damages. Yet, for a long time now, administrators of file-sharing sites have argued that as their servers do not hold any material, they should not be made liable for what circulates on the sites. As a case in point, the defendants could not be directly condemned for copyright infringement. Instead, the verdict was issued on the basis of 'contributory liability' to infringement (Manner et al., 2009: 200). Despite this verdict, and the many court injunctions issued against it, The Pirate Bay website still remains active today.

All of these cases illustrate that the concept of cyber law is highly problematic. So far, no legal system has been adequately applied to the internet. Governments are attempting to impose legislations that are, and have been, strongly challenged by users, including the early Telecommunication Act denounced by Barlow, the intellectual rights law used against the Atlanta Three, or the copyright laws restricting file-sharing services. These legislations all have in common the task to defend the economic interests and digital assets of major corporations.

For CAE, this situation represents the 'power-value' of digital information. Although the group does not provide a clear definition of the term, it argues that power-value can be measured by observing the level of punishment applied to protect digital assets, but also, the extent to which criminal laws are being modified and re-interpreted to enable prosecution. The premise is that governments and corporations will protect what they deem valuable, and severely punish any attempt to disrupt these assets. The fate of the Atlanta Three thus illustrates that 'the greater the intensity of defence and punishment, the greater the power-value' (CAE, 1996: 11).

Yet, far from suggesting a backtrack from the staging of digital action, CAE sees this conflict as a confirmation that cyberspace has indeed become the site for social and political contention. As a result, the group provides a new account of how digital resistance could be relocated in this sphere. This time, the aim is not to take control of digital bodies as in previous descriptions of virtual resistance. Instead, computer hacking is used to hold up access to digital information and to disturb the functioning of key institutions. The virtual protest takes the form of an electronic blockade, based on the assumption that 'blocking information access is the best means to disrupt any institution, whether it is military, corporate, or governmental. When such action is successfully carried out, all segments of the institution are damaged' (CAE, 1996: 13).

CAE's account reflects some of the philosophical and moral concerns of civil disobedience. The group is also clearer about the purpose and limits of its project, as shown by its detailed description of electronic civil disobedience:

> Activists must remember that ECD can easily be abused. The sites for disturbance must be carefully selected. Just as an activist group would not block access to a hospital emergency room, electronic activists must avoid blocking access to an electronic site that may have similar humanitarian functions. For example, let us assume that a profiteering pharmaceutical company is targeted. Care will have to be taken not to block the data controlling the manufacture and distribution of life-saving medications (no matter how bad the extortion profits might be from the drugs). Rather, once the company is targeted, activists would be wiser to select research

> or consumption-pattern databases as sites for occupation. Having the R&D or marketing division shut down is one of the most expensive setbacks that a company can suffer. The blockage of this data will give the resistant group a foundation from which to bargain without hurting those who are in need of the medications. Further, if terms are not met, or if there is an attempt to recapture the data, ethical behavior requires that data must not be destroyed or damaged. Finally, no matter how tempting it might be, do not electronically attack individuals (electronic assassination) in the company—not CEOs, not managers, not workers. Don't erase or occupy their bank accounts or destroy their credit. Stick to attacks on the institutions. Attacking individuals only satisfies an urge for revenge without having any effect on corporate or government policy.
>
> (CAE, 1996: 18–19)

Considering CAE's argument about the power-value of digital data, the type of resistance project described above is rather convincing. On the assumption that a limited denial of access can force companies to enter into negotiations, a digital activist movement which confronts capitalist interests by controlling the circulation of virtual assets could potentially modify power relations. The issue however is that this type of practice has serious legal implications, and CAE clearly identifies the central one:

> Forces, like the legal system, do not distinguish between actions in cyberspace on the basis of intent. Whether private information sources are accessed simply to examine the system, or whether the purpose is to steal or damage the source, these forces always assume that unauthorized access is an act of extreme hostility, and should receive maximum punishment.
>
> (1996: 14)

This implies that authorities will make no distinction in their sanctioning of online trespassing. As governments and corporations react strongly to the potential threat of financial loss, CAE's version of electronic civil disobedience will be considered as criminal, regardless of the motivations of the actors.

CAE's solution is to argue for a separate treatment of unauthorised access to digital data. The group contends that legal authorities need to assess the motivations behind digital disruptions. Governments will need to establish whether the act was performed as part of an activist protest, with the intent of making a social or political statement, or if it was for the sole purpose of carrying out criminal activities. The assumption is that if hacking is perceived as a form of social protest, the legal sanctions will presumably be less severe. This is ultimately the reason behind the reformulation of electronic disturbance as electronic civil disobedience. As the collective declares 'ECD is CD reinvigorated. What CD once was, ECD is now', and thus, 'the same legal penalties that apply to CD should also apply to ECD' (1996: 17–18).

Yet, there is a paradox between CAE's exposition of cyber power-value and the call for lenience towards digital activists. After all, if digital data has become a key economic good, it is bound to be protected against any type of threat, regardless of the motives. As mentioned before, in the absence of a tailored legal system, laws will be modified at ease, in order to criminalise any digital activities considered as a menace to capitalist values, this includes computer hacking and electronic civil disobedience. Indeed, it is *because* of its potential as a radical tactic that authorities are more likely to hamper the development of digital protest, and despite its many attempts to offer solutions, CAE is fully aware of this point. As they readily admit 'conflating electronic civil disobedience with criminal acts makes it possible to seal off cyberspace from resistant political activity' (1996: 17–18). In a way, this is where the legacy of civil disobedience becomes most palpable, that is to say that regardless of the many discourses and justifications, digital activists may need to accept the consequences of their social and political engagement.

Performers of Contention

The new framing of digital action as electronic civil disobedience explicitly reaffirms at least one element, the relationship between computer hacking and digital resistance. This association was already clear in CAE's rationale for the recovery of virtual sovereignty and the control of digital bodies. These actions were considered as central to electronic protest and were further described as recombinant theatre. Yet, with electronic civil disobedience, the relationship between digital action and theatrical performance disappears. CAE no longer mentions the creative and performative elements of electronic protest in its description. Instead, the collective re-centres the practice around computer hackers. As they describe, 'a small but coordinated group of hackers could introduce electronic viruses, worms, and bombs, into data banks, programs, and networks of authority, possibly bringing the destructive force of inertia into the nomadic realm' (1996: 25). We are far removed here from the activist performer who would get onto a stage to modify computer files before strolling the streets as part of a transgender performance.

The decision to present hackers as the central actors of electronic civil disobedience is also questionable. In the same way that the promotion of cyberspace as the unique site for dissent is problematic, this complete reliance on hackers to become digital activists seems reductive and antithetical, particularly since social mobilisation tends to encourage inclusion and mass participation. This issue is further complicated by CAE's conception of computer hackers. In one account, the group explains that the challenge in the development of electronic civil disobedience resides in the current profile of digital activists. Referring to hackers, CAE laments that:

> This is perhaps the one of the saddest chapters in the history of resistance in the US. Right now the finest political activists are children. Teen hackers work out of their parents' homes and college dormitories to breach corporate and governmental security systems.
>
> (1996: 15)

The group further argues that while they may be essential to digital action, hackers should not be left to their own device because of their general lack of political consciousness. Apparently, 'the problem of letting children act as the avant-garde of activism is that they have not yet developed a critical sensibility that would guide them beyond the first political encounter' (ibid.: 15). CAE also mentions hackers' 'youthful sense of immortality and 'their youthful fearlessness [which] tends to get them arrested' (ibid.).

While this *imaginaire* of the hacker as a lost hero is typical of science-fiction literature and movies, CAE's narrative of the 'technology-obsessed-secluded-white-teenage-male' is puzzling, particularly when related to digital activism. For one thing, hackers do not form a homogeneous group. While many would happily engage in hacking practices, certain ethics also discourage the blockage of digital information, as will be discussed in Chapter 5.

Perhaps this contradiction is what prompts CAE to later include a wider range of actors in the organisation of electronic civil disobedience. As a model and an alternative to mass mobilisation, the collective proposes the formation of microstructures or electronic civil disobedience cells. Accordingly, these activist cells should be constituted of four to ten people and allow for a mixture of various knowledge and skills. The group explains that:

> To be effective, the schism between knowledge and technical ability in the cell must be closed. (...) Avoid consensus through similarity of skills, since in order for the cell to be useful, different skills must be represented. Activist, theorist, artist, hacker, and even a lawyer would be a good combination of talents-knowledge and practice should mix.
>
> (CAE, 1996: 23)

This new cellular formation expands the type of activists that can be involved in electronic civil disobedience, but it does not resolve the dependency on computer hackers. What this new approach does, however, is to seemingly re-introduce creative practice by including the figure of the artist into the equation.

Throughout most of its writing, CAE meticulously avoids using the term 'artist'. The group refers to the 'cultural producer', the 'resistance cultural performer', the 'critical performer', or the 'resistant cultural worker', but it never mentions the term artist in isolation. This comes from CAE's endeavour to dissociate digital direct action from artistic practice. Yet, the limiting role given to artists as part of electronic civil disobedience is detrimental and counter-effective. As most accounts of social movements illustrate, artists and creative performers have played essential roles in the development of social mobilisation.

In their analysis of the relationship between art and social change, Bradley and Esche (2007) describe the engagement of modernist artists with the wider social world as a reflection of a desire to break away from art institutions. They argue that because artists are connected to society and social issues, 'art is always already politicised' (2007: 9). Bradley and Esche also state that social movements have adopted several creative practices, such as photomontage and performance, which initially developed within the context of contemporary art.

On the same issue, Feminist art critic Lucy Lippard describes activist art as a creative practice that develops in the 'outside wold', and requires that artists be directly involved with communities and political work (1984: 29). Art activist Gregory Scholette expands on this view, suggesting that activist artists play a central role in supporting direct action and raising social awareness. As he explains:

> To produce activist art is therefore to put one's political commitment to the test, first through non-institutional forms of cultural distribution and interaction – art for demonstrations and picket lines, mail art, on city walls or on the sides of buses, art in the middle of shopping malls and crowded plazas – and second to use that form of dissemination to speak about social injustices with an audience who presumably has little patience for refined aestheticism but does care about war, inequality, political freedom and protecting the environment.
>
> (Scholette, 1999: 49)

Considering this position, the origins of art activism as we know it today, can be traced back to the social and cultural developments of the mid-1970s. Until then, as art critic Nina Felshin argues, most of the (Western) art had been produced and consumed within the art world (1995: 10). The dominance of modernism confined art to its intrinsic aesthetic forms, or to the idea of art for art's sake. It is through the emergence of conceptual art, and its 'democratizing aesthetic tendencies' (ibid.), that activist art could begin to take shape. Felshin describes how the new practice materialised in public spaces through interventions, installations and performances. The collaborative element of art activism also became clear, with the direct involvement of actors from outside the art world, as well as public participants. In addition, activist artists embraced a wider range of media and technologies, focusing less on art objects and more on social processes.

Thus, in one way or another, artists have been actively engaged in most of the 20th-century social movements, including the civil rights, anti-war, feminist, LGBT, environmental, and alter-globalisation movements. Artistic productions have encompassed the creation of images, graphics, posters, photographs and sculpture, but also texts and manifestos in support of socio-political mobilisation.[3]

Alongside the visual arts, performance art also emerged as a central actor in social engagement. During the 1960s, artists were also interrogating the role of performance within wider society, and new tendencies started to develop that challenged the frameworks and spaces of traditional theatre. For example, the idea of 'happenings', as ephemeral artistic events and participatory performance, were put in practice and linked to social issues.

One key reference in the merging of theatrical performance and protest is the San Francisco Mine Troupe, an artistic group influenced by 16th-century Italian Commedia dell'Arte, Bertholt Brecht's epic theatre and Antonin Artaud. In the early 1960s, the group staged numerous politicised performance around the Bay Area. Founding member of the troupe, Ronald G. Davis, described their project as 'guerrilla theatre', a type of performance taking place in public spaces and aiming to change society. In the introduction of his manifesto, Davis explains that:

> The motives, aspirations, and practice of U.S, theatre must be re-adapted in order to:
>
> . teach
> . direct toward change
> . be an example of change
>
> to teach, one must know something.
>
> It is necessary to direct toward change because "the system" is debilitating, repressive, and non-aesthetic. (...)
>
> For those who like art pure of social issues, I must say - F*** ***! buddy, theatre IS as social entity. It can dull the minds of the citizens, it can wipe out guilt, it can teach all to accept the Great Society and the Amaaaaarican way of life (just like the moves, Ma) or it can look to changing that society ... and that's *political.* (original asterisk and original emphasis)
>
> (Davis, 1966: 131)

Guerrilla theatre is also described as a direct reference to the revolutionary figure of Che Guevara:

> Che Guevara tell us what do to about it: The guerrilla fighter needs full help from the people of the area... From the very beginning of the struggle he has the intention of destroying an unjust order and therefore an intention, more of less hidden, to replace the old with something new.
>
> (ibid.: 130)

This theatre is therefore a translation of guerrilla tactics, which redeploys small and mobile factions and shock methods, to create socio-political performances.

During its time of political engagement, the San Francisco Mine Troupe staged a series of mostly unauthorised plays in public parks throughout the city. The idea was to take theatre outside of playhouses and perform for new audiences. The plays feature satirical stories about racial issues, social discrimination and oppression. Despite its radical ambition, the initial practices of guerrilla theatre kept with many settings of traditional theatre, including the use of stages, props, scripts and professional actors.

It is only with the formation of other alternative troupes, such as The Diggers, that guerrilla theatre began to show its full potential. Historian Michael Doyle describes how this new group 'appropriated Davis's dramatic form of guerrilla theater and gave it a new twist. Where he had taken theater out of its traditional setting to stage it in the parks, the Diggers took theater into the streets' (2002: 80). With this example, Doyle identified a complete merging between protest and theatre. Guerrilla theatre no longer implied scripted plays performed in front of passers-by.

Instead, performers aimed to 'remove all boundaries between art and life, between spectator and performer, and between public and private' (ibid.).

In one of their most famous activist actions, The Diggers developed the concept of Free World which started with the daily provision of free food near the Golden Gate Bridge. They then run several free stores, where people could acquire all sorts of items for free. The anti-capitalist scheme expanded to offer free housing, free legal services and free medical care, but also free parties, street theatre and film screenings (Doyle, 2002: 81). Accordingly, this new performance tactic blurred the distinction between theatre and direct action, by doing away with any explicit references to theatricality. In this particular instance, protest fully became the performance of everyday life; and in this instance, a life opposed to capitalism.

The philosophy and tactics of guerrilla theatre are also evident in contemporary social movements' dramaturgic turn. In a recent analysis,

Juris (2014) examines the long history and legacy of protest theatre, from agitprop, street and puppet theatre, to guerrilla theatre, and later, media stunts and culture jams. Juris explains that usually protest theatre performances are 'more explicit in their adoption of the structure and format of theatre, including a clearer (but not complete) separation between the performer and the audience, greater level of previous rehearsing, and a more significant likelihood of repetition' (2014: 238). Juris further explains that these are often tactics for the disruption, interruption or hijack of contested events, although he also states that the distinction between theatrical protest and protest theatre is far from absolute. For example, guerrilla theatre was used during the 1960s by the Black Panthers and black power activists, who developed highly staged and televised performances that were meant to demonstrate their authority and their combative force (ibid.: 240). These elements led to the realisation that activists have an audience to perform to, and through these implied spectators, they become reflexive of their actions and performative potential.

Performance scholar Baz Kershaw also commented on this move away from 'the modernism notion of an attack on a known enemy towards a more improvisatory and hyper-real scenario style' (1997: 264). Kershaw's analysis of popular protests since the 1960s, confirmed that while resistance to the authority was still the main objective, protest also aimed to provide participants and spectators with a unique experience of freedom and power. As he explains:

> While earlier protests usually drew primarily on *political* sources for their dramaturgies, in the sense of political theory or ideologies, these later events derived much of their dramaturgical power from *theatrical* origins. This adjustment of focus opened up a much wider perspective on the potential of protest: in a sense the imaginary became more important than the possible, and the visionary more persuasive than the rational.
>
> (1997: 265)

This relation between street protest and protest theatre draws attention to the notion of reiteration. For instance, many historical demonstrations have used spectatorial aesthetics, including banners, slogans, chants, drums, music, and puppets. More specifically, Reed (2005) explains that music played a central role in the African American Civil Rights movement. In *The Art of Protest*, Reed posits that 'music was the key force in shaping, spreading, and sustaining the movement's culture and through culture its politics' (ibid.: 13). This is particularly relevant if we consider the historical importance of the Civil Rights movement. For Reed, it became the model, at least in the United States, of all subsequent social movements which were influenced by its 'tactics, strategies, style, vision, ideology, and overall movement culture' (ibid.: 2).

In this sense, there is a citationality to the performance of protest. This capacity for protesters to redeploy, or cite, resistance tactics is what makes protest recognisable. By adopting previous norms and strategies, including theatrical structures and creative performance, activists signal the nature of their engagement. While in some contexts, the repetition of norms can be considered regularising and constraining (Butler, 1993: 95), it is also the means through which street protest can be recognised as such. These citations allow for a historical continuity and geographical expansion that illustrate the power of contestation.

Following Derrida's proposition, and paraphrasing him, we can thus question whether social protest would 'succeed if its formulation did not repeat a 'coded' or iterable statement' (1982: 326). Indeed, the theatrical aesthetics of street marches, the inclusion of music, chants and performances, all contribute to the public perception and recognition of these actions as protest.

Some would argue that this repetition is double-edged. Certainly, reiteration can lead to the normalisation of protest, and facilitate the policing of activists. This may also support the argument that street protest has become standardised. Yet, once understood, it is difficult to refute the performativity of protest. In a Butlerian sense, 'every performance is an original and an imitation' (Denzin, 2003: 10). To extend on this point, the citationality of protest also functions as a safeguard. It is through this process that protesters have the potential to dissociate their practice from more controversial actions such as riots, or even, revolutions.

During the 1999 Seattle demonstrations, Wall (2003) identified one performing troupe, known as the Radikal Cheerleaders, which regularly participated in the marches. Wall describes how this group of young men and women, styled with pigtails and dressed up as sloppy cheerleaders, were chanting messages such as: '*The corporations have blood on their hands…. Stop corporate greed*' (ibid.: 41). Wall tells of the many fliers that depicted the protests as mass celebration and included statements such as '*Street festival to: End corporate rule. In unity and diversity there is strength … Music, giant puppets, theatre and you!!! Celebrate!*' (ibid.).

For the author, this type of performance was staged as much to protest as it was to attract spectators, resulting in a festive tone which dominated over the seriousness of the event. Similarly to the tactics of guerrilla theatre, the protest became a form of 'creative culture jamming', where 'resistance become a rave-like celebration', and the street performance seems to 'embody a postmodern political message; one challenging – not celebrating – capitalism's mass consumerism' (Wall, 2003: 42). The effectiveness of this performativity can be questioned of course, especially in comparison to the more radical performances that were also part of the spectacle, such as the acts of vandalism and the direct confrontations with the police. Yet, this joyful approach also meant that the protests could not be easily considered as threatening, due to the redeployment of recognisable performance tactics.

The relationship between creative performance and resistance is of course not limited to street demonstrations. A digital activist performance also took place during the Seattle protests. While the electrohippies were staging virtual sit-ins against the official website of the World Trade Organisation, the creative group, ®TMark (ArtMark), was generating additional confusion about the WTO. As part of its subversive project, ®TMark created an alternative version of the organisation website, called the 'World Trade Organization/GATT Home Page'. This rogue site was meant to confuse visitors as it contained satirical comments assigned to actual members of the WTO. Graham Meikle provides a detailed account of the prank in his analysis of digital activism:

> The gatt.org page offers quotes attributed to WTO Director-General Mike Moore. He says, for instance, that open trade 'leads to higher living standards for working families, which in turn leads to a cleaner environment'. The site also offers helpful commentary – 'This must be because working families are really dirty, and if you give them a little more money they clean themselves up and stop polluting everything'.
>
> (2002: 118)

Meikle explains that while gatt.org was a clone site that had no link with the WTO, the latter was still compelled to respond. The WTO released a statement in which director Mike Moore 'deplored the ®TMark site, saying "It's illegal and it's unfair"' (ibid.). For ®TMark this was a sign of victory as the target organisation was forced to publicly acknowledge, and to an extent, publicise the parody. This type of satirical performance eventually became the signature of ®TMark creative and political work and it likely opened the door to even more sophisticated digital pranks.

This style of digital activism is still far from the type of resistance anticipated by CAE. In the same way that it limits the role of artists in its resistance project, the collective would probably consider these opposition tactics as symbolic and ineffective. Yet, as will be examined in the chapters that follow, performance, citation and satire, happen to be the features that have come to shape digital direct action, giving it its unique quality and significance.

Conclusion

This chapter re-explored the rationale for digital protest by focusing on the conception of electronic civil disobedience. Abandoning its previous argument for the reclaim of individual sovereignty, CAE established digital resistance within the legacy of civil disobedience. The group built on the historical role and impact of this mode of action to propose the development of electronic blockades as core tactics. As part of this process, CAE used the story of three computer hackers to provide a convincing account of 'power-value' and the new dynamics of control and resistance in the virtual sphere. The group thus reinforced its claim that cyberspace should become the exclusive site of dissident action.

Yet, the status of electronic civil disobedience as a tactic is still to be established and early practitioners have had to extensively defend their virtual sit-ins, as in the case of the electrohippies and the Seattle protests. While digital activists insist on presenting cyberspace as a valid sphere for political dissent, they are also fully aware of the authorities' power to legislate against this claim, and CAE itself admits the limited scope of the project. In this sense, the use of the 'electronic civil disobedience' label may appear futile, at least from a legal point of view.

In addition, CAE's controversial placing of the computer hacker at the centre of the activist cell challenges the democratic assumption that anyone should be able to engage in social action. This position is further questioned with the forsaking of theatricality and performance. Countering the historical relation between creative practice and socio-political mobilisation, electronic civil disobedience implicitly discounts the legacy of performance in protest. Yet, as explained in this chapter, the use of theatrical structures and scenarios has strongly influenced the organisation, perception, and to some extent, validity of street demonstrations and social protest. As will be discussed in the forthcoming chapters, these performative elements do not disappear. Instead, they reclaim the central stage, as artists and activists embark on the practice of digital direct action.

Notes

1 Thoreau's essay was initially titled *Resistance to Civil Government*. Some doubts remain as to whether or not Thoreau himself changed it to *Civil Disobedience* at a later point.
2 For an extended account of this fascinating story see Sterling (1993).
3 For an account of the history of art and politics since 1945s see Mesch (2013).

4 'Not Found on this Server'
The Performance of Protest

> During the performance, the search for 'Human Rights' returned the following: 'Human Rights' not found on this server.
>
> —Carmin Karasic

On the 22nd of December 1997, in the small village of Acteal, Mexico, 45 indigenous people who gathered in a local church were killed by a group of paramilitaries. The victims belonged to the Tzotzil community considered to be sympathisers of the Ejército Zapatista de Liberación Nacional, EZLN (also known as the Zapatistas). While they did not all participate in the guerrilla, many of the Chiapas communities supported the Zapatista movement when it rose in 1994. The inhabitants of Acteal in the municipality of Chenalho were some of the supporters, and there are many reasons why their massacre became a turning point in the conflict.

With its abundant natural resources, Chiapas is one of the richest states of Mexico. It is also the home of the largest group of indigenous populations, with more than 10 ethnic groups and 50 languages spoken. Formed mostly of native Maya people, the Zapatistas entered into an armed conflict with the Mexican government, following decades of exploitation and discrimination. As mentioned in the Introduction, the group created an unprecedented political and social movement as part of its uprising. The EZLN and its supporters made extensive use of the World Wide Web to draw global awareness, creating in the process a unique wave of international solidarity.

The victims of Acteal belonged to the pacifist community of Las Abejas (The Bees) who had set up as an autonomous locality outside of Mexico's control. While they supported the Zapatistas's social and political project, Las Abejas were against violence and rejected the idea of an armed conflict. The community thus represented an ideal target to terrorise Zapatistas's sympathisers. While many reports from the local population and human right watchers indicated the presence of government-funded paramilitary groups, Mexico consistently denied any involvement. Yet, the massacre unravelled the authorities' real response to the conflict, that is, a low-intensity war waged by paramilitaries. The majority of the Acteal victims were women and children who had been displaced from their home following previous attacks. This aggression was the most violent perpetrated against civilians. It confirmed that the conflict had escalated and caused enough international uproar to pressurise the government to engage into a peace process.

The tragedy also triggered the first practical applications of electronic civil disobedience. In September 1998, the Electronic Disturbance Theater staged a virtual sit-in as part of the Ars Electronica Festival in Linz, Austria. This virtual theatre of resistance was performed to protest against the Mexican government and its American political and economic allies, but it also paid tribute to the Zapatista uprising and its many victims.

This chapter examines the case of the SWARM Project, Electronic Disturbance Theater's first attempt at digital direct action, with a focus on the practical and creative settings of the virtual performance. The analysis dwells on the challenges posed by the practice and begins to ascertain some of its central contradictions. The aim is to unfold the tensions between original conceptions and practical applications. For instance, while the SWARM performance created a unique space of solidarity and resistance, its renegotiation of radical action raises questions about legitimacy and globalised social movements. The other important issue relates to electronic civil disobedience as a simulation and a symbolic gesture. Through the reassertion of the theatricality of digital protest, Electronic Disturbance Theater offers a unique frame of action, but this position comes with its own sets of problems and opposition, which directly threatens the development of digital activism.

Digital Protest

In response to the tragedy of Acteal, the Anonymous Digital Coalition, an artistic collective based in Europe, announced its intention to organise a series of virtual actions to disrupt Mexican governmental websites. The coalition was effectively calling for the development of a protest within cyberspace. Following this call, American artist and activist Ricardo Dominguez joined arms with activist Stefan Wray and computer programmers Carmin Karasic and Brett Stalbaum. Together, they formed the US-based Electronic Disturbance Theater (EDT), and staged a series of digital direct action against the Mexican government, using the FloodNet programme. The project, known as the SWARM (stop the war in Mexico), ran for a year, with one intervention performed during the Ars Electronica festival in September 1998. The aim of FloodNet was to create digital disturbance. The application was designed to temporarily block access to websites and replicate the disturbance methods used during demonstration sit-ins. In the same way that activists physically block access to buildings to disrupt the flow of individuals, FloodNet was set up to block the flow of information.

Before the protest, participants were invited to download the programme onto their machines. The event was scheduled at a specific time so that users could participate in mass. The application was configured to request pages from the target websites every three seconds. It was expected that at some point, the hosting servers would slow down under the excessive number of requests, disturbing genuine access to the websites, and causing denial-of-services (DoS). During the Ars Electronica performance, FloodNet targeted the websites of the Mexican president, the Frankfurt Stock Exchange and the US Department of Defense.

Electronic Disturbance Theater explains that the SWARM protest was organised to 'demonstrate our capacity for simultaneous global electronic actions and to emphasize the multiple nature of our opponents' (EDT, 1998a: para. 5). The activists offered a clear rationale for their choice of targets. The Mexican government was targeted for its oppression of the Zapatistas and the US Pentagon website for its military and intelligence involvement in Mexico. The Frankfurt Stock Exchange was 'a less obvious choice, but one that makes sense as it is a key European financial site with high symbolic value, and as Germany is a major player in the global neoliberal economy' (ibid.)

While some reports suggested that the Mexican government website had experienced a reduction of its activity during the virtual protest, there was no evidence that the servers were ever at risk of shutting down (Fusco, 1999: para. 21). Similarly, the Frankfurt Stock Exchange's online services showed no delays or difficulties of access. This was mostly because all these servers were set up to support large numbers of online visits. They could therefore manage the increased amount of page requests sent through FloodNet. The virtual strike against the US Pentagon's website, on the other hand did not go unnoticed. According to Dominguez, in response to FloodNet, the Department of Defense sent its own counter-application, Hostile, which automatically returned empty browser windows to page requests. This allegedly disabled computers, forcing digital protesters to restart their machine. For this reason, Electronic Disturbance Theater treated the Pentagon's response as the first use of information war against a civilian server (Dominguez, 2014).

To this day, details regarding the virtual sit-ins are still limited but the organisers suggest that thousands of protesters took part in the event. Electronic Disturbance Theater member Stefan Wray (1999: 110) stated that 20,000 participants connected to FloodNet between the 9th and 10th of September. While the event may not have caused the level of public awareness that was expected, the SWARM Project should still be considered as the first official practice of electronic civil disobedience. The performance foretells the virtual protests staged against the World Trade Organisation in 1999, later becoming the privileged tactic of digital activists such as Anonymous.

Many aspects of the SWARM Project resonate with CAE's conception of digital resistance. First, by staging the protest against the websites of governments and financial institutions, the activists re-placed political action into cyberspace. Second, the focus on obstructing the flow of information (with the use of denial-of-services) created the type of disruption described in *Electronic Civil Disobedience*. Third, the event was the result of a long-term collaboration between activists, artists and computer experts.

At the same time, Electronic Disturbance Theater's project also contrasted with the core of electronic civil disobedience. In particular, it was not the type of action that could 'disrupt the institutions to such an extent that the occupants become disempowered' (CAE, 1996: 8). FloodNet strikes did not specifically disrupt the target institutions. Neither the Mexican government, nor the Pentagon, or the Frankfurt Stock Exchange were compelled to enter into negotiations with the cyber-activists in order to protect their digital assets. This suggests that the SWARM Project was first and foremost a symbolic act of resistance.

To be sure, Electronic Disturbance Theater explicitly positions its practice within a creative and activist framework. Ricardo Dominguez states that the project was a virtual performance of civil disobedience. FloodNet was used to create potential threat rather than actual technological damage. As Dominguez explains, denial of services are clearly inefficient as a means to shut down institutional websites. Instead, the purpose of the event was

> To create a platform where one didn't have to be a hacker or a cracker or a cyborg, that one could understand the most rudimentary language, HTML, and understand that there's this little button on the refresh, reload; all that this FloodNet did was count you and then how many people.
>
> (Dominguez, 2014)

Prior to the performance, Electronic Disturbance Theater set up a website to provide information about the event. The group issued an explicit notice about the contingency of virtual protest. As they downloaded FloodNet, participants were directed to an explicit disclaimer: 'WARNING: This is a protest, it is not a game, it may have personal consequences as in any off-line political manifestation on the street' (EDT, 1998b: para. 1). After inviting internet users to participate, the activists directed them to a page that listed the additional risks of engaging in the action:

> Your IP address will be harvested by the government during any FloodNet action.When you click and enter FloodNet your name and political position will be made known to the authorities. (Similar to having your picture taken during a protest action on the street.)

> 1 Possible damage to your machine may occur because of your participation in the FloodNet action. (Just as in a street action—the police may come and hurt you.)
>
> (ibid.: para. 2)

In this context, Wray (1998b) argues that electronic civil disobedience constitutes the first level of transgression which establishes the internet as a site for direct political action. It can therefore only be conceived as a symbolic gesture; a symbolism that establishes the distinction between protest and criminality. Yet, this separation between symbolic protest and more radical actions, such as the hacking of websites, has been rejected by CAE. While the group does not explicitly point to Electronic Disturbance Theater or the SWARM Project, the reference is obvious. CAE denounces those activists that use the Web to create:

> Hyperreal activist threats to fan the flames of corporate-state paranoia. Again, this is a media battle that will be lost. State panic and paranoia will be transformed through mass media into public paranoia, which will in turn only reinforce state power.
>
> (2001: 19)

CAE's dismissal is based on the argument that an action such as the SWARM does not produce the necessary disruption. For this to happen, the digital strikes should prevent the institutions from functioning or communicating, in the same way that physical blockades disrupt people's mobility and activities.

In addition to the symbolism of the event, the use of mass and public participation contradicts the principle of micro-activist cells involving a small number of activists (five or six, for CAE). This produces highly spectatorial events which again conflict with CAE's original project:

> CAE still believe that ECD is an underground activity that should be kept out of the public/popular sphere (as in the hacker tradition) and the eye of the media, and that simulationist tactics as they are currently being used by resistant forces are only modestly effective if not counterproductive.
>
> (1996: 14)

Thus, Electronic Disturbance Theater's practice refutes all the core assumptions of electronic civil disobedience, that is, the belief that digital resistance should exclusively take place in cyberspace, that it should create actual damage, and that its practice should develop anonymously and in small committee. Instead, SWARM emphasises the combination of activist tactics which includes virtual sit-ins and street demonstrations. Clearly, this dissonance raises many interrogations regarding digital action, and shows the complexity and ambiguity of the project.

One of the main questions that remains unresolved is the rationale for electronic civil disobedience. Following CAE's proposal, Electronic Disturbance Theater locates its activist practice within the framework of civil disobedience, but the activists do not dwell on the theoretical grounds of their project. Questions regarding the notion of disobedience in cyberspace or the justification for civil and legal engagements are not discussed. As such, a discussion about the legitimacy of the digital activists and the SWARM project is wanting.

The point is not just that specialist knowledge and apparatus are essential to the organisation of an event such as SWARM. Digital action raises questions about *who* can protest? for *what* cause? and on behalf of *whom*? As an illustration, several groups of Mexican activists actually objected to the SWARM Project and to electronic civil disobedience. They considered these practices illegal and non-justifiable. The activists questioned the impact of the virtual strikes and the possible response of the Mexican government, not against the digital protesters, but against the dissident populations. While there is no information about the protesters who took part in SWARM, it can safely be assumed that very few were located in the conflict area of Chiapas, or even in Mexico.[1] Hence, the SWARM action provided a platform and an opportunity to act, but only to those who had readily digital access. The consequence, perhaps unintended, was that the resistance project remained unaccessible to those directly affected by the events.

Following the first digital actions, Miguel Garcia Ramirez, member of the Mexican human rights organisation AME LA PAZ, wrote an open email to Electronic Disturbance Theater, describing what he considered to be 'a dirty war' (Ramirez, 1998). In his message, Ramirez voiced his concerns regarding the project of electronic civil disobedience, describing the possible effects of a remote, and paradoxically disengaged, form of resistance:

> Some months ago, someone from the USA told me about the idea of a kind of cybernetic guerrilla. I immediately said I was against it because the effect in short time can be the opposite of it was aimed to; mail bombers, hackers, can be a very exciting challenge for those doing that, it can mean for them a display of technology and knowledge. But a disaster for us who are in Mexico, and also for our communications in Internet and all around the world. It can be very exciting to trespass certain sites, for instance of big corporations. But for us who are talking to the world from Mexico it is not a very interesting idea; we don't care for big banks and corporations. Where we want to reach to is the minds and hearts of those navigating in the Web, those are the doors, less spectacular, we want to trespass.
> (1998: para. 14)

This comment is in startling contrasts with the appeal made by Electronic Disturbance Theater member Stephan Wray who encouraged participants to engage in the protest from home, work, university or anywhere with an internet connection (1998b: para. 17).

As a result of his assessment of the SWARM project, Ramirez directly questions the ideologies underlying the praxis of electronic civil disobedience:

> Did somebody ask the Zapatistas or Marcos? Did somebody tell us let's encourage hackers and mail bombers? Did somebody ask us, webmasters in Mexico that are dealing not one but various sites linked to the social movement, whether we considered such an action convenient? Did they consult it with anyone? Was their action supported by the NCDM in USA? It is not that we think a permission is necessary to take actions, but there must be a consensus about what can affect us all and especially if they are going to be taken in the name of the Zapatistas. Did anyone say: let's suggest without breaking the law actions that break the law or could destroy or saturate important segments of the Mexican state, banks and the stock market information system? Who can benefit from such actions when with antiterrorist laws in the USA whose target is foreigners? We, the Mexicans, need the world's solidarity, imagination and skills. We do not need to resurrect the monster of the metropolis and colony; an action such as the one suggested had to be consulted both with the Zapatistas and the organisations that have sites from Mexico. Or perhaps, immersed in the colonial perception, we are considered unable babies?
>
> (Ramirez, 1998: para. 18–20)

At the time that CAE was formulating the concept of electronic disturbance, less than 1% of the world population had access to the internet. It is true that the Zapatistas successfully created links with, and within, the virtual world; this is how the movement achieved global awareness. However, as Subcomandante Marcos's amusing story of the Zapatista cyber guerrilla suggests, militants did not use this access to engage in virtual strikes against the American and Mexican governments.[2]

The more contentious point of Ramirez's plea is the association made between electronic civil disobedience and Western imperialism. This is a reminder of the political inequality and socio-cultural domination entrenched in digital technologies. In the case of the SWARM Project, it becomes a form of resistance, whereby global participants can select social movements online and 'click to protest', from the comfort of their secured environment, unaware of, and unaffected by, the possible repercussions of their virtual engagement.[3] In a counter-productive way, the type of transnational solidarity developed through electronic civil disobedience may deny, or minimise, the importance of local populations and their distinctive social and political struggle.

The point made here is not, of course, that movements need to remain localised and self- contained. Rather, it is to highlight the consequences of the idealisation of transnational activism and the effects of the most utopian interpretations of digital technology. Since its inception, cyberspace has been advanced by enthusiasts as the most promising platform for freedom of expression and global democracy. Its construction as a revolutionary site for social change remains powerful, but it is also rooted in Western centric *cyber-imaginaires* that need to rethink worldwide relations between technology and political activism.

Performance Protest

The first day of the Zapatistas's insurrection was the day that the North American Free Trade Agreement (NAFTA), between Mexico, Canada and the United States, came into action. The Chiapas uprising started on the 1st of January 1994, a day that symbolised the pre-programmed destruction of Chiapas and its communities. To enter into the NAFTA trade, the Mexican government had to reform Article 27 of the Constitution, one of the most important for indigenous farming communities. This article originally prevented the privatization of communal lands but was revoked to enable the exploitation and expropriation of natural resources in abounding Mexican regions, such as Chiapas, mostly by American and Canadian corporations. The Zapatista movement therefore rose to fight against their subjugation but also against neoliberal ideology.

What made the movement unique is not only that it had remained unknown to the general public until it declared war against the Mexican authorities. It was also mainly formed of indigenous populations, from the Lacandon Jungle, who had been considered second-class citizens for most of their history. As John Holloway and Eloina Pelaez describe it, the perception was that:

> They should not be there, that they could not be there. And yet they were there, saying loudly and clearly 'here we are!' ... the 'here we are!' of all of us ... who have been told, in a million subtle or unsubtle ways, that we do not, or should not, exist. That is why the importance of the uprising stretches far, far beyond the state of Chiapas where it originated, far beyond Mexico, far beyond Latin America or the so-called 'Third World'.
>
> (1998: para. 1)

Indeed, this uprising against constant oppression and exploitation echoes the struggle of many other populations worldwide. The Zapatistas's demand for fundamental rights such as land, food, housing, healthcare and education is an illustration of the failure of current social and political systems.

Yet, the Zapatistas were not interested in power. In fact they rejected it. As members of the movement consistently declared, the aim of the uprising was not to overthrow the government and take power; it was to abolish power altogether. It is perhaps this radical stand, which suggested that the Zapatistas were not just a new guerrilla group fighting for power, that created large movements of solidarity and support from across the world. Again, Holloway explains the converging aspiration:

> What unites the Zapatista uprising in Chiapas or the Movement of the Landless (MST) in Brazil with the struggle of the internet workers in Seattle, say, is not a positive common class composition (as 'immaterial labour'?) but rather the community of their negative struggle against capitalism. The problem is not to understand our composition in the present paradigm but to understand our negativity as the substance of capitalist crisis.
>
> (2005: 164)

With this in mind, the Zapatistas developed a remarkable public campaign that raised awareness and explained the rationale of their uprising. What began as an armed conflict rapidly turned into a battle of communication. The confrontation with the Mexican authorities in San Cristobal de las Casas lasted just under 2 weeks, the Zapatistas having had no intention to wage a military conflict. Most of the political campaign therefore took place through countless communiqués issued by the Zapatistas. These were also distributed by the Mexican print press, mainly *La Jornada,* but most importantly, through the internet. In that same way, many of the international meetings organised by the Zapatistas, such as the 'Intergalactic Encounters', were coordinated using the internet.

Electronic Disturbance Theater Ricardo Dominguez explained his initial fascination for the movement and its unique form of social and political resistance:

> What was really fascinating to me was the poetics and aesthetics of the Zapatistas. ... they basically restructured the concept of what it meant to be in the 21st century seeking autonomy for an indigenous community under duress. ... This drove the [Mexican] government crazy, because instead of doing straight memos of declarations, 'We want this, this, this', they would send stories about kids with sticks, chickens with one leg, children's stories, erotica. So the government is going, 'well, you know, what is it they want?'
>
> (Dominguez, 2014)

The Zapatista built an impressive arsenal of stories, poems and fables about their historical struggle and resistance project. At the forefront of this literary arsenal is the prolific writing of Subcomandante Marcos. Many of the texts have now been published into compilation volumes. They are not, however, the typical political output that could be expected from a radical liberation movement. Instead, the stories of the Zapatistas are told through hundreds of compelling tales and conversations between the Zapatistas themselves and the imaginary characters they created. These stories come as part of the communiqués presented during the Zapatista gatherings.

According to Conant (2010), the distinct mode of communication of Zapatismo, which mixes both European and Mesoamerican tradition of storytelling, is what gives the movement its power and, to a certain extent, its endurance. This political strategy is even more layered if one considers that many of the stories about the living conditions and the demands of the indigenous communities are voiced through the accounts of Subcomandante Marcos, a *mestizo* (a term used to designate people from mixed European and Indigenous origins). Marcos often re-enacts his position as an outside-insider throughout his interactions with his fictional characters.

One of this early personage is Old Antonio, an elder indigenous man who follows Subcomandante Marcos in his many interrogations about life, oppression, rebellion but also about the rain, the wind, the fire and the clouds. Old Antonio often appears to teach lessons or to provide guidance to the younger Marcos, in wise and often poetic ways. In one story, Marcos recounts how Old Antonio shows up to help him decide the colour of their *pasamontañas*, or ski masks, which will become the notorious and symbolic attire of the movement's identity. As in most stories, this one begins with a conversation between Marcos and a few Zapatista officers:

> Another night, another rain, another cold. November 17, 1993. Tenth anniversary of the formation of the EZLN. The Zapatista General Command gathers around the fire. The general plans have been made and the tactical details worked out. The troops have gone to sleep, only the officers ranking above Major stay awake. There with us is Old Antonio, the only man who can breach all the Zapatista checkpoints and enter wherever he wants without anyone impeding his passage. The formal meeting ends and now, between jokes and anecdotes, we review plans and dreams. The issue of how we will cover our faces comes up again, whether with bandanas, or veils, or carnival masks. They all turn to look at me.
>
> "Ski masks," I say.
> "And how will the women manage that with their long hair?" asks Ana Maria.
> "They should cut their hair," says Alfredo.
> "No way man! What are you thinking? I say they should even wear skirts," says Josue.

"Your grandmother should wear skirts," says Ana Maria.
Moises looks at the roof in silence and breaks up the discussion with "and what color should the ski-masks be?"
"Brown… like the cap", says Rolando. Someone else says green.
Old Antonio makes a sign to me and separates me from the group. "Do you have that charred log from the other night?" he asks.
"Yes, in my backpack", I respond.
"Go get it" he says and walks toward the group around the fire. When I return with the bit of wood everyone is quiet, looking at the fire, as does Old Antonio, like that night of the white-tail deer.
"Here", I say, and place the black wood shard in his hand. Old Antonio looks at me steadily and asks, "Remember?" I nod in silence. Old Antonio puts the log on the fire. First it turns gray, then white, yellow, orange, red, fire. The log is fire and light. Old Antonio looks at me again and moves to disappear into the fog. We all stay watching the log, the fire, the light.
"Black", I say.
"What?" asks Ana Maria.
I repeat without taking my eyes from the fire, "Black. The ski masks will be black…" No one opposes the idea…
(Ejército Zapatista de Liberación Nacional, 1995: 77–78)[4]

Many have discussed the possibility that Old Antonio might have been a real person that Marcos met when he first arrived in Chiapas. Real or not, Old Antonio represents an important creative figure in the Zapatista political critique. His regular interactions with Marcos are captivating encounters that have fuelled the imaginary and performance of indigenous resistance.

The other recurrent character in Marcos's storytelling, who is more clearly imaginary, is Don Durito, the beetle with glasses, a smoking pipe and a strong personality. Don Durito de la Lacandona is perhaps the most rebellious personages of all, and his discussions with the Subcomandante provide the most comical and scathing commentaries on the human condition. Their interaction often mimics the relationship of Cervantes's characters Don Quixote de la Mancha and his subordinate Sancho Panza, with, of course, Marcos playing the role of Sancho.

The first encounter between him and the savvy beetle clearly signals the tone of their relationship and what is to come of their future interaction:

And you, what is your name?" I asked him.
"Nebuchadnezzar," he said, and continued, "but my friends call me Durito. You can call me Durito, Captain."
I thanked him for the courtesy and asked him what it was that he was studying.

"I'm studying neoliberalism and its strategy of domination for Latin America", he told me. "And what good is that to a beetle?" I asked him.

And he replied, very annoyed, "What good is it?! I have to know how long your struggle is going to last, and whether or not you are going to win. Besides, a beetle should care enough to study the situation of the world in which it lives, don't you think, Captain?"

"I don't know", I said. "But, why do you want to know how long our struggle will last and whether or not we are going to win?"

"Well, you haven't understood a thing", he told me, putting on his glasses and lighting his pipe. After letting out a puff of smoke, he continued, "To know how long we beetles are going to have to take care that you do not squash us with your big boots".

"Ah!" I said. "Hmmm," he said.

"And to what conclusion have you come in your study?" I asked him. He took out the papers from the desk and began to leaf through them. "Hmmm ... hmmm," he said every so often as he reviewed them. After having finished, he looked me in the eye and said, "You are going to win".

(Marcos, 2005: 42–43)

In an interview with Gabriel Garcia Marquez, Marcos concedes that Cervantes was indeed a major influence for him:

> Don Quixote is the best book out there on political theory, followed by Hamlet and Macbeth. There is no better way to understand the tragedy and the comedy of the Mexican political system than Hamlet, Macbeth and Don Quixote. They're much better than any column of political analysis.
>
> (Marcos *in* Márquez, 2001: para. 10)

Although, many of these stories have been widely translated and are now available in print, it must be understood that most of them are part of the orations delivered by Zapatistas in front of hundreds of members and sympathisers. As such, the performative elements of these stories cannot be overstated. They are meant to be heard, and listened to, as part of a performance that begins when members of the Zapatista National Liberation Army enter the presentation arena. The Zapatistas meetings often consist of talks delivered by the 'mesa directiva' (board of representatives), which represents the voices of the movement. Members usually sit at a large table, in order of speech, all wearing their *pasamontañas*. The encounters are often lengthy, and discussions often last hours, if not days. The fictional stories therefore become important moments of the conversations and they are much anticipated by the audience. The poetry and humour of these tales are central to the literary aesthetics and performance that has come to signify the Zapatistas uprising. It is not surprising therefore that, when engaging with the movement, activists also respond to this creative form of resistance.

As many socially engaged hackers and artists of that time, Electronic Disturbance Theater member Carmin Karasic was following the Zapatista solidarity movement that was growing on the internet. When she heard of the Acteal Massacre, she was convinced that more attention to the conflict was needed. This turns out to be the purpose of SWARM, to draw international attention to the conflict and call for justice. Karasic designed and coded the interface of the application and was in control of the servers that pointed to the target institutions. She was also behind the production of the technical instructions of how to use FloodNet (Vlavo, 2015).

During the SWARM performance, protesters could use one of the original features of FloodNet to send messages as part of the digital strikes. This function was later modified so that the names of the Acteal victims were entered in the search engine of the Mexican website. As they were requesting pages that did not exist, the site responded with default error pages. For example, a search for Paulina Hernandez, one of the victims of the massacre, returned the following phrase 'Paulina Hernandez not found on this server', metaphorically and symbolically suggesting her disappearance. Karasic describes how 'during the performance, the search for "Human rights" returned the following: "Human rights" not found on this server' (Karasic *in* Vlavo, 2015). It is unlikely that these messages of protest were seen by anyone else but the server's administrators, yet the imaginary logs represented a powerful and poetic textual symbol of the resistance. The event became what Karasic calls a 'hyper-monument'; a virtual monument of collective mourning and remembrance.

Paulina Hernandez died in the Acteal Massacre. She was 22 at the time, and her reappearance into the Mexican government website is a symbolic ceremony of remembrance and honouring. Through FloodNet, Paulina is temporarily resuscitated. The emergence and disappearance of her digital body with the loading of each browser page, is a symbol of her once existence and the reminder of her anonymous death. Paulina is both virtually present and physically absent. She is at once visible and invisible. Although she is dead, the performance re-inscribes her into the digital sphere as a virtual resistant body. As performance scholar Peggy Phelan stresses, 'the disappearance of the object is fundamental to performance; it rehearses and repeats the disappearance of the subject who longs always to be remembered' (1993: 147).

This development of digital resistance can also be read as a form of recombinant theatre. As a reminder, recombinant theatre is the theatre that unifies the space of everyday life, the space of traditional theatre, and the virtual space. It is the theatre that produces the sphere for radical resistance. Through the process of digital resuscitation, the victims 'come back' as dissident bodies to perform their own protest. This metaphorical performance acquires further significance by taking place within the space of the Mexican government. The Acteal victims occupy and disturb the virtual presence of the authority that has been rejecting them for centuries. While their physical death is evidence of the violence perpetrated against them, and all indigenous communities, their virtual counterparts take on new significance as bodies of resistance – bodies that should not, and cannot be ignored.

Ricardo Dominguez often compares the SWARM Project to the works of Bertolt Brecht and Augusto Boal. In the same way that Brecht and Boal advocate the revolutionary potential of art and theatre, Dominguez defends the power of digital performance through direct audience participation; hence the reason why Electronic Disturbance Theater rejects micro cells and anonymous actions. Electronic civil disobedience is a massively participatory project that requires a physical audience. According to Dominguez, the aim is to create:

> A type of interactive performance that would collapse the space of difference between the real body and the electronic body, between everyday life and everyday life online, between the activist and the hacker, the performer and the audience, individual agency and mass swarming.
>
> (Dominguez *in* Fusco, 2003: 152)

SWARM thus becomes a digital re-articulation of Augusto Boal's theatre of the oppressed which encourages members of the public to directly enact their resistance onto the digital stage.

Boal's work was of great influence in the conception of revolutionary political theatre. During the 1960s, he practised this form of theatre that encouraged members of the public to directly act on stage. To facilitate the process, the plays tackled contemporary social and political issues in Brazil. In his book, *Theatre of the Oppressed*, Boal proposes a rejection of Aristotle's classical drama in favour of Brecht's epic theatre, as a theatre which plays on illusion rather than realism to entice audience participation. He extended the critical thinking that Brecht imposes on the audience by suppressing the performer altogether. In other words, with Boal, Brecht's active spectator becomes an active participant. The theatre of the oppressed moves the traditional stage to the streets in an effort to encourage direct participation and active contribution to social change.

Hence, while CAE denies the potential theatricality of digital action, Electronic Disturbance Theater transforms the protest into political theatre. As Dominguez explains about the virtual strikes of the Mexican websites:

> Each performance has a very traditional three-act structure: act 1, the e-mail call to a core actor/audience network (you may also start to get responses from reporters for information and updates); act 2, the gesture itself, which is not very interesting to look at since you don't really see that much—you just click (click action); act three, you re-encounter your core actor/audience network to determine what might have occurred within your staging space, how many people participated, where they came from, what they might have said, and of course what has been reported about the performance.
>
> (ibid.: 156)

The idea of a digital theatre of the oppressed can be put forward as a radical interpretation of protest that allows the virtual formation of a collective memory of social movement.

There is still, however, the contention that, unlike Boal's proposition, the SWARM project does not give a direct voice to those at the forefront of the conflict. Effectively, the performances are still organised 'on behalf' of the oppressed populations, a practice that, as mentioned before, has been strongly contested. In subsequent performances of SWARM, and in response to the objection formulated by the Mexican activist group AMEL PAZ, Electronic Disturbance Theater redirects its virtual strike actions towards US-based websites (Dominguez, 2014). This move partially concedes to the limits of a globalised resistance project and points to the conceptual limitations of digital action.

Symbolic Protest

The SWARM Project was staged as a digital performance during Ars Electronica, one of Europe's most famous media art festival. The theme for the 1998 edition was INFOWAR. The programme focused on the role of computer technologies in socio-political conflicts and what the organisers termed, cyberguerrillas. It featured digital installations, network projects, and performances such as *Cyberwar is Coming!*, *Don't Panic Hack it!*, *Info Weapon Contest,* and Electronic Disturbance Theater's presentation *Digital Zapatismo* (Electronica, 1998). This staging of SWARM as part of an art festival was not essential for the activist project to succeed. CAE's idea of a small group of activists and hackers anonymously performing protest, was clearly achievable. Yet, Electronic Disturbance Theater, and later on the WTO digital activists, and the electrohippies, arranged for highly publicised and participatory events.

In addition, these groups all concurred that the virtual strikes were not meant to create actual damage or severe disruption.

Carmin Karasic who administrated FloodNet, explicitly states that the application was not designed to crash servers. She argues that while this was technically possible, it was not the purpose of the project. FloodNet had therefore not been programmed in this way (Vlavo, 2015). Similarly, the denial-of-service kit built by the electrohippies clearly detailed the conditions for staging electronic civil disobedience. All of these elements inevitably highlight the symbolic character of electronic civil disobedience. In a way, digital activists have conceded to the symbolic function of electronic civil disobedience, arguing that the aim is to demonstrate potential, as opposed to real threat. In particular, the framing of the SWARM Project as a theatrical performance suggests that digital direct action is both a political and creative gesture and should not be seen as a menace.

This vision is contradictory, however. While early practitioners assumed that the digital network should be more than a space for information and campaigning, to become the site for direct confrontation, problems emerged when these confrontations turn out to be symbolic, rather than actual. As Jordan and Taylor (2004) have argued, 'the style of electronic disobedience is almost wilfully contrary to the nature of cyberspace, in its desire to overcome the disembodied nature of cyberspace and to recreate the effects of a protest of many people' (2004: 73). This desire for mass participation implies that digital protest has to remain within an allegedly legal framework. The dilemma is that activists conceive electronic civil disobedience as an effective tactic for social change but their practice tends to turn it into a symbolic gesture. The reason for this approach is understandable, and non-negligible, but it still relays digital action to the domain of symbolic representation, as opposed to radical disruption.

In her analysis of Electronic Disturbance Theater's project, Lane (2003) proposes to evaluate the success of digital protest by measuring the symbolic, not technological efficacy of the event. This is a common argument used in the defence of SWARM, the fact that no data was damaged and that no servers were crashed. For Lane, FloodNet could be considered as 'the semantic structure through which thousands of global participants assembled to stage nonviolent protest in cyberspace' (2003: 139). Yet, probing this point further, it emerges that FloodNet did more than enabling a symbolic performance of resistance. It *simulated* these acts of disturbance. Due to the structure of the internet which makes it possible to damage websites and crash servers, defending the symbolic status of digital protest becomes problematic.

To grasp this important argument further we can refer to Jean Baudrillard's original conception of simulation. In *Simulation and Simulacra*, Baudrillard (1994: 3) describes simulation as the 'feign to have what one doesn't have'; a practice which according to him, has been dominating contemporary postmodern culture. A simulation is the generation of models that have no origin or reality; as such, they are 'hyperreal' (ibid.: 1). To explain this concept, Baudrillard uses the fable of Jorge Luis Borges about a detailed map that ends up covering the territory it is meant to represent. He argues that in this case, the map comes to precede and engender the territory. There is a shift from the reality of the territory to the hyperreality of the map. The map, which is initially meant to be a simulation of the territory, replaces the territory as the 'real' thing, and, in this process, makes the existence of the territory redundant. Baudrillard terms this shift 'the precession of simulacra', that is, a copy (or map) with no original (or territory).

The *imaginaire* of cyberspace is the archetype of Baudrillard's concept of simulation. Here is a virtual environment originally perceived as a digital map of the world with no borders. For some, this virtual world is open to conquest, others see it as the new home of virtual communities, while others still, conceive it as the site of radical action. Cyberspace thus appears as a simulation of the material world, with many characteristics that have no referents. Problems begin when these aspects lose their status as simulacra and start to be considered 'reality'. As Baudrillard warns 'the unreal is no longer that of dream or of fantasy, of a beyond or a within, it is that of a hallucinatory resemblance of the real with itself' (ibid.: 23).

In relation to digital action, a similar confusion, or conflation has occurred. Although activists have framed their practice as the simulation of server crashing, the potentiality of this happening is clear. As will be discussed in the next chapter, servers and websites have been shut down as a result of denial-of-service actions. Incidentally, CAE's original writings indirectly contributed to this conflation. Anyone reading *The Electronic Disturbance* or *Electronic Civil Disobedience* would be challenged to find references to the symbolic status of digital resistance. At no point does the collective suggest that disturbance should be simulated. In fact, the group argues quite the opposite. As a result, the distinction between 'real' actions and 'simulated' ones is no longer relevant. This is because 'simulation threatens the difference between the 'true' and the 'false', the 'real' and the imaginary' (Baudrillard, 1994: 3). The SWARM Project was not judged on the basis of what it *did,* but instead on what it *could* do, in other words, on its simulation of possible damage. In this paradoxical logic, digital protest effectively loses its symbolic status.

To be sure, a note warning against the potential of virtual actions was sent to the International Monetary Fund and the World Bank few years after the SWARM actions. The document was issued by the National Infrastructure Protection Center (NIPC), a federal agency responsible for monitoring the US infrastructure networks and systems. In its assessment, the centre gave a precise account of what it considered to be illegal digital activities:

> Hacktivism describes the convergence of political activism and computer attacks and hacking, where "hacking" refers to illegal or unauthorized access to, and manipulation of computer systems and networks. The use of hacktivism has been noted in protest activities since the EDT endorsed a series of so-called network-direct actions against web sites of the Mexican government in 1998. Although there has been no direct cyber threat against the International Monetary Fund (IMF) and World Bank meetings during the week of September 23, 2002, several hacker groups may attempt to conduct cyber protests during the meetings.
>
> (NIPC, 2002: para. 1)

The reference here is unambiguous. What Electronic Disturbance Theater and the electrohippies framed as symbolic activist performances was considered as unlawful cyber-attacks by the government. From this point, it is all too easy to position digital direct action as a national threat.

The NIPC warning was issued only few years after an important testimony given before the US House of Representatives, as part a panel about terrorism. In her function as information security expert, Dorothy Denning provided a definition of the term cyberterrorism. She defined it as:

> The convergence of terrorism and cyberspace. It is generally understood to mean unlawful attacks and threats of attack against computers, networks, and the information stored therein as well as in when done to intimidate or coerce a government or its people in furtherance of political or social objectives. Further, to qualify as cyberterrorism, an attack should result in violence against persons or property, or at least cause enough harm to generate fear.
>
> (Denning, 2000: para. 1)

In the testimony, Denning made explicit references to the practice of the Electronic Disturbance Theater and the electrohippies. While she admitted that their actions were not to be considered as cyberterrorism, because of their symbolic forms, she nevertheless suggested that they were 'something to watch and take reasonable precautions against' (ibid.: para. 10). In many ways, her comment was detrimental as it unwittingly associated electronic civil disobedience with cyberterrorism. As explained by Mathias Klang, once it is mentioned, the discourse of cyberterrorism becomes difficult to erase:

> When invoking the spectre of terrorism it is important to remember that today the relevance of the correct label in this case is far from

> academic. If the action of DoS is seen to be disobedience the courts may show tolerance; if it is seen to be criminal the courts will punish it; but if it is seen as terrorism then society will neither tolerate the actions nor forgive the proponents.
>
> (2005: 135)

Most supporters and performers of digital protest have been aware of the threat of the terrorist label. CAE itself had warned that governments would refer to terrorism in order to halt the development of digital direct action. Although, as they later admit, they did not fully measure the size of the problem:

> CAE noted that there was growing paranoia among U.S. security agencies about controlling the electronic resistance. Oddly enough, these agencies scared themselves with their own constructions of electronic criminality. It was much like Welles being scared of his own broad-cast. In that comic moment, CAE ironically suggested that ECD was successful without ever having been tried, and that merely announcing that some form of digital resistance could occur could have the effect of creating a panic in security agencies to such a degree that their primary focus would become locked in the hyperreality of criminal constructions and virtual catastrophe. This is a comment that CAE wishes it had never made...
>
> (2001: 19)

The collective reminds, in its third and last pamphlet, *Digital Resistance,* that the United States sanctioned trespass or blockage in cyberspace with disproportionate jail sentences. This amalgamate between electronic disturbance and cyberterrorism serves as a strategy to deny the 'right for people to use cyberspace as a location for political objection' (2001: 33). This is the reason why CAE encouraged activists to argue that cyberprotest and virtual sit-ins were acts of civil disobedience, and 'that a distinction [should] be made between trespass with political intent and trespass with criminal intent' (ibid.: 33–34). However, the group also warns of the danger of simulated digital actions (indirectly referring to SWARM Project) explaining that 'in the U.S., the voting public consistently supports harsher sentencing for "criminals", more jails, and more police, and it is this hyperreal paranoia that gets law-and-order politicians the votes needed to turn these directives into legislation' (2001: 19).

One of the issues is that since the mid-1990s, the United States have built on the discourse of cyberterrorism by publishing reports and statistics regarding cyberattacks, allegedly carried out by China, Cuba, North Korea and Libya (Vegh, 2002). Because cyberprotest and hacking can adopt similar tactics, critics have been inclined to link activism to computer crime. It is difficult to accept, however, that a project such as the

SWARM could genuinely be considered as cyberterror. There is indeed little doubt that this label serves a different purpose than raising the issue of national security.

According to Weimann (2005), the term *cyberterror* became very popular partly because of the anxiety it produced. As he explains, 'psychological, political, and economic forces have combined to promote the fear of cyberterrorism' (2005: 131). In addition, Weimann argues that 'the fear of random, violent victimization segues well with the distrust and outright fear of computer technology' (ibid.). The mass media have been stirring this fear, while politicians, law enforcement and security consultants have used it for their own agenda and benefit.

In opposition, many critics have challenged the concept of cyberterrorism. Conway (2002, 2011) not only argues that cyberterrorism has not, and will never occur, but she also explains why the term is not adequate. Looking at a wide range of media discourses, she contends that what is commonly referred to as 'cyberterrorism' is the use that terrorist groups make of the internet. She recognises the increasing and varied applications of networked technologies in relation to terrorism but still defends that these cases cannot be considered cyberterrorism, because in these instances, the internet is used as a *tool* for communication. Similarly, Green (2002: para. 5) argues that the emergence of the 'myth of cyberterrorism' demonstrates that 'Americans have had a latent fear of catastrophic computer attack ever since a teenage Matthew Broderick hacked into the Pentagon's nuclear weapons system and nearly launched World War III in the 1983 movie *WarGames*'.

Indeed, tracing the origin of the term *cyberterrorism* is akin to discovering a long-lost science-fiction novel. Barry Collin is often cited as the person who coined the term. Many studies mention that he first used the word around the 1980s, however, there is no evidence that *cyberterrorism* was used this far back. Instead, Collin's original statement first appeared in 1997, in a paper presented at the Eleventh Annual International Symposium on Criminal Justice Issues, a few years after the publications of CAE. This is important because, as evidenced by the extract below, the definitions that Collin proposes in his paper, 'The Future of CyberTerrorism', are based on a series of hypothetical accounts that make no references to recognised cyberterror attacks:

> A CyberTerrorist will remotely access the processing control systems of a cereal manufacturer, change the levels of iron supplement, and sicken and kill the children of a nation enjoying their food. That CyberTerrorist will then perform similar remote alterations at a processor of infant formula.
>
> A CyberTerrorist will place a number of computerized bombs around a city, all simultaneously transmitting unique numeric patterns, each bomb receiving each other's pattern.

> A CyberTerrorist will disrupt the banks, the international financial transactions, the stock exchanges.
>
> A CyberTerrorist will attack the next generation of air traffic control systems, and collide two large civilian aircraft.
>
> A CyberTerrorist will remotely alter the formulas of medication at pharmaceutical manufacturers. The potential loss of life is unfathomable.
>
> The CyberTerrorist may then decide to remotely change the pressure in the gas lines, causing a valve failure, and a block of a sleepy suburb detonates and burns.
>
> (Collin, 1997: para. 14)

These are the types of fictional scenarios of which Conway is very critical. The examples refer to the ways that terrorists could make use of the internet, in the same way that other telecommunication or devices could be used. The one exception is the reference to the disruption of banks, financial transactions and stock exchanges. While this may fit with more recent definitions of cyberterrorism, it still conflicts with the principle that cyberterrorism (or terrorism) induces a threat of physical violence, death or serious bodily harm (Badey, 1998). It thus seems difficult to maintain that any form of digital disruption could be terror, let alone cyberterrorism.

Since the term *cyberterrorism* was not part of the mainstream discourse at the time of the first virtual protests, it is evident that cyberprotest and cyberterror have been articulated to counter one another. Cyberprotest has been developed to disassociate internet-based protest from terrorism, and cyberterror has been articulated to frame digital direct action as a criminal activity. This explains the constant need to dissociate digital direct action from computer crime, because in the absence of a distinction, so-called real and simulated actions will be collapsed into a single, illegal practice.

For critic Feigenbaum (2012: 86), the terrorist discourse has been at the service of, on the one hand, a burgeoning market of digital security and electronic protection that recognises opportunities for cybersecurity solutions, and, on the other hand, it legitimates 'forms of surveillance, policing and prosecution that infringe individuals' civil liberties and apply terrorism legislation against a wide range of the population, particularly political protesters'. Hence, in this mixture of economic and political interests, the justification of electronic protest is clearly hampered.

In her defence of Electronic Disturbance Theater, Lane (2003) argued that the SWARM Project could not be considered as illegal since it did not involve unauthorised access to computer networks. For her, the group made use of 'the decidedly public spaces of the Internet ... to stake the important claim that cyberspace is public space and should be governed by the same social and legal norms that pertain in public spaces off-line' (ibid.: 139). Yet, and as will be examined in the next chapter, the many legal claims filed against participants of digital action, illustrate that legal systems can readily be changed to fit digital environments. As such, there is little doubt that targets of digital protest are already supported by a legal apparatus that can defend them, even if it includes the construction of *imaginaires* about terrorism and national threat.

Conclusion

The analysis of the virtual strikes against the Mexican government and the US Pentagon has revealed many facets of electronic civil disobedience. In particular, the SWARM Project has brought to the forefront the challenges of developing digital direct action. In contrast to CAE's original approach which advocates restricted activist cells and anonymous performance, activists have opted for mass participation, wide publicity and theatrical display of digital protest. In the case of SWARM, resistance included the re-appropriation of the concept of recombinant theatre, but also the performative strategies of the Zapatistas. Electronic Disturbance Theater rejected the idea of provoking technological damage, in favour of a poetical performance of virtual mourning and resistance. In doing so, digital activists gave political theatre and theatricality a central role.

Yet, at the same time that it opens up creative and artistic possibilities, this approach exposes the symbolic performance of electronic civil disobedience, putting into question its potential effectiveness. On the one hand, digital action appears as a symbolic gesture that creates little tension and offers even less scope for political negotiation. On the other hand, it is also perceived as a serious threat that should be eradicated. As the distinction between 'reality' and simulation collapses, digital protest is assessed on the potential damage that it can produce, as opposed to what activists engage into. The threat of criminal charge has haunted activists since the inception of digital activism and many discursive strategies have been developed to counter accusations. None of them have deterred the conflation between virtual protest and criminality, however, and the task has become even more challenging with the formulation of the *imaginaire* of cyberterrorism.

While this chapter has explained how these processes of conflation and dissociation occur, it is important to remember that the bundling of criminality and digital action is not inevitable. As with any form of resistance, this decision remains deeply entrenched in politics of control. Indeed, activists cannot readily expect that legitimacy will be granted by the authorities they are opposing, and in many ways, addressing and exposing the performativity and theatricality of their practice seem to be the solution to countering the amalgamate. This does not signal the end of digital action, however. As will be examined in the next chapter, digital protest continues to develop through other new forms, but also, at other new costs.

Notes

1 According to ITU reports, in 1998, the estimated number of internet users in Mexico was 1,350 m. The figures were 8,000 m in the United Kingdom and 60,000 m in the United States. ITU, *Yearbook of Statistics: Telecommunication Services Chronological Time Series 1989–1998,* International Telecommunication Union, Geneva, 2000.

2 See Introduction in this book.

3 This issue becomes prominent with the advent of social media and the rise of what critics have termed 'clicktivism' or 'slacktivism' (for more details, see Gladwell, 2010; Morozov, 2011).

4 Original Spanish source from EZLN (1995), English translation from Conant (2010: 125).

5 'I Did It for the Lulz'

The Humour of Disturbance

'I Did It for the Lulz'.

—Anon.

In December 2010, the websites of several major companies were briefly taken down following a series of denial-of-service (DoS) strikes. Among others sites, MasterCard, Visa, PayPal and Amazon experienced the wrath of the internet activist movement known as Anonymous. The event was named 'Operation Avenge Assange' but is often referred to as Operation Payback, in reference to the strategy of retaliation developed by Anonymous since its formation.

The revenge operation was in response to the US government's attempt to stop the electronic release of confidential information by WikiLeaks. Right before the digital actions, the whistleblower organisation had published hundreds of thousands of diplomatic cables from the US Department of Defense, in association with international newspapers, including *The Guardian*, *The New York Times*, *Der Spiegel*, *Le Monde* and *El Pais*. Most of these cables contained information deemed confidential and many were considered state secrets. Under the pressure of the US government, several commercial companies withdrew their services to WikiLeaks. Amazon discontinued its hosting of WikiLeaks's website, and PayPal and Visa rejected all electronic donations sent to the organisation.

In addition, WikiLeaks founder Julian Assange was arrested, under a separate accusation, and faced extradition for trial. Considering these events as a threat to civil liberties, Anonymous officially declared its support to Assange. In a statement published on the Web, the collective announced its intention to strike back at the attackers:

> Julian Assange deifies everything we hold dear. He despises and fights censorship constantly, is possibly the most successful international troll of all time, and doesn't afraid [*sic*] of fucking anything (not even the US government). ...

> Therefore, Anonymous has a chance to kick back for Julian. We have the chance to fight the oppressive future which looms ahead. We have a chance to fight in the first infowar ever fought.
>
> 1 Paypal is the enemy. DDoS'es will be planned, but in the meantime, boycott everything.
>
> (Anonymous, 2010c: para. 1–4)

Notably, this grandiloquent message was introduced by yet another grandiloquent statement, from no one else but John Perry Barlow, who declared: 'the first serious infowar is now engaged. The field of battle is Wikileaks. You are the troops' (ibid.). With this, Barlow suggested that he had finally encountered, in Anonymous, the cyber warriors that could defend his digital cause.

This chapter examines the activist practice of Anonymous and considers its relationship with the politics of technology and information. While Anonymous movement emerged from a hacker milieu, and thus greatly differs from Electronic Disturbance Theater and the electrohippies, there is no doubt that its activist philosophy is rooted in *cyber-imaginaires*. The endorsement of John Perry Barlow may be incidental, but the influence is evidenced by Anonymous's belief in the freedom of information and its opposition to state control.

The discussion in this chapter retraces the path of Anonymous, from its origin as a group of trolls and pranksters to its public rise as a fierce digital activist movement. Despite dominant representations, Anonymous is far from being an unruly and juvenile group of hackers who create chaos on the internet. Instead, it is a heterogeneous and malleable collective of people who tend to share similar ethos, supporting free access to digital information and abhorring any form of censorship. In many ways, the movement has produced a new anti-capitalist *imaginaire* of the digital space that is much more compelling than that of earliest cyber-enthusiasts.

While technology is at the core of Anonymous's political engagement, the influence of art and creative practice is undeniable. Aside from the re-appropriation of denial-of-service, the collective has committed to the development of highly creative and performative actions. This approach is rooted in the constant quest for mischievous humour or, as the group calls it, 'lulz'. The chapter will explore this central element in relation to the historical practice of combining humour and protest.

Finally, the chapter discusses the core challenges faced by Anonymous which are related to the use of its main resistance tool, LOIC, as well as the increasing prosecution of digital activists. What will become clear is that, as most activist groups before it, and despite developing various discourses and strategies, Anonymous has not fully succeeded in legitimising its activist project.

Anonymity of Disturbance

A few years after entering the public scene, Anonymous published a video which answered the question that many had had on their minds since 2008. Who was the organisation behind the scorning of the Church of Scientology? And why was it now striking multinational corporations? Anonymous's response was rather singular. The video recording featured a computerised voiceover bluntly declaring that Anonymous did not exist. Anonymous was just an idea, 'an internet meme – that can be appropriated by anyone, anytime, to rally for a common cause that's in the benefit of humankind' (Anonymous, 2010d: para. 4). This type of explanation is what turned Anonymous into the most appealing and powerful activist movement of the last two decades.

Throughout its brief existence, Anonymous's activist project has remained highly controversial and often misunderstood. This is mostly because the group does not seem to have a 'consistent philosophy or political program' (Coleman, 2012: para. 5). As a result, many have described the movement as chaotic, anarchist or criminal. Yet, expert research has provided more useful accounts of the phenomenon. Anthropologist Gabriella Coleman has produced an extensive analysis about the activist movement, which provides a better understanding of its origin. In one study, she explains that 'Anonymous is no different from us. It simply consists of humans sitting at their glowing screens and typing, as humans are wont to do at this precise moment in the long arc of the human condition' (Coleman, 2014: 115). This point goes against the dominant idea that Anonymous is a secluded movement. Coleman confirms that the easiest way to reach Anonymous members (or Anons) is to visit the digital platforms where they meet and exchange ideas; the most popular one being IRC (Internet Relay Chat).

Yet, Anonymous also emerged from a unique context that shaped its activist ideology and practice. While it is influenced by the hacker culture, which can be traced as far back as the 1960s, the movement is commonly linked to 4chan, a popular online bulletin board set up in 2004. For over a decade, 4chan has been providing anonymous users a virtual social space where they can gather and share material about a wide range of interests, including manga, anime, games, food or cats. Over time, the site has become particularly (in)famous for the success of its 'random'/b/board where users can post uncensored and often offensive images; all of this, again, anonymously.

Prior to becoming involved in digital direct action, Anons were thriving on 4chan, engaging in the random pranking and trolling of unsuspecting internet users. These mischievous practices essentially consisted in the disruption of anything, or anyone, using any means that could generate laughter. Some of the pranks performed included sending unpaid pizzas to the home of targeted individuals, revealing private or false information about people, highjacking social media accounts, disrupting virtual communities, defacing websites, and spreading hateful speech and images. These actions varied in their level of deviance, but they were all intended to be funny, and cause what is known as 'lulz'.

Originally derived from the acronym lol (laughing out loud), Coleman defines lulz as 'a deviant style of humor and a quasi-mystical state of being', which has been with Anonymous since its formation (2014: 2). Lulz can be considered as a nasty version of lol, with the idea that the laugh often happens at the expense, and through the humiliation, of somebody else. As Anonymous itself declares:

> We laugh at the face of tragedy. We mock those in pain. We ruin the lives of others simply because we can ... A man takes out his aggression on a cat, we laugh. Hundreds die in a plane crash, we laugh. We are the embodiment of humanity with no remorse, no caring, no love, and no sense of morality.
>
> (Anonymous *in* Coleman, 2014: 1)

Many of the pranks performed by Anonymous require advanced computer skills, which is also why generating lulz is different from creating simple lol. Pranksters and trolls often have a better command of the technology and the most praised pranks are often linked to programming exploits. As Coleman (2014) argues, the obvious pleasure that is derived from the creation of lulz is deeply rooted in hacker culture.

This does not mean, however, that Anonymous is exclusively formed of computer hackers. Coleman's work also challenges this preconception, and she explains that the origin of Anonymous lays within the geek culture as well as the hacker culture. Hackers tend to be self-identified programming experts, but this is not always the case for geeks. Although they do share passionate interests for computers and digital communication, geeks may not themselves be involved in programming (Coleman, 2011: 512–513). While the difference between the two groups is not set in stone, it helps understanding the variety of people and skills involved in the activist project of Anonymous. Geeks and hackers also have in common a commitment to information freedom. This philosophy is often expressed through the development of digital technology, for example with the production of open source software, but also through the free sharing of information, including material that others would perceived as being private or copyrighted.

The same philosophy is at work within Anonymous, and when the group eventually became famous it was directly related to its fierce campaign against digital censorship. In 2008, the Church of Scientology attempted to stop the circulation of a controversial video featuring its leading member Tom Cruise. Anonymous considered this as an explicit case of digital censorship which threatened the free flow of information. As a reaction, the movement set up a digital direct action against the church. Named Project Chanology (in reference to its birth on the 4chan board) the activist campaign first started on the internet before spawning international street demonstrations that aimed to publicly discredit the Church of Scientology.[1] The operation, which in digital activism contexts was a grand success, demonstrated the technological mastery and political engagement of those who consider themselves as 'citizens of the Internet' (Anonymous, 2010b: para. 1).

While a technological drive is at the core of Anonymous's political engagement, the influence of *cyber-imaginaires* is also evident, particularly in the construction of the internet as a model of freedom. In a video press release issued against anti-piracy law, one Anonymous branch in the Netherlands explains that 'the Internet has given us freedom, the freedom to gain the education and information we need and deserve' (Anonymous Netherlands, 2012: para. 5). This position implies that Anonymous will oppose anyone who wants to 'take that freedom away by calling it piracy' (ibid.).

This vision clearly echoes the dichotomy established by the Digerati and the *Declaration of Independence of Cyberspace*, that is, a split between internet users, corporations and governments. As discussed in Chapter 1, this binary vision is problematic because it minimises the role, and thus the power, that corporations and states can exert over the internet. When Anonymous (2010b: para. 1) opens its call for direct action with the assertion that 'the time has come to reclaim what's ours', it is still not clear what the group is referring to as 'theirs'. To adopt this position, one needs to embrace the *imaginaire* of the free and open world, in other words, to adopt the Barlowian utopia of cyberspace.

Anonymous does produce a new *cyber-imaginaire* however, one that is much more compelling than the early discourses developed by the virtual elite. Its anti-capitalist stand promotes an approach to digital information that contrasts with the digerati entrepreneurial ambition. For instance, in one of the many statements explaining its campaign, Anonymous argues that the new piracy legislation is a way to give full control to corporations and to public broadcast companies that are financed by taxpayers' money. This is when the group famously declared, 'they call it piracy, yet we call it freedom' (Anonymous Netherlands, 2012: para. 4). This difference in vision comes from the influence of the hacker and geek free culture, but also, from the global scope of the movement, which goes far beyond the dominance of US capitalistic ideology.

The real novelty and challenge however, is that Anonymous does not associate with a single political agenda. One of the premises of the movement is that anyone can create an operation using the pseudonym. This means that the digital actions can cover a range of different issues, depending on who is organising them. Anonymous makes this point very clear:

> So you want to join Anonymous? You can not join Anonymous. Nobody can join Anonymous. Anonymous is not an organization.

> It is not a club, a party or even a movement. There is no charter, no manifest, no membership fees. Anonymous has no leaders, no gurus, no ideologists. In fact, it does not even have a fixed ideology.
> (Anonymous, 2012: para. 1)

These are the types of comments that have frustrated the media and fuelled the idea that Anonymous is a group of vindictive anarchists. Yet the story is much more complex. The position described by Anonymous is actually a hard line. It is not just that the movement claims to have no leaders, gurus or ideologists, Anons have developed a strategy against anyone who would attempt to position themselves as spokesperson for the movement, particularly in front of the media.

The strategy consists in exposing and banning anyone who is perceived as trying to gain special status or recognition. Coleman (2014) provides a detailed account of this practice in her book on Anonymous. In the chapter titled 'Moralfaggotry', she describes how participants that consider themselves core to Anonymous can be summarily banned from the IRC channels, and effectively from the community, if others establish that they have engaged in any form of personal promotion. Within Anonymous, this tendency is considered taboo and most Anons carefully avoid possible accusations. Coleman describes the threats as 'tactics for enforcing the ideal of egalitarianism' (ibid.: 189). This also reflects some of the principles of the hacker culture, whereby hackers do not generally introduce themselves as hackers, until others in the community recognise them as such.

Yet, this does not mean that the system is without hierarchy or control. The power to oust participants still belongs to those in control of the communication channels; more often than not, they are those with higher status and skills. There may not be leaders in the traditional sense, but network operators do control who can and cannot have a voice within specific contexts. These power dynamics are not unique to Anonymous of course; they are at the core of any social and political movement. As in most collective formations, administrators or moderators acquire the power to include and exclude, but not to the point where there remains no one to dialogue with, or to participate in the actions. For instance, protest such as Operation Payback required the central involvement of hackers, but those with less advanced technical skills and authority were still crucial to the project. These members run chatrooms meetings and discussions, they create videos and press releases, and they administer websites and communication portals. This way of dividing tasks is similar to other social movements where people use their skills to contribute to the general campaign, without the need for traditional leadership.

Along with the leaderless ethos, the rule for anonymity is also, evidently, core to Anonymous. This convention is facilitated by the absence of public leaders and the premise that anyone can join the movement. It means that beyond the virtual interactions, no one knows who the others are, as members rarely use or reveal their legal identity.

The story of how anonymity became key and how Anonymous got its name, again illustrates the humoristic overtone of the movement. In her book, *We Are Anonymous*, journalist Olson (2012) describes how Christopher Poole, the founder of 4chan, was convinced to allow anonymous posting instead of enforcing the use of nicknames. As Poole agreed, 4chan abandoned nicknames and imposed anonymity on several of its boards. This new system was not to everyone's taste however, and soon, users began to clash. Those in favour of nicknames use tripcodes, a function that enables user identification, as a way to override anonymity. As Olson recounts:

> Supporters of anonymity and tripcodes started creating separate threads, calling on anyone who supported their own view to post a message and demonstrate support, or starting "tripcode vs. anon" threads. The tripfags began mocking the anonymous users as a single person named "Anonymous", or jokingly referring to them as a hive mind. Over the next few years, however, the joke would wear thin and the idea of Anonymous as a single entity would grow beyond a few discussion threads.
>
> (2012: 28)

Thus, what was first and foremost a mockery became pseudonymous to one of the most omnipotent group of digital activists.

Initially, the plea for anonymity was based on the assumption that by using 'Anon', all participants would be kept at the same level, with no direct means to achieve individual popularity or form clans. Yet, this commitment later became paramount, especially to those engaging in digital direct action. As evidence, Anonymous promptly published a series of guidelines on how to remain anonymous and retain privacy.

In the video release, *How to join Anonymous – A beginners guide*, potential newcomers were given detailed advice about protecting their identity on the internet. Anonymous encouraged members to create new digital personas, using multiple email addresses and social media accounts. It also recommended the use of encryption programmes to achieve higher level of security if needed. More importantly however, Anonymous reminded viewers that anyone could become part of the movement. As a consequence, the rule for anonymity first and foremost prevailed within Anonymous itself:

> If you talk to another Anonymous, you will never know who he is. He may be a hacker, cracker, phisher, agent, spy, provoker—or just the guy from next door. ... We will always respect your need for

> privacy. We will never ask for your personal information. If we do, we will not expect a truthful answer; And neither should you.
>
> (Anonymous, 2012: para. 5–6)

In this complex and deceptive context, it seems difficult to imagine that Anonymous could ever undertake successful digital activist campaigns, and yet, the movement carried out a series of remarkable actions that have reshaped the scope of contemporary social mobilisation. In the process of creating digital disturbance, Anonymous redeployed the tactics of past activists, such as the use of denial-of-services, as well as the performance of highly theatricalised events. The movement also adopted the cellular formation envisioned by CAE, placing hackers at the core of the project. In addition, and against CAE's vision of hackers as apolitical and awkward youngsters, those involved in Anonymous's digital actions were often highly engaged in the politics of information and, wittingly outspoken about it.

Performance of Disturbance

Operation Payback is the story of a vengeance, and as all great vengeance stories, it contains all the suspense, tension and twists necessary to its unfolding. Without doubt, the actions of Anonymous could have easily come out of a Hollywood film studio. Following the best-selling format of a trilogy, the first movie features an exhilarating revenge against a religious group; the second segment is a remorseless strike against copyright supporters; and the third episode is a merciless retaliation against corporate domination.[2]

While the project of early digital activists is more easily associated with theatrical performance, the work of AnonOp, the branch of the movement that engages more specifically with direct action, incorporates a wider range of tactics. These new creative and performative possibilities offer a fascinating picture of some of the newest aesthetics of resistance.

To fully understand the third and infamous episode of Operation Payback (the digital strike in support of WikiLeaks), it is useful to retrace the origin of the vengeance narrative created by Anonymous. In September 2010, several Anons came across the news story of Aiplex, a company based in India, whose director proclaimed to have used denial-of-service tactics against file-sharing sites. The Pirate Bay was one of the targets, and a controversy arose when it appeared that Aiplex had been contracted by copyright holders that included Hollywood film studios (Norton, 2012). Considering the legal battles related to the use of DoS, and the many hackers that faced prosecutions, it seemed outrageous that private corporations could resort to similar tactics in all impunity.

Anonymous's answer was instant, and few days later, Aiplex's website was taken down by a distributed denial of services (DDoS) strike. The operation was so brief that the group decided to target more organisations. The action was therefore extended to the website of the Motion Picture Association of America (MPAA), a company that was believed to be a client of Aiplex. Anons then decided to hit the Recording Industry Association of America (RIAA), and the International Federation of the Phonographic Industry. The group named the strike 'Operation: Payback is A Bitch', a very catchy and movie-like title which echoed the hacker logic of 'you DDoS me, I DDoS you' (Olson, 2012: 103).

This revenge scenario would have been rather conventional if it were not for the highly entertaining performance prepared by Anonymous. On the surface, the group follows one of the key principles of electronic civil disobedience, that is, the prior public disclosure of a digital action. However, Anonymous does not just send simple warnings to companies. Instead, the group creates a series of sophisticated digital items, which include posters, notices, images and videos. These function as both warnings addressed to the targets, but also as recruitment tools for participants. Many of the images sport the logo of Anonymous, a black-and-white headless figure wearing a suit and a tie. A question mark signals the absence of a head, referring to both principles of anonymity and leaderlessness. The logo also often includes, a spheric shape surrounded by two tree branches, which clearly echoes the emblem of the United Nations. Another re-appropriated symbol is the Guy Fawkes masks that often covers the faces of members making video appearances.

Mostly, posters are used to provide practical information about the operations, such as the date and time of actions, list of targets, the various platforms where planning and discussions take place, and the sites where activists tools can be downloaded. All of these are carefully crafted along with the insertion of private jokes or humoristic comments that add to the creative and performative function of the material. In many ways, the protest and the lulz both begin before any digital strikes actually start.

The design produced for the operation against Aiplex's website also harbored the logo of The Pirate Bay, a black-and-white pirate ship with a cassette tape on its sail (replacing the usual skull), in solidarity with the anti-copyright campaigners. Ironically, this advertising poster also revealed that the target had already been taken down and that the digital strike would move to a new target:

> How fast you are in such a short time! Aiplex, the bastard hired gun that DdoS'd TPB [The Pirate Bay]' is already down! .... Now we have our lasers primed, but what do we target now? We target the bastard group that has thus far led this charge against our websites, like The Pirate Bay. We target MPAA.ORG!
>
> (Anonymous, 2010a)

Before wishing a 'good hunting' to its members, Anonymous (ibid.) warned its opponents that the strike would be 'a calm, coordinated display of blood' and that it would 'not be merciful'; a rather humorous threat, considering that the whole confrontation was to take place exclusively on the internet. Yet, after the hype and excitement generated by the plan, the premature collapse of Aiplex website was clearly a letdown, which explains the immediate pursuit of new digital targets.

This is when the twist of the story occurs. In the general excitement, no one thought it relevant to confirm the story behind the operation. In particular, there was no proof that MPAA was a client of Aiplex. The firm had been hired by movie companies to perform anti-piracy actions, but there was no mention of the involvement of the American film industry. A new story later confirmed that, instead, Aiplex had been working on behalf of Bollywood companies (Norton, 2012; Coleman, 2014). This means that Anonymous's grandiloquent revenge scenario had been played out against the wrong targets.[3] Whether the confusion was genuine or not is a question that remains unanswered. What is clear is that Anonymous convinced many to take part in the operation, and at least 700 followed its development on the internet (Coleman, 2014: 96). In addition, the digital action successfully caught the attention of the mainstream media, a key player in Anonymous's subsequent campaigns.

As with most trilogies, the success of this Operation Payback was a direct effect of the previous episode which generated the initial enthusiasm and support for the movement. Many of those who took part in the demise of Aiplex, and its alleged patrons, had already experienced Anonymous's activism through its notorious campaign against the Church of Scientology. With Project Chanology in mind, many Anons may have readily got on board, eager to experience more fun, or in this case, more lulz.

The story goes that in the early days of 2008, the Church of Scientology was attempting to prevent the circulation of a leaked video featuring a rather proselytic Tom Cruise. In a complacent moment, the institution went as far as threatening with legal action anyone who did not comply. Many outlets conformed and removed the recording, until one source, the US blog site Gawker, decided to publish it, declaring: 'it's newsworthy; and we will not be removing it' (Denton, 2008: para. 3).

For any Anons directly emerging from 4chan, the bulletin board that allows anything and everything to circulate on its forums, the persecution of the Church was simply unconceivable. This digital censorship was against the notion of free flow of information, particularly when the information involved a famous actor making a fool of himself. Within few weeks, Anonymous had crashed the website of the Church with DDoS strikes, and was preparing to 'expel from the Internet and systematically dismantle the Church of Scientology in its present form' (Anonymous, 2008).

Again, Anonymous provided plenty of warning to the Church, including a dramatic threat, issued through an equally dramatic recording. This first video, published on YouTube, was more than a simple warning. It was the detailed trailer of a forthcoming strike, and as such, it featured all the ingredients of a classic action movie. To begin, the video which opened on a cloudy sky, presaged the coming of apocalyptic times; a crescendo soundtrack created an unbearable suspense; and an unrecognisable and intimidating voiceover elaborated on the consequences of the coming menace. Even the two-minutes length of the recording complied with the standard format of a trailer. The video functioned as the synopsis of the imminent wrath of Anonymous, which would result in the destruction of its ultimate enemy the Church of Scientology. It also ended with the now famous Anonymous signature statement: 'Knowledge is free. We are Anonymous. We are Legion. We do not forgive. We do not forget. Expect us' (Anonymous, 2008).

The video was also an example of the kind of activist work that does not require programming or hacking skills. It was created by a group of Anons with video editing skills and lots of creativity, as Olson describes:

> The group spent the next several hours finding uncopyrighted footage and music, then writing a video script that could be narrated by an automated voice. The speech recognition technology was so bad they had to go back and misspell most of the words—destroyed became "dee stroid," for instance—to make it sound natural. The final script ended up looking like nonsense but sounding like normal prose.
>
> (2012: 71)

Clearly, Anonymous had fun producing this humoristic video. After all, the group openly admitted to the Church that its destruction would be 'for the good of your followers; for the good of mankind; and for *our own enjoyment*' (Anonymous, 2008, added emphasis). This is perhaps the one defining feature of Anonymous activist practice; the humour that it promotes, but also, the humour that its audience actively seeks, and that its targets eventually come to fear.

As mentioned before, this particular type of humour is known as 'lulz', and it is an intrinsic part of Anonymous's culture. Mixing pranking, hoaxing and trolling, lulz can be seen as mischievous, when it is not outrightly vicious. In one case, an Anon set up a harsh prank by posting flashing images onto the site of the Epilepsy Foundation. The images ended up provoking seizures amongst some of the epileptic visitors (Coleman, 2014: 69). While the action was clearly condemnable, and many Anons did so, others would have considered this as a typical case of lulz seeking; a quest often self-justified by the Anonymous prankster's statement: 'I did it for the lulz' (ibid.: 8). The act was indeed a sharp reminder that before engaging in political digital action, Anonymous was first and foremost about pranking and trolling, and anyone contesting this facet could be easily proven wrong.

The trolls and pranksters within Anonymous may have considered the group's political engagement as deprived of proper lulz, but in terms of its practice, there is no doubt that Anonymous has developed a unique form of digital protest that incorporates humour, irony and parody. After all, it is to provoke laughter that Anonymous produces comical artefacts and performances as part of its digital campaigns. This strategy clearly fits into the historical tradition of combining socio-political activism with humour.

In her research about humour and protest, social historian Hart (2007) argues that humour and laughter can be used as powerful communication tools. Hart examines the use of humour within the context of various social movements, and confirms its role in the development of collective identity and the empowerment of lower social groups. Referring to the work of Mikhail Bakhtin on popular culture in the medieval and modern periods, Hart suggests that even at that time 'political protest was possible, as long as it was done by joking' (2007: 4). Anonymity also played an important role, as 'the masquerades of religious festivals often hid the identity of the participants', and members of the lower classes could use this 'to express their hostility towards the ruling oligarchy', albeit under the veil of general amusement (ibid.). Throughout the centuries, humour made direct and indirect appearances in social and political dissent, and it also functioned as a strategy to avoid repression.

Likewise, laughter had a role in the social movements of the 1960s. The humour developed in some social protests functioned as a non-violent tactic that aimed to expose and challenge the authorities, but it also worked as a way to create and sustain social groups. In a comment that echoes Reed's account of freedom song singing, Hart suggests that

> The impact of humour (brought about by laughing with one another) can strengthen and forge long-term responses like feelings of affection, solidarity, and loyalty among activists. In this regard, laughing together has similar bonding powers like marching, dancing, or singing together. Combining marching and humorous singing is an effective tactic to create solidarity, like chants during a demonstration, which often use the rhythm and accentuation of popular songs. (2007: 12)

In the case of Anonymous, the performance of humoristic stunts was as important as the political cause that was defended. Many of its digital actions were staged as grand spectacles for Anonymous's own pleasure, as well as the entertainment of its followers and the mainstream media.

This approach closely resembles the type of *situations* championed by the Situationist International in the 1960s. Led by Guy Debord, this

European radical movement notoriously declared its opposition to capitalism and the society of spectacle. Directly influenced by Marxism and avant-garde theories, the Situationists aimed to challenge the alienation created by modern capitalism through the staging of radical *situations*. As Debord explains in the pamphlet, *Report on the Construction of Situations*:

> We must call attention, among the workers parties or the extremist tendencies within those parties, to the need to undertake an effective ideological action in order to combat the emotional influence of advanced capitalist methods of propaganda. On every occasion, by every hyper-political means, we must publicize desirable alternatives to the spectacle of the capitalist way of life, so as to destroy the bourgeois idea of happiness.
>
> (Debord, 1957: 43)

The Situationists thus concluded on the need to devise a new society. They proposed a radical programme designed around the concept of *détournement,* which they defined as 'the integration of present or past artistic productions into a superior construction of a milieu' (Situationist International, 1958: 52).

In his analysis of the movement, Wark (2011) expands on the concept, suggesting that the key purpose of détournement is to challenge private property. As he explains, 'détournement attacks a kind of fetishism, where the products of collective human labor in the cultural realm can become a mere individual's property' (ibid.: 40). In this context, situationism becomes about the re-appropriation, recuperation, highjack or theft of any cultural artefact with the aim of altering its meaning and purpose. This echoes the Situationists's claim that 'there can be no situationist painting or music, but only a situationist use of those means' (Situationist International, 1958: 52). Wark further observes that 'key to any practice of détournement is identifying the fragments upon which it might work. There is no particular size or shape. It could be a single image, a film sequence of any length, a word, a phrase, a paragraph' (2011: 40).

Anonymous's activism clearly functions within these situationist terms, but it also distorts the initial conception of *détournement*. While *détournement* aimed to alert to the commodification of everyday life and denunciate capitalist spectacles, Anonymous's re-appropriation of the codes of mass communication, advertising and news report, both celebrated and challenged this idea. For sure, the collective made full use of spectacle for its political agenda but also for its own amusement. Hence, and contrary to Situationist International's (1958) statement that 'the victory will go to those who are capable of creating disorder without loving it', Anonymous not only created disorder, it *loved* doing so.[4]

By the time Anonymous announced Operation Avenge Assange, the movement was well versed into the performance of 'constructed situations', or what the Situationist International described as 'a moment of life concretely and deliberately constructed by the collective organization of a unitary ambience and a game of events' (1958: 52). The digital strike of December 2010 closely adhered to a script inspired by the successful campaigns waged against the Church of Scientology and Aiplex. As before, the main poster contained the rationale for the operation, it listed the targets and also functioned as a direct recruitment tool, encouraging readers to 'Protest. Inform. Enquire. Fight' (Anonymous, 2010c). In addition, the poster harboured Anonymous's signature logo of a headless and suited figure, as well as a shorter version of its now famously threatening motto.

As described before, Anonymous's third revenge episode targeted several major commercial groups that had halted the financial support of whistleblower WikiLeaks. One of these institutions was the credit card company MasterCard. MasterCard.com was hit on December 8, as part of a direct action using the tactic of denial-of-service. As a result, the site of one of the largest financial institutions remained inactive for 12 hours (Olson, 2012: 436).

While demonstrating the power of digital action, the event also generated a good dose of humour, or lulz. Following the successful crash of the MasterCard's site, one statement which rapidly circulated on the web cleverly mocked MasterCard's famous *Priceless* slogan. The original statement which read '*There are something's money can't buy. For everything else there's MasterCard*', was parodied by the new phrase, '*Freedom of Speech is priceless. For everything else there's MasterCard*' (Al Jazeera, 2010).

In one of her many conversations with Anonymous, Coleman was reminded of the power and potential of humour. As one member mentioned to her, 'it's that idea of humor and irreverence which is at the heart of this ...: it's what will stop it ever being able to be labeled terrorist' (2014: 15). As discussed in Chapter 4, the terrorist accusation was already present when Electronic Civil Disobedience and the electrohippies performed electronic civil disobedience. While these actions were far from humoristic, they nevertheless managed to overturn the cyberterrorist discourse. Anonymous's mixing of Hollywood aesthetics and irreverent humour has certainly contributed to further dismiss the idea of cyberterrorism. Yet, there is another threat that its tactics have been less successful at deflecting, that is the label of criminality; and unfortunately, Anonymous's activist tools have been far from foolproof and have substantially affected the movement.

Politics of Disturbance

Anonymous's activist philosophy and politics may greatly differ from that of Electronic Disturbance Theater and the electrohippies, but the three share a predilection for the spectacular staging of denial-of-service strikes. For Anonymous, this is not surprising considering the technological milieu within which it emerged and evolved, and the movement did not wait long before creating its own version of DDoS tools. The main one was named LOIC, Low Orbit Ion Cannon, in reference to a fictitious weapon featured in the video game, *Command and Conquer* (NS, 2011). LOIC functioned in the same way that FloodNet did, by sending large amount of information requests to target servers in order to block access to websites. Technically, these actions are known as distributed denial of services (DDoS) as they are performed by multiple machines. Also like FloodNet, LOIC did not require advanced technical skills. This contributed to its success and popularity amongst digital activists. LOIC was used during Anonymous's key campaigns including the operations against the Church of Scientology, the software company Aiplex, and the Operation Payback.

In her detailed analysis of the digital tool, Sauter (2013) explains that LOIC had several versions designed by different hackers, which provided various level of use. One basic level enabled participants with little knowledge to run the programme and engage in direct action. For these users, the only task was to indicate the URL or IP address of the target server. Other levels enabled more experienced participants to modify the software for their convenience. Whereas FloodNet remained under the supervision of Electronic Disturbance Theater during the actions, LOIC remained open-source and rapidly became usable on many devices and with various operating systems. This effectively expanded the pool of potential participants.

Similar to its predecessor, LOIC could be used to send messages as part of the digital actions. It is likely however that these were still visible only to the administrators of the servers. On a different level, the tool was true to Anonymous's strive for self-entertainment, and LOIC's user interface contained many references inherited from 4chan. A recurrent one was the phrase "IMMA CHARGIN MAH LAZER" which labelled the launching button of DDoS on the programme page. These type of expression, familiar to most Anons, worked as direct reminders of the lulz. New references were also created which explicitly stated the political function of LOIC. As Sauter explains:

> The changes made by New EraCracker also heighten the explicit and overt political value of the tool. Whereas "A cat is fine, too" and "Desudesudesu" are relatively nonsensical in the context of an adversarial DDOS attack, "U dun goofed" is explicitly confrontational. It accuses the target of making a grave error and implies that he or she is now, or shortly will be, suffering the consequences of his or her actions.
>
> (2014: 126)

These statements clearly fit within Anonymous's grand revenge narrative, and considering the efficacy of LOIC, there were certainly reasons to fear the wrath of the collective.

Yet, despite its great usability, LOIC had a major flaw: it did not provide anonymity to users. Participants to digital actions could easily be traced through their IP addresses. Whether they had downloaded the programme onto their devices, or accessed it from a web page, activists had their IP information recorded each time they pressed the strike button.

During Operation Payback, PayPal installed a programme that collected data from the traffic logs of its website. As it turned out, these reports contained the IP addresses of machines that had accessed the site during the DDoS strikes. At the same time, the US Federal Bureau of Investigation (FBI) was monitoring the press releases and social media interactions of Anonymous. With these details, the authorities matched their information about digital operations with the data from PayPal's logs (Poulsen, 2011: para. 4). From there, obtaining the real names and home addresses of the IP owners was pure formality.

This led to the massive arrest and prosecution of Anonymous's members. According to one source, 'it was easy to distinguish the packets coming from [LOIC] because they contained strings like "wikileaks," "goof," and "goodnight,"' (ibid.: para. 7). Ironically, the anonymity of Anonymous was erased by its insatiable need for lulz, turning the movement's signature trait into its Achilles' heel.

It may initially seem that, like Achilles, Anonymous had no reason to believe in its vulnerability. First, its notorious collective identity, as well as enforced anonymity, constructed the mystical *imaginaire* that members were untraceable. The assumption was that anyone joining the movement would inherit this invisibility, provided they did not purposefully revealed personal information. Second, the use of LOIC did not require advanced technical knowledge and participants were not expected to know about systems of web traffic monitoring. The third issue was much more problematic, however. Many contradictory accounts circulated about the security issue of LOIC. At the height of Operation Payback, several hackers began to alert members that the programme was not safe. However, these warnings were often ignored, or downplayed by participants who believed in the trope of 'safety in numbers'.

In her account of the PayPal strikes, Olson (2012) recounts a revealing chat between users:

> "Can I get arrested for doing this?" a person called funoob asked in the #setup channel on December 8.
>
> "Nah, they won't arrest you," answered someone called Arayerv. "Too many people. You can say you have spyware. They can't charge you."

> Another called who cares concurred: "If you get arrested just say you don't know but it's probably a virus."
>
> (2012: 127)

Predictably, those who ended up being arrested for Operation Payback were participants who were not able to fully cover their tracks, or were not even aware that they needed to do so in the first place.

This issue is in sharp contrast with Electronic Disturbance Theater's approach to digital protest. As a reminder, the group had issued an explicit warning to participants explaining to them that the protest was not a game, and that governments would collect the IP addresses of any machines making use of FloodNet. The activists even suggested the possibility of future arrests. This warning was posted on the web page that contained the downloading link to FloodNet. It was therefore impossible for participants to miss it. While this may sound as a harsh judgement, it could be said that had some of Anonymous activists been knowledgeable about the original use of DoS in digital protest, they might have responded differently to the first concerns raised about LOIC's security, or lack thereof.

Members of Anonymous who were less knowledgeable about computers probably also missed the use (and existence) of botnets as part of DDoS strikes. The term *botnet* combines the words *robot* and *network*, and refers to a large number of connected computers that communicate through the internet. Botnets are made out of thousands of machines that often become infected through malicious code or software. Most people unknowingly become part of these when they download unknown files or images from the internet. The malware remains dormant on their computer, until they are activated to perform DDoS, often without the owner's knowledge or consent (Coleman, 2014: 93).

Botnets are often controlled by a single hacker who tends to have more authority and power because of this tool. These hackers effectively have under their control 'an army of zombie computers' ready to strike at their command (ibid.: 60). Many believed that Anons were behind each single computer that was striking PayPal and MasterCard, but in fact, botnets were the ones taking down the companies' websites (Olson, 2012). Thus, the idea of mass participatory action was undermined by the use of botnets, and many of those who knew about their existence remained discreet about it (ibid.). Yet again, there is no doubt that, had participants known that a large amount of their fellow activists were in fact robots, their reliance on 'safety in numbers' would have been called for.

Despite these twists, when the time for repression arrived, there were enough Anonymous that had voluntarily taken part in digital actions and could face prosecution, once they were identified by the government. In another study, Sauter (2014) details the cases of Anons that were jailed for taking part in digital action against the Church of Scientology. More members were convicted in relation to the Operation Avenge Assange. Most of them pleaded guilty to charges of access to, or damage of protected servers. The main issue, however, was the application of the US Computer Fraud and Abuse Act (CFAA). In a context which echoes the court cases of the Atlanta Three hackers, this more recent act allows claimants to request financial restitution. Plaintiffs such as PayPal can therefore claim unspecific damage and loss of income from the defendants. The outcomes are usually excessive fines and prison sentences that do not reflect the political character of the digital actions. As Sauter concludes:

> When used to prosecute activist DDoS actions, the CFAA directly gives the targets of protest the ability to extort payments from activists for their dissent and disruption. When coupled with the innovative reality of online activism, the CFAA literally renders the Internet a space where you can be charged hundreds of thousands of dollars for participating in a collective protest.
>
> (2014: 144–145)

This is the situation that CAE had been trying to avoid since it first conceived of digital direct action. The group went as far as constructing the concept of electronic civil disobedience to claim similar legal treatment as traditional disobedience. In its last pamphlet published in 2001, the collective reiterates this stand:

> We must demand that a distinction be made between trespass with political intent and trespass with criminal intent. For civil disobedience in physical space the penalty in the U.S., if one is arrested at all, is usually a $25 fine and a night in jail with one's fellow demonstrators. The state can be generous here, since such tactics are purely symbolic in the age of nomadic capital. Such generosity is not shown when the political action could actually accomplish something. This is a situation that must be changed.
>
> (CAE, 2001: 33–34)

The outcome of Anonymous's trials was not inevitable, however. A previous court case could have acted as a precedent. In 2001, a German activist group, known as Libertad, staged a digital disruption of the Lufthansa airline website. This was to protest against the role of the airline in the deportation of asylum seekers. According to the activist group, over 13,000 internet participants joined the digital protest (Bendrath, 2006). As a result the leader of the movement Andreas-Thomas Vogel was prosecuted. It took over five years for a Criminal Chamber Court in Frankfurt to deliberate and rule that the cyberprotest was not illegal (ibid.). Initially, Vogel had been condemned by a lower justice court who ruled that the digital blockades had damaged the airline and was therefore illegal. The activist was found guilty and ordered to pay a fine equivalent to 90 days of detention. Yet, following an appeal, Vogel was cleared of all charges. The German Higher Court ruled that the demonstration against Lufthansa was not violent and did not involve any form of coercion. This practice of influencing public opinion was therefore considered legitimate (ibid.).

This case takes on further meaning in the context of subsequent practices of criminalisation. In November 2006, the British legal system made the use of denial-of-service a criminal offence. The new legislation came into action after 18-year-old David Lennon was brought to court for his alleged breach of the Computer Misuse Act of 1990. Following a dispute with his former employer, Lennon resolved to overflow the company's server by sending several million e-mail messages (Kirk, 2006). Incidentally, and like German activist Andreas-Thomas Vogel, Lennon faced trial twice. In the first instance, his lawyers successfully argued that the accusation of 'unauthorized modification of the contents of any computer' was not applicable to the case. Their argument was that sending and receiving e-mail messages was the very purpose of a server and as such 'sending a flood of unsolicited emails would not cause unauthorised access or modification' (Espiner, 2005: para. 6). The court thus ruled that denial-of-service actions could not be prosecuted under the Computer Misuse Act, and Lennon was found not guilty. The prosecutors appealed against the decision however, and Lennon was retried a year later.

Between the time of the two trials, the British Parliament passed a new Police and Justice Act which condemned 'unauthorised acts with intent to impair operation of computer' (UK Parliament, 2006). With this new act in place, the court was able to find Lennon guilty. Through this process, the use of denial-of-service was officially criminalised, and additionally, the maximum sentence for carrying out denial-of-service actions was increased from 5 to 10 years of imprisonment.

The court cases of Vogel and Lennon clearly demonstrate the lack of consensus regarding the validity of digital direct action. In particular, it seems difficult to believe that the British Police and Justice Act 2006 was decreed independently of the fact that DDoS was used by digital activists such as Anonymous. Many activists believed that the German verdict was an important step and that Vogel's case would become jurisprudence. After all, he had achieved what digital activists had been campaigning for decades, but while the German court opted for human civil rights, the UK legal system chose to favour economic interests. As a result, the recognition of digital direct action as a valid form of activism is still pending; and with the dissemination of the discourse of global war against terror, one can easily predict that fewer governments will show understanding or lenience.

As most digital activists before them, Anonymous has been aware of the necessity to dissociate its practice from cybercriminality and alleged cyberterrorism. One strategy has been to inform its members that supporting the movement remains a legitimate act:

> It is not illegal to be Anonymous. Nor is it illegal to wear Guy Fawkes masks. Keep that in mind. If you personally have not been involved in illegal activities, you have nothing to worry, no matter whom you talk to; If you have, it is wise not to talk about it. To no one.
>
> Anonymous (2012)

Another, more recent, strategy has been for some Anons to officially request that DDoS be considered as free speech. In early 2013, and as a response to an increasing number of arrests, a petition was launched on the 'We the People' website, which demanded that the US government recognise the practice as a valid form of protest. The argument used by Anonymous is familiar to most digital activists: digital disruption through DDoS is similar to street demonstrations and the occupation of public spaces, and this should qualify it as civil disobedience (Li, 2013: 304). Predictably, the petition did not reach the 25,000 signatures required for consideration by the White House, and some commentators highlighted the irony of this request, coming from a movement that appeared anti-government and anti-establishment (O'Neil, 2013).

The other issue is that the practice of DDoS has been strongly challenged within the hacker community itself. Since its use by Electronic Disturbance Theater and the electrohippies, many hackers have criticised denial-of-service, arguing that it contradicts the ethic of free flow of information so central to the hacking culture. Wark (2004) summed up the essence of this point in his text, *A Hacker Manifesto*, which famously claims that 'information wants to be free but is everywhere in chains' (2004: para. 126). This statement has become the footing of opposite stands about digital activism. On the one hand, those rejecting the practice of electronic disturbance argue that information should remain free and accessible at all time. On the other hand, those supporting digital protest defend their action as a way to free information, and to strike anyone attempting to withhold its flow.

One vocal opponent to DDoS was Oxblood Ruffin, lead member of the Cult of the Dead Cow hacker group, who responded to the digital actions of the electrohippies back in the 1990s, with the following statement:

> Denial of Service attacks are a violation of the First Amendment, and of the freedoms of expression and assembly. No rationale, even in the service of the highest ideals, makes them anything other than what they are—illegal, unethical, and uncivil. One does not make a better point in a public forum by shouting down one's opponent. Say something more intelligent or observe your opponents' technology and leverage your assets against them in creative and legal ways.
>
> (Ruffin, 2000: para. 15)

Against the practice of digital disturbance, Ruffin promoted computer programming and the development of open-source systems, as a legal form of activism.[5]

Despite this controversy, it should be reminded that a DDoS action does not inflict permanent damage to the target websites, nor does it result in the loss of data. In fact, some of the digital strikes staged by Anonymous failed to create any disturbance due to the high level of security applied to the servers, for instance Amazon.com (Halliday, 2010). More importantly, Anonymous developed its own ethics regarding its practice of digital direct action, and members have issued a series of guidelines that reflected the movement's strategic stand. The key principles are clearly spelt out:

> Anonymous is a non-violent resistance movement consisting of a global collective of autonomous individuals who adhere to these basic principles:
>
> 2 Do not attack the media. (This includes main stream, independent, and social media)
> 3 Do not attack critical infrastructure. (Such as communications networks, power grids – or hospitals)
> 4 Work for Justice and Freedom. (Especially with regards to freedom of information and the internet)
>
> ANYONE anywhere can initiate an Anonymous operation, action, or group – and so long as they adhere to these basic principles they are as much Anonymous as anyone.
>
> EVERYONE is Anonymous.
>
> (Anonymous, 2013)

These points directly echo the recommendations that Critical Art Ensemble had also made in its account of practical electronic civil disobedience. As a reminder, the collective also insisted that the strikes should not target individuals and that no essential information should be damaged. CAE's assumption was that these ethos would help dissociate digital direct action from criminal intent. In the end, however, the fate of the Anonymous serving jail sentences brings this rationale down, challenging in the process the future of digital protest.

Conclusion

This chapter examined the digital practice of Anonymous. The aim of the discussion was to retrace the emergence of an activist project that focuses on the politics of digital technology. While Anonymous remains a controversial and perhaps misunderstood movement, the analysis here has demonstrated that its activism directly relates to early conceptions of digital disturbance, including those elaborated by Critical Art Ensemble.

In addition, Anonymous's practice exposes the dynamics of information as a politics, in particular through its engagement against censorship and its support of whistleblowers and anti-copyright campaigners.

Central to Anonymous's practice is an original take on the power of humour and laughter as communication tools. In the backdrop of its trolling and pranking history, the collective has developed a unique aesthetic of resistance which has expanded the performative repertoire of digital direct action. Mixing its signature lulz with cinematographic parody and grand visual spectacles, the resistance of Anonymous has attracted the attention of mainstream media, and through this, many sympathisers who would have otherwise missed the movement. As many activists before them, Anonymous has been aware, and has made full use, of the effects of creative and performative inputs on the social framing of political mobilisation, and few commentators have actually use the spectre of cyberterrorism to discuss the movement.

The collective has not been so successful at wavering the charge of cybercriminality, however. By considering the legal treatment of the Anonymous arrested for taking part in digital actions, as well as the court cases of other DDoS users, the chapter has confirmed the process of criminalisation that began with the prosecution of computer hackers in the early 1990s. The contention, which was already exposed in Chapter 3, is that the recent ban of DDoS actions is responding to the threat perceived against digital commerce. The constant decree of new legislations has also been a way to hamper the development of digital direct action. This remains the most challenging issue for all digital activists, as no collective has managed, so far, to effectively legitimise digital direct action.

Notes

1 For detailed accounts of Project Chanology, see Coleman (2014) and Olson (2012).
2 For the purpose of this book, the discussion will be limited to these digital campaigns although Anonymous staged many more actions throughout the years. For an in-depth analysis of these other operations, see Coleman (2014).
3 The story goes, however, that by then, anti-piracy companies had been suspected of engaging in similar practices as their Indian counterparts.
4 No doubt that the Situationists and Debord would have come to appreciate Anonymous's *détournement* of their *détournement*!
5 For a full account of the concept of digitally correct hacktivism, see Jordan and Taylor (2004).

Conclusion

Tactical Performance

> The streets are always alive. There can still be resistance; any space is open to contestation. Virtual intervention in and of itself is not enough.
>
> —Critical Art Ensemble

In December 2010, a young Tunisian named Mohamed Bouazizi set himself on fire to protest against the rampant violence and the social oppression he had experienced throughout his life. Following his tragic death, the Tunisian people massively descended into the streets, demanding social justice and the end of the political repression. This became the most important social mobilisation of the country in decades, and it forced the ruling president to resign. It also brought a new wave of political changes in Tunisia, before culminating in a series of mass protests, commonly referred to as the 'Arab Spring', which transformed the political landscape of North Africa and the Arab region.

These radical movements against disavowed governments were not merely symbolic. Protesters did not march only to return to their home in the evening. Instead, they occupied the streets and public squares, in a direct confrontation with the authorities. As an illustration, the occupation of the Tahrir Square (Liberation Square) in the centre of Cairo, Egypt, is now seminal in the history of social movements. The uprising, which saw the fall of the president, lasted for almost three weeks, at which point reports stated that the number of protesters had reached one million (Al Jazeera, 2011). More occupations and protests occurred in nearby countries, including Libya, Yemen, Algeria, Morocco, Iraq and Syria, often with tragic consequences.

The significance of the North African and Arab Spring was such that many European countries witnessed the re-emergence of large-scale protests. These demonstrations first began in the South of Europe, the part most affected by the financial and economic crisis, and similarly relied on the occupation of public squares and city centres. One of the largest gatherings was the Spanish *Indignados* movement (the Indignants), initiated in May 2011, with the occupation of La Puerta de Sol in Madrid. More occupations were staged at the Lisbon Parliament in Portugal, and the Syntagma Square in Athens, Greece. As part of the mobilisation, protesters organised regular assemblies to discuss the movements, as well as possibilities for new social organisations. From this, the term and social movement, 'Occupy' came into being, and rapidly spread across the world.

This concluding chapter revisits the central themes examined in the course of this book, in light of recent developments in social mobilisation. In particular, the chapter reaffirms the role of performance as a key tactic for direct action. As demonstrated throughout this study, the reading of protest as performance is not a new proposition. The role of the body in the performance of resistance was examined in Chapter 2, as was the theatricalisation of direct action in Chapter 3. In addition, and core to the investigation, the performativity of digital protest was established in Chapters 4 and 5, with the analysis of the work of Electronic Disturbance Theater and Anonymous.

Yet, the role of performance in social mobilisation has been re-ignited by recent protest movements, with the renewed practice of space occupation. More specifically, cases such as the Egyptian uprising and the Occupy Wall Street movement have reinstated occupation as a radical protest tactic. In both instances, space occupation becomes a claim for the re-appropriation of public space, a claim for social justice, but also, a claim for the very right to protest. As will become evident in this final account, this renewal does not displace digital direct action, far from it. In the context of alienating discourses of terror and criminality, space re-appropriation, both physical and virtual, confirms the importance of performance tactics in the pursuit of social change.

A Return to Space

Among the many civil protests that formed the African and Arab Spring, notably in Iran, Tunisia, Algeria and Jordan, the contestation movement that received the largest media attention was the Egyptian uprising and its occupation of Tahrir Square, the historical centre of Cairo. As the symbol of the Egyptian uprising, protestors occupied the emblematic place, in direct confrontation with the regime for over 18 days. In the course of the protests, Tahrir Square was transformed into what Hussam Salama describes as 'an urban utopia, a place of community engagement, collective projects, social discourse, and most importantly, freedom of speech and expression' (2013: 133). As Salama further explains, until then, many Egyptians carried the assumption that public space was first and foremost government space – that is, a space owned and controlled by the state. In addition, Egyptian emergency laws prevented public gatherings of more than five people, to prevent the formation of protest, while the government assigned secret police to surveil public spaces (ibid.: 128). The decision to occupy Tahrir Square in 2011 therefore required a commune re-conception of public place as a legitimate sphere of dissent.

As for many socio-political mobilisations, the choice of Tahrir Square (Liberation Square in English) was not random. Along with its historical role in the revolution movements of the 20th century, the square is considered to be the geographical centre of Cairo. Many of the important streets of the capital converge towards the square, making it the ideal meeting point of marches from all corners of the city. In late January 2011, people began to gather in these surrounding streets. The Egyptian police initially considered the various formations as small isolated movements, until protesters all converged towards the city centre. Faced with an unprecedented flow of people, the authorities had no means to control access to the square (Salama, 2013: 133). Protesters thus began their occupation of Tahrir Square. In situations where contestation has no prior legitimacy, the appropriation of public space becomes the contention itself, the tactic is crucial to the mobilisation as protesters need to take, but also to keep control of the re- appropriated space, as a symbol of their opposition to the authorities.

Despite its remarkable organisation, this occupation of the Tahrir Square was not a first. In 1919, the place, previously known as Ismailiya Square, became the terrain of the Egyptian revolution that overthrew the British ruling. After this, the square turned into the central location of public protest, including the 1952 revolution against the King; the 1967 march in support of the president, and the 1977 Egyptian Bread Riots (Salama, 2013). As social movement historian Tilly (2008: 4) confirms, collective contentions belong to a repertoire of 'learned and historically grounded performances', and with this latest uprising, Egyptians were clearly reaching into their own historical repertoire. This time however, the square witnessed a protest formation that shifted from mass demonstration to mass occupation.

Tahrir Square was redesigned into a large protest camp, sectioned to accommodate various areas so that protesters could sleep, eat, and pray, but also organise public discussion and debates. The place included essential facilities such as a childcare area, restrooms and first aid clinics. In addition, spaces were designated for bloggers and media reporting, and for creative and art display. Small stages were also used for evening concerts (BBC, 2011). As mentioned before, the Egyptians needed to re-envision Tahrir Square, not as a government-controlled space but as a city centre that belonged to the people. This was a necessary shift for protesters to stage and maintain the occupation – that is, a core belief in their right to be there and their right to remain indefinitely. In this original setting, protesters created, or rather performed, a microcosm that echoed their vision of a liberated Egypt.

The encampment became the performative space, of not only protest and resistance, but also of aspiring liberation and freedom. As they chanted throughout the revolt, 'we won't leave; he should leave' (referring to the disavowed president), Egyptians were reclaiming their *space* and *place* before the state, and before the world. Their occupation effectively became a performance, one that allowed them to enact forms of freedom and social order so far forbidden. As explained by Mathijs van de Sande, Egyptians were engaging in prefigurative politics, that is, a social practice where 'certain political ideals are experimentally actualised in the 'here and now', rather than hoped to be realised in a distant future' (2013: 230).

Indeed, through the staged transformation of the square, protesters acted as the citizens of a re-imagined Egypt:

> Tahrir Square witnessed the generation of new forms of public organization and administration that were not common in Egypt. Committees were formed and discussion assemblages between diverse political, religious and social groups emerged in the square. These nodes of socio-political discourse were trigged spontaneously in response to rapidly changing dynamics of the square. However, they gradually constructed the organizational structure of the place.
> (Salama, 2013: 136)

The performativity of the occupation becomes even more tangible when considering the surroundings of Tahrir Square. Following the initial confrontations with the police, a degree of safety was maintained in the square, but occupiers had to erect barricades and checkpoints to protect the camp against police invasion. Meanwhile, on the outskirts, the uprising remained violent and deadly as hundreds of protesters were losing their lives in direct confrontation with governmental forces (Abul-Magd, 2012). Tahrir Square was therefore a unique performative space where a different social order prevailed. In this sense, the performance of prefigurative politics enabled the social (re)construction of the square as a liberated space, one that was immune to state repression.

While this social reconfiguration of Tahrir Square meant that immediate and forced eviction could not take place, its status as a public space also played an important role. During the post-revolution era of the 1950s, the Egyptian government embarked on the nationalization of all public places, and through this, transformed the notions of public and private property. As Salama explains,

> The experience of Cairo was in fact a reversed process of the widely discussed concept of "privatization of Public Space" ... Many of the public spaces that were limited to social elites were either fully or partially transferred to the government. For the majority of Egyptians, this act was a victory against the Feudal System that controlled that controlled the country for decades.
> (2013: 130)

Egyptians had initially conceived public spaces as controlled and surveilled by the state, but their ultimate rejection of the government made the re-appropriation of the square possible, and essential, as a symbolic reclamation of sovereignty.

A year later, recognising these new social and political dynamics, the first freely elected president of the country took the decision to pledge his allegiance, not in front of the parliament, but in Tahrir Square. In June 2012, before the thousands of Egyptians gathered in the square, the president declared: 'You are the source of legitimacy and power, above all' (Ramadan, 2012: 145). Although the aftermaths of the elections led to further conflicts, this occupation of Tahrir Square certainly infused the new *imaginaire* of social protest across the world.

To be sure, the wave of social mobilisations that later spread across Europe and the United States adopted similar occupation tactics. As a key example, the Occupy movement, which began with Occupy Wall Street in September 2011, was one of the largest political protests to take place in the United States in a decade. On Saturday 17th, thousands of people convened towards the financial district of Manhattan, to occupy Zuccotti Park. The mobilisation aimed to challenge the increasing social and economic inequality in the country. With the slogan 'We are the 99%', protesters were drawing attention to the blatant disparities between the poor majority and a wealthy minority.

Imitating the type of occupation previously staged across the globe, US activists arranged for the takeover of Zuccotti Park. The site was not the original choice. Occupy Wall Street (OWS) was redirected to Zuccotti Park after the police received words of the original location. The particularity of the park was its legal status as a privately owned public space. This means that, in line with the New York City legislation, the police could neither prevent access to the park, nor its occupation. Protesters could also not be evicted without the authorisation of the park owners. Occupy Wall Street movement thus re-appropriated the space, transforming it into a public sphere where people could assemble and protest.

One of the early OWS participants, David Graeber, explains that after considering the occupation tactics used in Tunisia, Egypt and in Europe, US activists wanted to 'occupy a public space to create a New York General Assembly, a body that could act as a model of genuine, direct democracy to contrapose the corrupt charade presented to us as "democracy" by the US government' (2011a: para. 7). The popularity of OWS was such that thousands of people initiated their own occupation protest. New movements emerged in Atlanta, Chicago, Philadelphia, San Francisco, Seattle, and Washington DC, among other cities. Significantly, these protests developed at a time when demonstrations in the United States had been considered institutionalised, if not obsolete.

Clearly, the wave of mobilisations reminded us that urban streets have always played a central role in social and political activism. Even Critical

Art Ensemble recognised the importance of the streets, suggesting that its controversial statement 'The streets are dead capital', had been too often misinterpreted to mean that 'the streets are dead'. As Kurtz defends:

> We didn't mean that at all. The streets are always alive. There can still be resistance; any space is open to contestation. Virtual intervention in and of itself is not enough. There has to be a synthesis of a variety of strategies and tactics.
>
> (Vlavo, 2014)

All significant social movements have involved marches and demonstrations, and have turned turned the streets into concrete spaces of contestation. Many mobilisation campaigns, such as the civil rights, anti-war, feminist, or LGBT movements, owed much of their success to their use and control of public space, and recent demonstrations have reiterated this reclamation of space. This re-conception of the city street is what Saskia Sassen theorises as the 'global street', a street that can be 'conceived as a space where new forms of the social and the political can be *made*' (2011a: 574; original emphasis). In this redefined urban space, Sassen recognises a shift whereby powerless people practice new politics, by claiming 'rights to the city and to the country rather than protection of property' (ibid.).

Clearly, the occupation of Zuccotti Park was a direct challenge to the laws that prohibit spontaneous mass gathering, but it also signalled a refusal to engage with the bureaucracy of legal demonstrations. As many protesters argued:

> [Zuccotti Park is] a public space; we were the public; the public shouldn't have to ask permission to engage in peaceful political assembly in its own park; so we didn't. ... For those who desire to create a society based on the principle of human freedom, direct action is simply the defiant insistence on acting as if one is already free.
>
> (Graeber, 2011a: para. 17)

Against the mediatic memory of a violent police eviction a few months after the start of the protest, images of a well-organised occupation still prevail. Zuccotti Park was re-arranged as a camp that accommodated facilities such as sleeping areas, food services, medical care and social support, but also a public library and a Wi-Fi hotspot. Like protesters in Cairo, the occupiers engaged in a performance based on the practice of prefigurative politics. For instance, regular daily assemblies were organised to discuss the occupation and to explore various forms of social organisation. In particular, the principle of consensus-based politics was experimented, and discussions on social issues were given hours if not days of debate. This practice, inspired by anarchist precepts, refuses to recognise the legitimacy of existing political and legal orders. In this way, 'Zuccotti Park, and all subsequent encampments, became spaces of experiment with creating the institutions of a new society' (Graeber, 2011b: para. 13). As such, OWS participants were engaging in acts of civil disobedience by refusing to obey a legal system they deemed unacceptable. Through the occupation, they aimed to (re)place themselves at the top of the democratic process, openly rejecting the downwards of neoliberal politics.

The US government had a different view on this however. As mentioned before, Zuccotti Park was a privately owned public space, which means that the site was legally required to be open to the public. City plazas and shopping centres often have this status which can keep them out of immediate police control. For this reason, Occupy Wall Street protesters were not expelled at first. Yet, the park was still private, and it took no time before property laws were enforced.

After nearly two months of occupation, the New York police raided Zuccotti Park and dismounted the camp. The site later re-opened but under strict policing and surveillance to prevent re-occupation (*The Guardian*, 2011).

Analysing the context of the eviction, Kohn (2013) suggests that the action was made possible through a re-conceptualisation of public space. She explains that the US court authorised the dismantling of the camps based on the rationale that 'the occupation of parks and plazas was an illegitimate privatization of public space' (ibid.: 100). This means that by setting up their encampment in Zuccotti Park, protesters were somehow engaging in private activities that conflicted with the public status of the park. This judgement effectively reconfigured the notion of private and public, and by doing so, it challenged the status of space occupation as a protest tactic. It also confirmed the constant regulation of public spaces in United States, as illustrated by the declaration of the New York City Mayor, who, at the height of the Occupy Wall Street movement, stated that: 'people have a right to protest, and if they want to protest, we'll be happy to make sure they have locations to do it' (IBTimes, 2011: para. 11). In other words, people can engage in protest, as long as this takes place in designated areas, and with little disruption or impact on the daily functioning of the city.

Ultimately, the forced removal of the Zuccotti Park protesters illustrates the ongoing and methodical privatisation of cities performed by the state, with the support of the judicial system. It also indicates that in reaction, protesters invariably need to reformulate, or reiterate, their right to assemble, to march, or to occupy, as part of their dissident practice. In this process, understanding and manoeuvring the politics of shifting discourses is of primary concern to all activists, digital or not.

A Return to Discourse

While the emergence of the Occupy movement re-ignited debates about the value of street protest in social movement, it also spotlit a privatisation of city streets that echoes the privatisation of the digital space. The treatment of the Zuccotti Park occupation can easily be compared to the treatment of the Atlanta three hackers or the anti-copyright group The Pirate Bay, examined in Chapter 3. In both cases, the strategy to control the environment was to invoke private property laws, and each time the aim was to protect economic interests. As previously established, the core of Critical Art Ensemble's call for resistance was based on a persuasive prediction that neoliberal politics would inevitably lead to this process of privatisation. As evidence, the US authorities have been as eager to prevent digital direct action as they have been to suppress recent street protests.

If these practices of control need to be further illustrated, then the revelation that OWS activists were closely surveilled by secret services is another evidence. Since the end of the Occupy movement, several sources, such as the Partnership for Civil Justice Fund (PCJF), have revealed that the FBI considered the Occupy movement as 'a potential criminal and terrorist threat even though the agency acknowledges in documents that organizers explicitly called for peaceful protest and did "not condone the use of violence" at occupy protests' (PCJF, 2012: para. 1). The organisation goes on to list several documents attesting that the surveillance programme had been rolled out across the country. Political critics also commented on the military approach chosen by the authorities to deal with the protestors. For Saskia Sassen, these practices were specific to the US government, as she notes that:

> Unlike Spain, Germany, and other European countries with social uprisings, the United States has deployed anti-terrorism units from local police departments and the federal Department of Homeland Security to "keep order." These are civic protests—not attempts to destroy or take over the government. With these anti-terrorist measures, the US government re-marks the civic as a threat to national security.
>
> (2011b: para. 18)

From there, it is hard not to draw a comparison with the ways in which the discourse of cyberterrorism has been deployed against digital activists. Occupy protesters may not have been aware of the risk at the time, but there is no doubt that the threat of terrorist accusations alters the dynamics of social mobilisation.

As a case in point, it is worth mentioning that while the Occupy Wall Street movement consisted in the occupation of the New York financial district, the initial call for disruption was issued on the internet.[1] Many Anonymous responded to the proposal by digitally spreading the information, and the group eventually published one of its signature videos, announcing a plan for direct action. The statement seemed to imply, however, that unlike previous campaigns, members would engage in street occupations, rather than in digital direct action:

> Anonymous will flood into lower Manhattan, set up tents, kitchens, peaceful barricades and occupy Wall Street for a few months. Once there, we shall incessantly repeat one simple demand in a plurality of voices. We want Freedom. This is a Non Violent protest, we do not encourage violence in any way.
>
> (Anonymous, 2011)

It is not clear if denial-of-service strikes were eventually staged, but if so, they occurred on a different, minor scale than Anonymous's previous campaigns.

One reason why the digital engagement of Anonymous during the OWS movement may have been limited, is no doubt related to the systematic prosecution of those who participated in the Payback operations. As examined in Chapter 5, many Anonymous activists were tracked down and sentenced to prison and hefty fines. This process was facilitated by the legal modifications that enabled the prosecutions, such as the implementation of the US Computer Fraud and Abuse Act, and the British Police and Justice Act. The concept of cyberterror was never explicit in these legal actions, but the discourse still played a role in the treatment of digital direct action; one that CAE had accurately anticipated in its proposal for electronic protest.

In the third and final pamphlet published on the topic, *Digital Disturbance*, CAE recounts an early conversation occurring at the London Institute of Contemporary Art, back in 1994. During the talk, one member in the audience hailed the collective, claiming that electronic civil disobedience was 'pure terrorism' (CAE, 2001: 30). At the time, the group provided a seemingly logical answer:

> How can terror happen in virtual space, that is, in a space with no people—only information? Have we reached a point in civilization where we are capable of terrorizing digital abstractions? How was it that this intelligent person had come to believe that electronic blockage equaled terror?
>
> (ibid.: 31)

Back then, the very notion of cyberterrorism clearly belonged to a science-fictional *imaginaire*. The incident still prompted CAE to reflect on their original proposal and attempt to further dissociate electronic resistance from what they called 'the mythology of terrorism on the net' (ibid.: 29). The collective went on to deconstruct the discourse of terrorism and to conclude that 'electronic resistance has no relationship to terrorism in any tactical sense—no one dies, no one is under any threat' (ibid.: 36). The problem with this argument was that it did not foresee the extent to which governments and corporations would go to protect digital assets, including producing a discourse of cyberterrorism.

To this day, the power of the terror discourse has been such that no legal institution or government has recognised the validity of digital direct action. The only exception, which did not become a precedent, was the 2001 judgment of the German Higher Court in favour of the activist group Libertad. As discussed in Chapter 5, the German activists were cleared of criminal charges because the judges evaluated that the disruption of the Lufthansa airline website was a form of free speech, but more importantly, they considered the action as non-violent, and of little financial damage to the company. As the computer hacker, and former Electronic Disturbance Theater, Carmin Karasic points out:

> If the consequence of a denial-of-service is that a server goes down, it is not that it can never come back. The strike doesn't turn the server into cinders. It does reboot. It's a very reasonable form of self-expression that should not become a criminal act.
>
> (Vlavo, 2015)

This principle should be contrasted with a type of digital activities whereby substantial damage is inflicted to digital infrastructures. For example, in 2007, the Estonian government reported that the country's internet had experienced severe cyber-attacks. According to the authorities, the virtual strikes began after the removal of a Soviet war memorial from the capital city Tallinn. This led Estonia to believe that Russia had orchestrated a cyberware (BBC News, 2007). If this is the case, then it would be difficult to conceive that the Russian hackers had engaged in electronic civil disobedience. First, because there was no official announcement prior to the strikes, and thus no socio-political justification, and second, because the disruption created was not symbolic or simulated; it actually affected the country's infrastructure for several weeks. Since then, several reports have suggested that many countries regularly engage in cyber-attacks against their so-called enemies. For obvious reasons, these actions usually remain hidden from the general public and the mainstream media.

However, one important case, Stuxnet, made it to the open. Stuxnet was a cyber-attack staged against Iran's nuclear project in 2009. While this was never formally acknowledged, many sources concur that Stuxnet was jointly planned by the Americans and the Israelis, to compromise the machines that controlled Iran's nuclear programme. The software, which functioned like a virus, was introduced on the plant using a USB stick (Falliere et al., 2011). In his analysis, warfare scholar Rid (2012), confirms that the sophistication of the attack implies that the project had been funded by several states. Yet, against popular views, Rid rejects the claim that Stuxnet was akin to cyberwar. With the same arguments used to counter the discourse of cyberterror, he dismissed the term 'cyberwar', suggesting that 'an offensive act has to meet certain criteria in order to qualify as an act of war. Any act of war has to have the potential to be lethal; it has to be instrumental; and it has to be political' (2012: 6). For Rid, no single case of cyber-attack has ever caused the loss of human life or even damaged a building. Instead, he argues that cyber-attacks can be classified as updated versions of previous warfare tactics, such as subversion, sabotage and espionage. These categories include Stuxnet and the strikes against Estonia, which both qualify as acts of sabotage, rather than so-called cyberwar.

Against this stand, the logic of cyberterrorism assumes that all digital strikes are terrorist acts; from multi-millions and state-funded attacks, to DDoS strikes or websites defacements. This is why the discourse of cyberterror, with all of its legal threats, operates as an effective deterrent for digital activists. Most practitioners have been aware of the risks and many have inscribed their activist practice within CAE's concept of electronic civil disobedience, including Electronic Disturbance Theater, the electrohippies, and more recently Anonymous. Yet, this discursive positioning has had little success, and the framing of digital action as electronic civil disobedience may have become altogether redundant. As Steve Kurtz recently conceded:

> It's the disobedience part that CAE is unsure about. We still believe the ideas of digital activism and digital resistance have a lot of currency. But the disobedience part—it's like you were saying, it's a history that's been lost for most people. As a tactic, it's more dangerous to employ because governments and businesses have invested a lot of time and money in creating laws to make sure that such expression is heavily criminalized.
>
> (Vlavo, 2014)

The legal outcome of Anonymous's digital campaign against PayPal confirms these points, along with the more recent case of computer hacker and Anonymous member Jeremy Hammond. In November 2013, Hammond was found guilty of leaking confidential information retrieved from the US private intelligence firm Stratfor. During his sentencing statement, Hammond explained that his action against Stratfor was an act of civil disobedience. As he proclaimed, 'the hypocrisy of "law and order" and the injustices caused by capitalism cannot be cured by institutional reform but through civil disobedience and direct action' (2013: para. 23). This argumentation did not affect the outcome of the case as Hammond was condemned to 10 years of imprisonment. Instead, it confirmed CAE's early suspicion that electronic civil disobedience would be difficult to legally justify. The fact that Hammond used the hacking of private servers as a tactic, rather than the more common use of denial-of-services certainly affected his defence, but the disbelief came more from the excessiveness of his prison sentence, which clearly illustrates the continuous use of utilitarian punishment to protect digital economies.

The analysis of Anonymous's practice in this book did not cover the use of cracking and information leaking by smaller factions, such as Lulzsec and AntiSec. This decision was mostly due to the complex legal issues brought up by these practices. Nonetheless, Hammond's case was worth mentioning for its aftermath. Several months after his conviction, a leaked document revealed that the Federal Bureau of Investigation (FBI) had placed Jeremy Hammond on a list of "possible terrorist organisation member". The document was stamped with the statements: "destroy after use" and "do not advise this individual that they are on a terrorist watch lists" (Pilkington, 2015).

This clearly echoes the revelation that Occupy Wall Street protesters had been under special surveillance as potential terrorist threats. As Hammond himself declared:

> We are condemned as criminals without consciences, dismissed as anti-social teens without a cause, or hyped as cyber-terrorist to justify the expanding surveillance state. But hacktivism exists within the history of social justice movements. Hacktivism is still the future, and it's good to see people still doing something about it.
>
> (Hammond, 2014)

The comment is even more salient, considering that the question of blatant entrapment was excluded from Hammond's court case (Lennard, 2013). It also confirms that governments have become much more successful at framing digital direct action and prosecuting activists, partly by shifting from the discourse of cyberterror to that of cybercrime. To a large extent, digital activists have managed to repel the first label, they now need to focus on the second one; a more complex task that no doubt requires the production and dissemination of new narratives. As defended in this book, one way will be to re-position digital direct action as a cultural and creative practice.

A Return to Performance

The aim of this book was to explore the performative and aesthetic features of the developing practice of digital direct action. The rationale for this focus was that these creative aspects had been so far under-examined within digital media scholarship. Throughout this study, I have established that the role of performance, and performativity within social and political protest has also been underestimated. To be sure, the discursive processes that have seen the conflation of digital action and terrorism have not sustained close scrutiny, and despite the pervasiveness of the cyberterror discourse, collectives such as Electronic Disturbance Theater, the electrohippies and Anonymous, have been predominantly described as activists. As concluded in the discussion of Anonymous's practice, many activists believe that the movement's unique stand on humour, or lulz, has helped deflecting the suspicion that the group may be engaging in terrorist activities.

The second important conclusion is that with the increasing value of digital information, activists cannot assume that governments and corporations will acknowledge their resistance practices, or that legal courts will show clemency in their judgement. As a result, and as for most activists, digital protesters will need to formulate new narratives that explicitly state their social and political engagement.

All of the collectives examined in this book have participated in this task, in one way or another, beginning with the main theorists of digital resistance. In *Digital Resistance*, Critical Art Ensemble proposes an ultimate framework to position the practice of digital action. For the collective, ECD belongs to the field of tactical media. This is a retrospective link which clearly aims to address the challenges of ECD practice by connecting electronic disturbance to the tactical use of media. The concept first came into general use during a series of conference festivals in Amsterdam, in the mid-1990s. The events, known as Next 5 Minutes (N5M), were organised to host creative exhibitions and to host debates about the merging of art, politics and media. As part of the movement, Theorists Geert Lovink and David Garcia presented their manifesto, *The ABC of Tactical Media*, in which they refer to the concept as 'media of crisis, criticism and opposition', led by a variety of typical heroes such as 'the activist, nomadic media warriors, the prankster, the hacker, the street rapper, the camcorder kamikazes' (1997: para. 3).

This definition, or lack thereof, certainly allows for the integration of digital resistance in its various forms, including hacktivism, denial-of-service attacks, digital hijacks, or collaborative software (Raley, 2009: 6). The absence of an explicit definition also leaves the field opened to all practices. As Mackenzie Wark playfully declares, 'the most tactical thing about tactical media is the rhetorical tactic of calling it tactical' (2002: para. 12). Even so, the main focus of tactical media is in the interactions between media and technologies, and while CAE's re-appropriation seems justifiable, it eludes the key feature examined in this book, that is, the role of performance in digital direct action.

Throughout its writings, the one framework that CAE never fully acknowledges is the framework of performance. Yet, performance is the one feature that connects resistance practices as diverse as civil rights movements, indigenous insurrections, anti-copyright strikes or censorship disputes. As examined in this study, these protest movements harbour unique creative and performative qualities illustrated by the use of theatrical staging, the production of lyrical texts, or the re-appropriation of popular culture. In the process, they also echo, or directly cite, historical activist movements. The Seattle demonstrations stood in the long tradition of US social mobilisation, to include the staging of virtual sit-ins. The narratives of the Zapatista uprising were inherited from the revendications of the Mexican Revolution. More recently, the Occupy movement experimented with strategies inspired by the African and Arab Spring. The point is that this citationality, which is facilitated by performative attributes, is a way to ensure that social protest is identified as social protest.

In this context, the concept of 'tactical performance' can be used to refer to the specificity of these activist practices, including digital direct action. Tactical performance identifies a type of activism which develops, or re-appropriates distinct performative features. Performance is therefore not simply a tool, or an event in the protest, it is protest itself. As activists engage in the creative staging of opposition, performance becomes the tactic of resistance, with all of its potential for subversion, re-appropriation and coercion; in other words, with all of its performativity. Contrary to the tendency to distance the study of performance from theatrical and artistic contexts, the analysis here explicitly displayed there-appropriation of theatricality. Whether it relates to CAE's transgender hacking, Electronic Disturbance Theater's recombinant theatre or Anonymous's cinematic revenge, tactical performance virtually offers new spaces of contention.

Moreover, performance is the tactic against terror, *par excellence.* At the time when CAE's was publishing its first pamphlets, the contention that governments would frame digital protest as a criminal act was still hypothetical. Two decades later, the threat was acted upon with the first arrests and prosecutions of digital activists. All the same, direct action continued to develop as a main form of protest. As argued before, the creative and performative aesthetics of digital action have been best at dismissing the label of cyberterror. The poetics and playfulness of the SWARM Project or the Operation Payback cannot compare to the digital strikes organised against Estonia or the attempted sabotage of Iran's nuclear plant: here lays the performativity of tactical performance.

In another famous example, the concept of electronic civil disobedience was also displaced as the main theoretical framework of digital direct action. In 1999, a legal and virtual battle opposed eToys.com and etoy.com. The first one was a large American toy company, and the second one, a collective of media artists from the Netherlands. A few weeks before its most important sales period, eToys.com decided to file a lawsuit against the group of artists, over the content and name of their website. The toy company was claiming inappropriate competition and effectively wanted to buy out the collective. Following an injunction that required them to shut down their website, etoy.com decided to retaliate by staging a public virtual strike against eToys.com. The collective recruited hundreds of activists, artists, lawyers, celebrities and journalists, 'to join the playful TOY.army' (etoy.com, n.d.). For the 2 months surrounding the Christmas period, the toy company witnessed the continuous disruption of its website and the collapse of its market shares. Faced with imminent bankruptcy, the company eventually abandoned the lawsuit against etoy.com (Grether, 2000).

Although the artists-activists deployed the classic tools of digital direct action, it seems difficult to classify the project as electronic civil disobedience. In fact, the group made no reference to the concept. Instead, the project was named TOYWAR and described as 'the most expensive performance in art history' (etoy.com, n.d.). The term *tactical media* could also be used to explain TOYWAR but it remains too unspecific. After all, what the artists had purposefully engaged in is the tactical performance of a digital revenge; one that aimed to challenge capitalistic corporate control. In this sense, the artists and the performance predicted and enacted on the increasing power of digital data.

Perhaps, the best example of tactical performance was CAE's reinterpretation of the body without organs. This original *cyber-imaginaire* which (re)positions the body within digital action was explored in detail in Chapter Two. The analysis unravelled the relationship between digital technology, body and power, which signals the formation of new regimes of control, facilitated by the aggregation of electronic data. In 1984, Jean-Francois Lyotard predicted that 'the nation-states will one day fight for control of information, just as they battled in the past for control over territory, and afterwards for control of access to, and exploitation of, raw materials and cheap labor' (1984: 5). Ten years later, Critical Art Ensemble identified this struggle as the loss of digital sovereignty and called for the re-appropriation of digital bodies. The proposition entailed the staging of digital plays and of hacking performances. Through this, CAE called for the emergence of a new virtual theatre that could challenge nomadic powers within cyberspace. In a discursive sense, there was no requirement for these accounts to adopt a performance repertoire, but with it, electronic disturbance inherited the power of performative utterances; and in the process it became a tactical discourse with a compelling *imaginaire* of resistance and freedom, readily embraced by digital activists.

It is therefore unfortunate that CAE should later abandon this trail, in favour of the concept of electronic civil disobedience. Indeed, the tensions related to the data body and the loss of individual sovereignty could not be more closely associated to the issues raised by the recent scandals of governmental surveillance programmes. As illustrated by the projects of artists such as Hasan Elahi and David Kemp, discussed Chapter 2, the power of data to affect our very existence cannot be minimised. The uncontrollable accumulation of information originally described by CAE, has now given room to the systematic recording of data on everything, and on everybody. This is no longer a simple plot by marketing companies to boost commercial sales. Virtually every institution, public and private, is engaged in the senseless collection of data, often without the informed consent of the population.

In her recent study on governance and biopolitics, Ajana (2013) explains why we should be concerned with the practice and technology of data collection. Focusing on biometric identity systems that facilitate the identification of people using physical and biological information (for example, fingerprints, facial recognition, iris recognition, and DNA), Ajana argues that the dangers far exceed common concerns about access, privacy or data protection. Instead, she points to the current technologies of measurement that are affecting the very ontology of human existence. For Ajana, biometrics are directly linked to politics of control and power, and she recognises the central role of bodies in the biologisation and informatisation of identity and citizenship.

As expected, most governments have been prompted to assert the advantages of biometrics systems, notably in relation to dealing with national security, criminality, employment and other social organisations. However, questions about the ethics and supervision of surveillance and the misuse of data have remained mostly unanswered. This is where the relevance of what CAE's termed digital sovereignty resurfaces. The main argument that we have been denied the right to control our data, or virtual body, is still pertinent today. Most advocate of digital rights would argue that there is little transparency, and that we are prone to face further challenges with the growth of data collection processes. In addition, most recognise that information has become politics, or as described by Tim Jordan, 'one of these ongoing conflicts of exploitation and liberation as part of a multiple politics' (2015: 2). While these important questions are beyond the scope of the present book, the point is to reiterate the intrinsic relationship between bodies, space and information politics.

The central proposition of this book was that by examining the performativity of digital action, the dynamics of social and political struggles could be clarified. To this end, the analysis has ascertained the divergent conceptions of digital technologies that are placing governments, corporations and citizens in the midst of escalating conflicts, as well as the many defensive strategies used by all parties. What must be retained is that despite many contradictions in the *imaginaire* of digital action, bodies and spaces, physical and virtual, will need to remain the core focus, and as confirmed by the long historical tradition of protest, tactical performance will no doubt play a major role in this project.

Note

1 The call for the organization of a massive protest in Wall Street New York was first published on the internet by the Canadian Anti-advertising and culture jamming magazine Adbusters.

Bibliography

Abul-Magd, Zeinab (2012) 'Occupying Tahrir Square: The Myths and the Realities of the Egyptian Revolution', *The South Atlantic Quarterly*, 111 (3), pp. 567–572.

Ajana, Btihaj (2013) *Governing Through Biometrics: The Biopolitics of Identity*. London: Palgrave Macmillan.

Al Jazeera (2010) *Hactivists' Wage War for WikiLeaks*, 9 December 2010. Available from: http://www.aljazeera.com/news/europe/2010/12/201012916376458396.html [Accessed 30 October 2016].

Al Jazeera (2011) *Protesters Flood Egypt Streets*, 1 February 2011. Available from: http://www.aljazeera.com/news/middleeast/2011/02/2011215827193882.html [Accessed 21 July 2016].

Anonymous (2008) *Message to Scientology*. Available from: https://www.youtube.com/watch?v=JCbKv9yiLiQ [Accessed 30 October 2016].

Anonymous (2010a) *Operation Payback is a Bitch Poster Image*. Available from: http://www.plughitzlive.com/theupstream/856-operation-payback.html [Accessed 30 October 2016].

Anonymous (2010b) *Press Release*, 9 December 2010. Available from: https://www.youtube.com/watch?v=8Zsf1JM2yLk [Accessed 30 October 2016].

Anonymous (2010c) *Operation Avenge Assange*. Available from: https://web.archive.org/web/20101213031528/https://uloadr.com/u/4.png [Accessed 30 October 2016].

Anonymous (2010d) *What is Anonymous? - Understand Us!* Available from: https://www.youtube.com/watch?v=7cqP8qqqfI0 [Accessed 30 October 2016].

Anonymous (2011) *Hello Wall Street - We Are Anonymous*. Available from: https://www.youtube.com/watch?v=T-eFxCDx7Yw [Accessed 30 October 2016].

Anonymous (2012) *How to Join Anonymous - A Beginners Guide*. Available from: https://www.youtube.com/watch?v=ZdL3aU0yZBE [Accessed 30 October 2016].

Anonymous (2013) *What Is Anonymous?* Available from: wedonotfogivewedonotforget.blogspot.com/ [Accessed 30 October 2016].

Anonymous Netherlands (2012) Message to Alberto Stegeman. Available from: https://www.youtube.com/watch?v=654QQUnpp3A [Accessed 30 October 2016].

Ante, Spencer E. (2000) 'Against All Odds, Napster's Beat Goes On', *BusinessWeek*, 3 October, 2000.

Ars Electronica (1998) *Festival Catalog 98*. Available from: http://www.aec.at/festival/en/archiv/ [Accessed 11 June 2016].

Artaud, Antonin (1958) The *Theatre and Its Double*. New York: Grove Press.

Austin, John L. (1975) *How to Do Things with Words*. Cambridge, Mass: Harvard University Press.

Badey, Thomas J. (1998) 'Defining International Terrorism: A Pragmatic Approach', *Terrorism and Political Violence*, 10 (1), pp. 90–107.

Baudrillard, Jean (1994) *Simulacra and Simulation*. Ann Arbor: University of Michigan Press.

Barbrook, Richard & Cameron, Andy (1995) *The California Ideology*. Available from: www.hrc.wmin.ac.uk/theory-californianideology-main.html [Accessed 25 March 2016].

Barlow, John Perry (1990) *Across the Electronic Frontier*. Available from: http://w2.eff.org/Misc/Publications/John_Perry_Barlow/HTML/eff.html [Accessed 15 June 2016].

Barlow, John Perry (1996) *A Declaration of the Independence of Cyberspace*. Available from: https://www.eff.org/cyberspace-independence [Accessed 25 March 2016].

Battlestar Galatica (2004) [TV Series] creator: Glen A. Larson. United States: British Sky Broadcasting.

Bell, David (2001) *Introduction to Cyberculture*. London: Routledge.

Bendrath, Ralf (2006) 'Frankfurt Appellate Court says Online Demonstration is not Coercion', *EDRi*, 7 June 2006. Available from: https://edri.org/edrigramnumber4-11demonstration/ [Accessed 30 October 2016].

Bennahum, David (1996) 'United Nodes of Internet: Are We Forming a Digital Nation?' In: Ludlow, P. (ed.) (2001) *Crypto Anarchy, Cyberstates, and Pirate Utopias*. Cambridge, Mass.: MIT Press, pp. 39–45.

Boal, Augusto (1985) *Teatro del Oprimido (Theatre of the Oppressed)*. Mexico: Nueva Imagen.

Bradley, Will & Esche, Charles (2007) *Art and Social Change: A Critical Reader*. London: Tate Publishing.

Brand, Steward (1968) *Purpose of the 1968 Whole Earth Catalog*. Available from: http://www.wholeearth.com/issue-electronic-edition.php?iss=1010 [Accessed 25 March 2016].

British Broadcast Corporation (2007) 'Estonia hit by 'Moscow Cyber War'', *BBC News Europe*, 17 May 2007. Available from: www.bbc.co.uk/2/hi/europe/6665145.stm [Accessed 13 June 2016].

British Broadcast Corporation (2011) 'Egypt unrest', *BBC News Middle East*, 11 February 2011. Available from: http://www.bbc.co.uk/news/world-12434787 [Accessed 12 November 2016].

Brockman, John (1996) *Digerati: Encounters with the Cyber Elite*. London: Orion Business Books.

Buchstein, Hubertus (1997) 'Bytes That Bite: The Internet and Deliberative Democracy', *Constellations*, 4 (2) pp. 248–263.

Bukatman, Scott (2007) 'Cyberspace'. In: Bell, D. & Kennedy, B. M. (eds.) *The Cybercultures Reader*. New York: Routledge, pp. 80–105.

Butler, Judith (1990) *Gender Trouble: Feminism and the Subversion of Identity*. New York: Routledge.

Butler, Judith (1993) *Bodies That Matter: On the Discursive Limits of Sex*. New York: Routledge.

Carlson, Marvin (1996) *Performance: A Critical Introduction*. London, New York: Routledge. Castells, Manuel (1997) *The Power of Identity*. Oxford: Blackwell Publishers.

Chesher, Chris (1994) 'Virtual Reality: Construction of the Discourse of Virtual Reality 1984–1992', *Cultronix*, 1 (1). Available from: http://cultronix.eserver.org/chesher/ [Accessed 25 March 2016].

Christiansen, Adrienne E. & Hanson, Jeremy J. (1996) 'Comedy as Cure for Tragedy: ACT UP and the Rhetoric of AIDS', *Quarterly Journal of Speech*, 82 (2), pp. 157–170.

Coleman, Gabriella (2011) 'Hacker Politics and Publics', *Public Culture*, 23 (3), pp. 511–516.

Coleman, Gabriella (2012) 'Our Weirdness Is Free, The Logic of Anonymous—Online Army, Agent of Chaos, and Seeker of Justice', *Triple Canopy*, 15. Available from: https://www.canopycanopycanopy.com/issues/15/contents/our_weirdness_is_free [Accessed 30 October 2016].

Coleman, Gabriella (2014) *Hacker, Hoaxer, Whistleblower, Spy: The Many Faces of Anonymous*. New York: Verso.

Collin, Barry C. (1997) 'The Future of Cyberterrorism: The Physical and Virtual Worlds Converge', *Crime and Justice International*, 13 (2), pp. 15–18. Available from: http://www.crime-research.org/library/Cyberter.htm [Accessed 13 June 2016].

Conant, Jeff (2010) *A Poetics of Resistance: The Revolutionary Public Relations of the Zapatista Insurgency*. Oakland, CA, Edinburgh, UK: AK Press.

Conquergood, Dwight (2002) 'Lethal Theatre: Performance, Punishment, and the Death Penalty', *Theatre Journal*, 54 (3), pp. 339–367

Conway, Janet (2003) 'Civil Resistance and the Diversity of Tactics in the Anti-Globalization Movement: Problems of Violence, Silence, and Solidarity in Activist Politics', *Osgoode Hall Law Journal*, 41 (2, 3), pp. 505–530.

Conway, Maura (2002) 'Reality Bytes: Cyberterrorism and Terrorist "Use" of the Internet', *First Monday*, 7 (11). Available from: http://firstmonday.org/article/view/1001/922 [Accessed 13 June 2016].

Conway, Maura (2011) 'Against Cyberterrorism', *Communications of the ACM*, 54 (2), pp. 26–28.

Critical Art Ensemble (1994) *The Electronic Disturbance*. New York: Autonomedia.

Critical Art Ensemble (1996) *Electronic Civil Disobedience*. New York: Autonomedia.

Critical Art Ensemble (2001) *Digital Resistance*. New York: Autonomedia.

Cronon, William (1987) 'Revisiting the Vanishing Frontier: The Legacy of Frederick Jackson Turner', *The Western Historical Quarterly*, 18 (2), pp. 157–176.

Davis, Mike (1993) 'Virtual Light', *Artforum*, 32 (4), pp. 10–12.

Davis, R. G. (1966) 'Guerrilla Theatre', *The Tulane Drama Review*, 10 (4), pp. 130–136.

Dean, Jodi (1997) 'Virtually Citizens', *Constellations*, 4 (2), pp. 264–282.

Debord, Guy (1957) 'Report on the Construction of Situations'. In: Knabb, K. (ed.) (2006) *Situationist International Anthology*. Berkeley, Calif.: Bureau of Public Secrets. pp. 25–43.

Deleuze, Gilles & Guattari, Felix (1987) *A Thousand Plateaus: Capitalism and Schizophrenia*. Minneapolis: The University of Minnesota Press.

Deluca, Kevin M. (1999) 'Unruly Arguments: The Body Rhetoric of Earth First!, ACT UP, and Queer Nation', *Argumentation and Advocacy*, 36 (1), pp. 9–21.

Denning, Dorothy (2000) *Cyberterrorism*. Testimony before the Special Oversight Panel on Terrorism Committee on Armed Services U.S. House of Representatives, 23 May 2000. Available from: stealth-iss.com/documents/pdf/CYBERTERRORISM.pdf [Accessed 13 June 2016].

Denton, Nick (2008) 'The Cruise indoctrination video Scientology tried to suppress', *Gawker*, 15 January 2008. Available from: http://gawker.com/5002269/the-cruise-indoctrination-video-scientology-tried-to-suppress [Accessed 30 October 2016].

Denzin, Norman K. (2003) 'The Call to Performance', *Symbolic Interaction*, 26 (1), pp. 187–207.

Derrida, Jacques (1982) *Margins of Philosophy*. Chicago: University of Chicago Press.

Derrida, Jacques (2002) *Negotiations: Interventions and Interviews, 1971–2001*. Stanford, California: Stanford University Press.

Diamond, Elin (ed.) (1996) *Performance and Cultural Politics*. New York: Routledge.

Dominguez, Ricardo (2014) *Interview with Electronic Disturbance Theater*. 18 August 2014. Fidèle Vlavo, Ann Arbor, MI.

Doyle, Michael William (2002) 'Staging the Revolution: Guerrilla Theater as a Countercultural Practice, 1965–1968'. In: Braunstein, P. & Doyle, M. W. (eds.) *Imagine Nation: The American Counterculture of the 1960s and '70s*. New York: Routledge, pp. 71–98.

Earl, Jennifer & Kimport, Katrina (2013) *Digitally Enabled Social Change: Activism in the Internet Age*. Cambridge, Mass.: MIT Press.

Ejército Zapatista de Liberación Nacional (EZLN) (1995) 'La larga traversía del dolor a la esperanza' ('The long journey from despair to hope'), *Documentos y Comunicados*, 2, pp. 49–79.

Ejército Zapatista de Liberación Nacional (EZLN)/SupMarcos (2013) *Them and Us VI. The Gaze 4: To Look and Communicate*. Available from: http://enlacezapatista.ezln.org.mx/2013/02/17/them-and-us-vi-the-gaze-4-to-look-and- communicate/ [Accessed 12 November 2016].

Elahi, Hasan (2014) 'I Share Everything. Or Do I?', *Ideas.Ted.Com*. Available from: http://ideas.ted.com/i-share-everything-or-do-i/ [Accessed 19 May 2016].

Electronic Disturbance Theater (1998a) 'FloodNet warning', *Thing.net*. Available from: http://www.thing.net/~rdom/zapsTactical/warning.htm [Accessed 13 June 2016].

Electronic Disturbance Theater (1998b) 'September 9—Advance release', *Thing.net*. Available from: http://www.thing.net/~rdom/ecd/September9.html [Accessed 13 June 2016].

Espiner, Tom (2005) 'British Teen Cleared in 'e-mail bomb' Case', *ZDNet*, 2 November 2005. Available from: http://www.zdnet.com/article/british-teen-cleared-in-e-mail-bomb-case/ [Accessed 30 October 2016].

etoy.com (n.d) *TOYWAR*. Available from: http://toywar.etoy.com/ [Accessed 1 March 2017].

Fairclough, Norman (1992) *Discourse and Social Change*. Cambridge: Polity Press.

Falliere, Nicolas, Murchu, Liam O., & Chien, Eric (2011) *W32. Stuxnet Dossier* (Version 1.4). California: Symantec.

Feigenbaum, Anna (2012) 'Security for Sale! The Visual Rhetoric of Marketing Counter-Terrorism Technologies', *The Poster*, 2 (1), pp. 75–92.

Felshin, Nina (1995) *But Is It Art?: The Spirit of Art as Activism*. Seattle: Bay Press.

Finlayson, James G. (2005) *Habermas: A Very Short Introduction*. Oxford: Oxford University Press.

Flichy, Patrice (1999) 'The Construction of New Media', *New Media and Society*, 1 (1), pp. 33–38.

Flichy, Patrice (2007) *The Internet Imaginaire*. London: MIT Press.

Foster, Susan L. (2003) 'Choreographies of Protest', *Theatre Journal*, 55 (3), pp. 395–412.

Foucault, Michel (1977) *Discipline and Punish*. London: Allen Lane.

Foucault, Michel (1990) *The History of Sexuality: An Introduction*. Vol. 1. New York: Vintage.

Foucault, Michel (1992) 'What is an Author?' In: Harrison, C. & Wood, P. (eds.) *Art in Theory, 1900–1990: An Anthology of Changing Ideas*. Oxford: Blackwell, pp. 923–1015.

Fusco, Coco (1999) *Electronic Disturbance Ricardo Dominguez Interviewed by Coco Fusco*. London, Institute of International Visual Arts, 25 November 1999, London, UK. Available from: http://subsol.c3.hu/subsol_2/contributors2/domingueztext2.html [Accessed 13 June 2016].

Fusco, Coco (2003) 'On-Line Simulations/ Real-Life Politics', *The Drama Review*, 47 (2), pp. 151–162.

Garcia, David & Lovink, Geert (1997) *The ABC of Tactical Media*. Available from: http://www.nettime.org/Lists-Archives/nettime-l-9705/msg00096.html [Accessed 30 October 2016].

García Márquez, Gabriel & Marcos, Subcomandante (2001) 'A Zapatista Reading List', *The Nation*, 2 July 2001. Available from: http://www.thenation.com/article/zapatista-reading-list/ [Accessed 13 June 2016].

Geertz, Clifford (1973) *The Interpretations of Cultures*. New York: Basic Books.

Gibson, William (1984) *Neuromancer*. London: Gollancz.

Gibson, William (1986) *Count Zero*. London: Gollancz.

Gibson, William (1996) *Idoru*. London: Viking.

Gladwell, Malcolm (2010) 'Small Change: Why the Revolution will not be Tweeted', *The New Yorker*, 4 October 2010. Available from: http://www.newyorker.com/magazine/2010/10/04/small-change-malcolm-gladwell [Accessed 30 October 2016].

Godwin, Mike (1994) 'When Copying Isn't Theft: How the Government Stumbled in a "Hacker" Case. Available from: http://w2.eff.org/Misc/Publications/Mike_Godwin/phrack_riggs_neidorf_godwin.article [Accessed 21 July 2016].

Goffman, Erving (1982) [1967] *Interaction Ritual: Essays in Face to Face Behavior*. New York: Pantheon Books.

Goldsmith, Jack & Wu, Tim (2006) *Who Controls the Internet?: Illusions of a Borderless World*. New York: Oxford University Press.

Goldstein, Emmanuel (1990) 'Hacker view of the "Legion of Doom" sentencing in Atlanta', *The Risks Digest*, 10 (65) 6 December 1990. Available from: http://catless.ncl.ac.uk/Risks/10/65 [Accessed 10 September 2016].

Gould, Jonathan (2014) 'Insurance Firms Turn to Big Data to Help Identify Risks', *Daily Mail*. Available from: http://www.dailymail.co.uk/wires/reuters/article-2759511/Insurers-turn-big-data-help-identify-risks.html [Accessed 30 October 2016].

Graeber, David (2009) *Direct Action: An Ethnography*. Edinburgh; Oakland: AK Press.

Graeber, David (2011a) 'On Playing by the Rules: The Strange Success of #OccupyWallStreet', *Naked Capitalism*, 19 October 2011, (blog entry). Available from: http://www.nakedcapitalism.com/2011/10/david-graeber-on-playing-by-the-rules-%e2%80%93-the-strange-success-of-occupy-wall-street.html [Accessed 21 July 2016].

Graeber, David (2011b) 'Occupy Wall Street's anarchist roots', *Al Jazeera*, 30 November 2011, (opinion). Available from: http://www.aljazeera.com/in-depth/opinion/2011/11/2011112872835904508.html [Accessed 21 July 2016]

Green, Joshua (2002) 'The Myth of Cyberterrorism', *Washington Monthly*, 34 (11) (November), pp. 8–13.

Grether, Reinhold (2000) 'How the etoy Campaign Was Won: An Agent's Report', *Leonardo*, 33 (4), pp. 321–324.

Guevara, Alberto (2008) 'Pesticide, Performance, Protest: Theatricality of Flesh in Nicaragua', *InTensions*, 1, pp. 1–23.

Gunderson, Laura (2013) 'Equifax must pay $18.6 million after failing to fix Oregon woman's credit report', *The Oregonian*. Available from: http://www.oregonlive.com/business/index.ssf/2013/07/equifax_must_pay_186_million_a.html [Accessed 19 May 2016].

Habermas, Jürgen (1991) *The Structural Transformation of the Public Sphere: An Inquiry into a Category of Bourgeois Society*. Cambridge, Mass.: MIT Press.

Hamman, Robin (1996) Rhizome@Internet using the Internet as an example of Deleuze and Guattari's "Rhizome", *Cybersociology Magazine*. Partially available from: https://selforum.blogspot.mx/2005/09/ [Accessed 12 May 2017].

Hammond, Jeremy (2013) 'Sentencing Statement', *Sparrow Project*, 15 November 2013. Available from: http://www.sparrowmedia.net/2013/11/jeremy-hammond-sentence/ [Accessed 7 July 2015].

Hammond, Jeremy (2014) 'I'm an Anonymous Hacker in Prison, and I am not a Crook. I'm an Activist', *The Guardian*, 18 December 2013. Available from: http://www.theguardian.com/commentisfree/2014/dec/18/anonymous-hacker-prison-jeremy-hammond-hacktivism [Accessed 7 July 2015].

Halliday, Josh (2010) 'Operation Payback Fails to Take Down Amazon in WikiLeaks Revenge Attack', *The Guardian*, 9 December 2010. Available from: https://www.theguardian.com/media/2010/dec/09/operation-payback-wikileaks-anonymous [Accessed 30 October 2016].

Hands, Joss (2011) *@ Is for Activism: Dissent, Resistance and Rebellion in a Digital Culture*. London: Pluto Press.

Hart, Marjolein'T. (2007) 'Humour and Social Protest: An Introduction', *International Review of Social History*, 52 (S15), pp. 1–20.

Hohle, Randolph (2009) 'The Body and Citizenship in Social Movement Research: Embodied Performances and the Deracialized Self in the Black Civil Rights Movement 1961–1965', *The Sociological Quarterly*, 50 (2) pp. 283–307.

Holloway, John & Pelaez, Eloina (1998) *Zapatistas! Reinventing the Revolution in Mexico: Introduction*. Available from: http://www.korotonomedya.net/kor/index.php?id=10,46,0,0,1,0 [Accessed 13 June 2016].

Holloway, John (2005) *Change the World Without Taking Power: The Meaning of Revolution Today*. London: Pluto Press.

I, Robot. (2004) [film], director: Alex Proyas. United States: Twentieth Century Fox Film Corporation.

IBTimes New York (2011) 'Occupy Wall Street' to Turn Manhattan into 'Tahrir Square', 17 September 2011. Available from: http://www.ibtimes.com/occupy-wall-street-turn-manhattan-tahrir-square-647819 [Accessed 21 July 2016].

International Telecommunication Union (ITU) (2000) *Yearbook of Statistics: Telecommunication Services Chronological Time Series 1989–1998*. Geneva: International Telecommunication Union.

International Telecommunication Union (ITU) (2010) *The World in 2010: ICT Facts and Figures. Geneva:* International Telecommunication Union.

Jordan, Tim (1999) *Cyberpower: The Culture and Politics of Cyberspace and the Internet*. London: Routledge.

Jordan, Tim & Taylor, Paul A. (2004) *Hacktivism and Cyberwars: Rebels with a Cause?* New York: Routledge.

Jordan, Tim (2015) *Information Politics: Liberation and Exploitation in the Digital Society*. London: Pluto Press.

Joyce, Mary (2010) *Digital Activism Decoded: The New Mechanics of Change*. New York: International Debate Education Association.

Juris, Jeffrey S. (2014) 'Embodying Protest: Culture and Performance within Social Movements'. In: Baumgarten, B. Daphi, P. & Ullrich, P. (eds.) *Conceptualizing Culture in Social Movement Research*. UK: Palgrave Macmillan, pp. 227–246.

Karatzogianni, Athina (2015) *Firebrand Waves of Digital Activism 1994–2014: The Rise and Spread of Hacktivism and Cyberconflict*. Basingstoke Hampshire: Palgrave Macmillan.

Kemp, David (2009) *Data Collection* – Artist Statement. Available from: http://davekemp.ca/xhtml/datacollection/data_collection_stmt.htm [Accessed 19 May 2016].

Kershaw, Baz (1997) 'Fighting in the Streets: Dramaturgies of Popular Protest, 1968–1989', *New Theatre Quarterly*, 13 (51), pp. 255–276.

King, Martin L. Jr. (1963) 'Letter from a Birmingham Jail'. Available from: http://www.africa.upenn.edu/Articles_Gen/Letter_Birmingham.html [Accessed 1 March 2017].

Kirk, Jeremy (2006) 'UK Teen Pleads Guilty to DOS e-mailattack', *InfoWorld*, 24 August 2006. Available from: http://www.infoworld.com/article/2658828/applications/uk-teen-pleads-guilty-to-dos-e-mail-attack.html [Accessed 30 October 2016].

Klang, Mathias (2005) 'Virtual Sit-Ins, Civil Disobedience and Cyberterrorism'. In: Klang, M. & Murray, A. (eds.). *Human Rights in the Digital Age*. Cavendish Publishing: London, pp. 135–146.

Kohn, Margaret (2013) 'Privatization and Protest: Occupy Wall Street, Occupy Toronto, and the Occupation of Public Space in a Democracy', *Perspectives on Politics*, 11 (1), pp. 99–110.

Kravets, David (2012) 'Supreme Court Lets Stand $675,000 File-Sharing Verdict', *Wired*, 21 May 2012. Available from: http://www.wired.com/2012/05/supreme-court-file-sharing/ [Accessed 21 July 2016].

Kroker, Arthur & Weinstein, Michael A. (1994) *Data Trash: The Theory of Virtual Class*. Montreal: New World Perspectives.

Landow, George P. (2006) *Hypertext 3.0: Critical Theory and New Media in an Era of Globalization*. Baltimore: Johns Hopkins University Press.

Lane, Jill (2003) 'Digital Zapatistas', *The Drama Review*, 47 (2), pp. 129–144.

Lefebvre, Henri (1991) *The Production of Space*. Oxford: Blackwell.

Lennard, Natasha (2013) 'Jeremy Hammond: Stung or Entrapped?', *Salon*, 18 November. 2013. Available from: http://www.salon.com/2013/11/18/hammond_stung_or_entrapped/ [Accessed 7 July 2015].

Levy, Steven (1984) *Hackers: Heroes of the Computer Revolution*. London: Penguin.

Li, Xiang (2013) 'Hacktivism and the First Amendment: Drawing the Line between Cyber Protests and Crime', *Harvard Journal of Law & Technology*, 27 (1), pp. 301–330.

Licklider, J.C.R. (1960) *Man-Computer Symbiosis*. Available from: http://groups.csail.mit.edu/medg/people/psz/Licklider.html [Accessed 19 May 2016].

Lievrouw, Leah A. (2011) *Alternative and Activist New Media*. Cambridge; Malden, MA: Polity.

Lippard, Lucy (1984) *Art & Ideology*. Available from: http://archive.newmuseum.org/index.php/Detail/Object/Show/object_id/6450 [Accessed 10 September 2016].

Lister, Martin, Dovey, Jon, Giddings, Seth, Grant, Ian, & Kelly, Keiran (2003) *New Media: A Critical Introduction*. London: Routledge.

Lockard, Joe (2000) 'Babel Machines and Electronic Universalism'. In: Kolko, B. *et al* (eds.) *Race in Cyberspace*. New York: Routledge, pp. 171–189.

Lyotard, Jean-François (1984) *The Postmodern Condition: A Report on Knowledge*. Minnesota: University of Minnesota Press.

Manner, Mikko, Siniketo, Topi & Polland, Ulrika (2009) 'The Pirate Bay Ruling—When the Fun and Games End', *Entertainment Law Review*, 20 (6), pp. 197–205.

Marcos, Subcomandante (2005) *Conversations with Durito: Stories of the Zapatistas and Neoliberalism*. New York: Autonomedia.

McCarthy, John D. & McPhail, Clark (1998) 'The Institutionalization of Protest in the US'. In: Meyer, D. & Tarrow, S. (eds.) *The Social Movement Society: Contentious Politics for the New Century*. Lanham, Maryland: Rowman and Littlefield, pp. 83–110.

McCaughey, Martha & Ayers, Michael D. (eds.) (2003) *Cyberactivism: Online Activism in Theory and Practice*. New York: Routledge.

McLaren, Margaret (2002) *Feminism, Foucault and Embodied Subjectivity*. Albany: Suny.

Meikle, Graham (2002) *Future Active: Media Activism and the Internet*. New York: Routledge.

Meikle, Graham (2008) 'Electronic Civil Disobedience and Symbolic Power'. In: Karatzogianni, A. (ed.) *Cyber-conflict and Global Politics*. London: Routledge, pp. 177–187.

Mesch, Claudia (2013) *Art and Politics: A Small History of Art for Social Change since 1945*. London: I.B. Tauris.

Metropolis (1927) dir. Fritz Lang, Germany.

Miller, Laura (1995) 'Women and Children First: Gender and the Settling of the Electronic Frontier'. In: Brook, J. & Boal, A. I. (eds.) *Resisting the Virtual Life: The Culture and Politics of Information*. San Francisco: City Lights, pp. 49–57.

Mondo 2000 (1990) 'The Rush Is On! Colonizing Cyberspace', *Mondo 2000*, 2 (Cover).

Morozov, Evengy (2011) *The Net Delusion: The Dark Side of Internet Freedom*. New York: Public Affairs.

Murphy, Jeffrie G. (1971) *Civil Disobedience and Violence*. Belmont: Wadsworth Publishing.

National Infrastructure Protection Center (NIPC) (2002) *Activism in Connection with Protest Events of September 2002*, 23 September 2002. Available from: http://www.iwar.org.uk/infocon/assessments/2002/02-002.htm [Accessed 13 June 2016].

Norton, Quinn (2012) 'How Anonymous Picks Targets, Launches Attacks, and Takes Powerful Organizations Down', *Wired*, 3 July 2012. Available from: http://www.wired.com/threatlevel/2012/07/ff_anonymous/ [Accessed 30 October 2016].

Olson, Parmy (2012) *We Are Anonymous: Inside the Hacker World of LulzSec, Anonymous, and the Global Cyber Insurgency*. New York: Little, Brown and Company.

O'Neil, Lorraine (2013) 'Anonymous wants DDoS attacks legalized as form of protest', *CBC News*. Available from: http://www.cbc.ca/newsblogs/yourcommunity/2013/01/anonymous-wants-ddos-attacks-legalized-as-form-of-protest.html [Accessed 30 October 2016].

O'Neill, Gerard K. (1977) *The High Frontier: Human Colonies in Space*. London: Cape.

Oppenheimer, Martin & Lackey, George (1965) *A Manual for Direct Action: Strategies and Tactics for Civil Rights and All Other Nonviolent Protest Movements*. Chicago, IL: Quadrangle Books.

Partnership for Civil Justice Fund (2012) *FBI Documents Reveal Secret Nationwide Occupy Monitoring*. Available from: http://www.justiceonline.org/fbi_files_ows [Accessed 1 March 2017].

Phelan, Peggy (1993) *Unmarked: The Politics of Performance*. London: Routledge.

Pilkington, Ed (2015) 'FBI put Anonymous 'hacktivist' Jeremy Hammond on Terrorism Watchlist', *The Guardian*, 2 February 2015. Available from: http://www.theguardian.com/us-news/2015/feb/02/fbi-anonymous-hacktivist-jeremy-hammond-terrorism-watchlist [Accessed 7 July 2015].

Poulsen, Kevin (2011) 'In Anonymous raids, feds work from list of top 1,000 protesters', *Wired*, 26 July 2011. Available from: http://www.wired.com/threatlevel/2011/07/op_payback/ [Accessed 30 October 2016].

Raley, Rita (2009) *Tactical Media*. Minneapolis: University of Minnesota Press.

Ramadan, Adam (2012) 'From Tahrir to the World: The Camp as a Political Public Space', *European Urban and Regional Studies*, 20 (1), pp. 145–149.

Ramirez, Miguel G. (1998) 'A Dirty War in Internet (analysis)', *Thing.net*, 27 April 1998, Available from: http://www.thing.net/~rdom/ecd/amelapaz.html [Accessed 13 June 2016].

Rawls, John (1971) 'Definition and Justification of Civil Disobedience'. In: Bedau, A. H. (ed.) (1991) *Civil Disobedience in Focus*. London: Routledge, pp. 103–121.

Raymond, Eric (ed.) (1991) *The New Hacker's Dictionary*. Cambridge, Mass: MIT Press.

Reed, T. V. (2005) *The Art of Protest: Culture and Activism from the Civil Rights Movement to the Streets of Seattle*. Minneapolis, MN: University of Minnesota Press.

Reinelt G. Janelle (2002) 'The Politics of Discourse: Performativity Meets Theatricality'. *SubStance*, 31 (2), pp. 201–215.

Rheingold, Howard (1991) *Virtual Reality*. New York: Summit Books.

Rid, Thomas (2012) 'Cyber War Will Not Take Place', *Journal of Strategic Studies*, 35 (1) pp. 5–32.

Robocop (1987) [film], director: Paul Verhoeven. United States: Orion Pictures.

Ruffin, Oxblood (2000) *'Valid Campaign Tactic or Terrorist Act?': The Cult of the Dead Cow's response to client-side distributed denial-of-service*. Available from: http://w3.cultdeadcow.com/cms/2000/07/hacktivismo.html [Accessed 30 October 2016].

Salama, Hussam Hussein (2013) 'Tahrir Square a Narrative of a Public Space', *Archnet-IJAR*, 7 (1), pp. 128–138.

Sassen, Saskia (2011a) 'The Global Street: Making the Political', *Globalizations*, 8 (5), pp. 573–579.

Sassen, Saskia (2011b) 'The Global Street Comes to Wall Street', *Possible Futures*, 22 November 2011. Available from: http://www.possible-futures.org/2011/11/22/the-global-street-comes-to- wall-street/ [Accessed 1 March 2017].

Sasson-Levy, Orna & Rapoport, Tamar (2003) 'Body, Gender, and Knowledge in Protest Movements the Israeli Case', *Gender and Society*, 17 (3), pp. 379–403.

Sauter, Molly (2013) 'LOIC Will Tear Us Apart', *American Behavioral Scientist*, 57 (7), pp. 983–1007.

Sauter, Molly (2014) *The Coming Swarm: DDOS Actions, Hacktivism, and Civil Disobedience on the Internet*. New York: Bloomsbury.

Schechner, Richard (2006) *Performance Studies: An Introduction*. New York: Routledge.

Scholette, Gregory (1999) 'News from Nowhere: Activist Art and After', *Third Text*, 13 (45), pp. 45–62.

Seattle Municipal Archives (n.d.) *World Trade Organization Protests in Seattle*. Available from: http://www.seattle.gov/cityarchives/exhibits-and-education/digital-document-libraries/world-trade-organization-protests-in-seattle [Accessed 21 July 2016].

Situationist International (1958) 'Definitions'. In: Knabb, K. (ed.) (2006) *Situationist International Anthology*. Berkeley, Calif.: Bureau of Public Secrets. pp. 51–52.

Solomon, Alisa (1998) 'AIDS Crusaders ACT UP a Storm'. In: Cohen-Cruz, J. (ed.) *Radical Street Performance*. London: Routledge. pp. 42–50.

Solove, Daniel J. (2004) *The Digital Person: Technology and Privacy in the Information Age*. New York: New York University Press.

Sterling, Bruce (1993) *The Hacker Crackdown: Law and Disorder on the Electronic Frontier*. New York: Bantam Books.

The Bionic Woman (1976) [TV Series], creator: Kenneth Johnson. United States: Harve Bennett Productions.

The electrohippies collective (2000) *Cyberlaw UK: Civil Rights and Protest on the Internet*. Communiqué December 2000. Available from: http://www.iwar.org.uk/hackers/resources/electrohippies-collective/comm-2000-12.pdf [Accessed 10 September 2016].

The electrohippies collective DJNZ and the Action Tool Development Group (2001) 'Client-Side Distributed Denial-of-Service: Valid Campaign Tactic or Terrorist Act?' *Leonardo* 34 (3), pp. 269–274.

The Guardian (2011) 'Occupy Wall Street: Zuccotti Park Re-opens – as it Happened', *World blog*, 15 November 2011. Available from: https://www.theguardian.com/world/blog/2011/nov/15/occupy-wall-street-zuccotti-eviction-live [Accessed 12 November 2016].

The Matrix (2000) [film], director: Andy & Larry Wachowski. United States: Warner Bros.

The Net (1995) [film], director: Irwin Winkler. United States: Columbia Pictures Corporation.

The Pirate Bay (n.d) *About*. Available from: https://thepiratebay.org/about. [Accessed 21 July 2016].

The Six Million Dollar Man (1974) [TV Series], producer: Kenneth Johnson. United States: Harve Bennett Productions.

The Terminator (1984) [film], director: James Cameron. United States: Hemdale.

The War of the Worlds (1953) [film], director: Byron Haskin. United States: Paramount Pictures.

Thompson, Clive (2007) 'The Visible Man: An FBI Target Puts His Whole Life Online', *Wired*. Available from: http://www.wired.com/2007/05/ps-transparency/ [Accessed 19 May 2016].

Thoreau, Henry D. (1888) *Yankee in Canada. With Anti-slavery and Reform Papers*. Boston: Houghton, Mifflin.

Tilly, Charles (2008) *Contentious Performances*. New York: Cambridge University Press.

Tomas, David (1991) 'Old Rituals for New Space: Rites de Passage and William Gibson's Cultural Model of Cyberspace'. In: Benedikt, M. L. (ed.) *Cyberspace: First Steps*. Cambridge, Mass: The MIT Press, pp. 31–48.

Turner, Frederick J. (1921) *The Frontier in American History*. New York: Holt.

Turner, Fred (1999) *Cyberspace as the New Frontier?: Mapping the Shifting Boundaries of the Network Society*. Paper presented at the *International Communication Association*, 27–31 May 1999, San Francisco, CA.

Turner, Fred (2006) *From Counterculture to Cyberculture: Stewart Brand, the Whole Earth Network and the Rise of Digital Utopianism*. Chicago: Chicago University Press.

Turner, Victor (1982) *From Ritual to Theatre: the Human Seriousness of Play*. New York: Performing Arts Journal Publications.

UK Home Office (2010) *identity-theft.org.uk*. Webpage archived from original site on 15 July 2006. Available from: http://webarchive.nationalarchives.gov.uk/20060919103940/identity-theft.org.uk/ [Accessed 19 May 2016].

United Kingdom Parliament (2006) 'Police and Justice Act 2006'. Available from: http://www.legislation.gov.uk/ukpga/2006/48/contents [Accessed 30 October 2016].

van de Sande, Mathijs (2013) 'The Prefigurative Politics of Tahrir Square– An Alternative Perspective on the 2011 Revolutions', *Res Publica*, 19, pp. 223–239.

Vegh, Sandor (2002) 'Hacktivists or Cyberterrorists? The Changing Media Discourse on Hacking', *First Monday*, 7(10). Available from: http://firstmonday.org/htbin/cgiwrap/bin/ojs/index.php/fm/article/view/998/919 [Accessed 13 June 2016].

Vlavo, Fidèle (2014) (unpublished) *20 Years of the Electronic Civil Disobedience: Interview with Steve Kurtz.*

Vlavo, Fidèle (2015) (unpublished) *Hacking Performance and Digital Mourning: Interview with Carmin Karasic.*

Wall, Melissa A. (2003) 'Press Conferences or Puppets', *Javnost the Public*, 10 (1), pp. 33–48. Wark, McKenzie (2002) 'Strategies for Tactical Media', *RealTime*, 51 (Oct-Nov) p. 10.

Wark, McKenzie (2004) *A Hacker Manifesto*. Cambridge, Mass: Harvard University Press.

Wark, McKenzie (2011) *The Beach Beneath the Street: The Everyday Life and Glorious Times of the Situationist International.* London: Verso.

Weimann, Gabriel (2005) 'Cyberterrorism: The Sum of all Fears?', *Studies in Conflict & Terrorism*, 28 (2), pp. 129–149.

Wetherell, Margaret, Taylor, Stephanie & Yates, Simeon J. (2001) *Discourse Theory and Practice: A Reader.* London: SAGE.

Wilbur, Shawn P. (2000) 'An Archaeology of Cyberspaces: Virtuality, Community, Identity'. In: Bell, D. & Kennedy, B. M. (eds.) *The Cybercultures Reader.* New York: Routledge, pp. 45–55.

Winston, Brian (1998) *Media Technology and Society: A History: From the Telegraph to the Internet.* London: Routledge.

Wray, Stefan (1998a) 'Rhizomes, Nomads, and Resistant Internet Use', *Thing.net*. Available from: http://www.thing.net/~rdom/ecd/RhizNom.html [Accessed 13 June 2016].

Wray, Stefan (1998b) 'Electronic Civil Disobedience and the World Wide Web of activism', *Switch*, 2 (4). Available from: http://switch.sjsu.edu/web/v4n2/stefan/ [Accessed 13 June 2016].

Wray, Stefan (1999) 'On Electronic Civil Disobedience', *Peace Review*, 11 (1), pp. 107–111.

Yang, Guobin (2011) *The Power of the Internet in China: Citizen Activism Online.* New York: Columbia University Press.

Yen, Alfred C. (2002) 'Western Frontier or Feudal Society?: Metaphors and Perceptions of Cyberspace', *Berkeley Technology Law Journal*, 17, pp. 1207–1263.

Index

4chan 111

Abul-Magd, Zeinab 134
ACT UP 52–53
Acteal 86–87
activist art 79–80
aesthetics 9, 13–14, 82–83, 94
African and Arab Spring 131–32, 144
Ajana, Btihaj 146
Al Jazeera 122, 131
Anons (activists) 111
anonymity 111, 114–15, 124
Anonymous 110, 114, 116–19
Anonymous Netherlands 113
Ante, Spencer E. 74
Ars Electronica 87, 88, 100
Artaud, Antonin 41, 47, 80
artist 12, 55, 57, 78
The Atlanta Three 71–73
Austin, John L. 7, 8, 30
Ayers, Michael D. 5

Badey, J. Thomas 106
Barbrook, Richard 18, 19, 30
Barlow, John Perry 15–16, 23–27, 55, 110; *see also the Declaration of Independence*
Battlestar Galatica 54
Baudrillard, Jean 101, 102
Bell, David 30
BellSouth computers 71
Bendrath, Ralf 126
Bennahum, David 27
biometrics 146
The Bionic Woman 54
blockades 52, 85, 90, 126
Boal, Augusto 99, 100
body: performance 46; resistance 53; sovereignty 40
'body without organs' 40–46, 60–61
Bradley, Will 79
Brand, Steward 18, 68
Brecht, Bertolt 80, 99
BBC 133, 140
British Police and Justice Act 127
Brockman, John 17–20, 38
Buchstein, Hubertus 69
Bukatman, Scott 22
Butler, Judith 7, 9, 83

Californian Ideology 19
Cameron, Andy 18, 19, 30
Carlson, Marvin 7
Castells, Manuel 2
Chesher, Chris 22, 23
Chiapas 86, 93
Christiansen, Adrienne 52
Church of Scientology 112–13, 118
citationality 14, 83, 144
civil disobedience 48, 62–67, 75, 85
Civil Rights movements 49–50, 65, 82
Coleman, Gabriella 111, 112, 122
Collin, Barry C. 105–06
Conant, Jeff 95, 108
Conquergood, Dwight 7
contention 62, performers 77; strategies 63
Conway, Janet 66
Conway, Maura 105–06
creative practice 79, 85, 110
Critical Art Ensemble 11–12, 30, 63, 131, 138, 143, 145
Cronon, William 24
cyber-imaginaire 14, 23, 38, 93, 113, 145
cyberactivism 5
cybercriminality 127, 130
cyberprotest 104, 106

cyberspace 11–13, 16–23
cyberterrorism 103–07
cyborg 54

data body *see* digital body
Davis, Mike 21, 22
Davis, R. G. 80
Dean, Jodi 69
Debord, Guy 120–21, 130
The Declaration of Independence 23, 27, 29
Deleuze, Gilles 34, 41
Deluca, Kevin M. 61
denial-of-service 67, 70, 88–89, 101–02, 109–10, 127–28
Denning, Dorothy 103
Denton, Nick 118
Denzin, Norman K. 83
Derrida, Jacques 23, 30, 83
détournement 121, 130
Diamond, Elin 7
digerati 17
digital activism 3–10, 14, 58, 74, 84, 141; activists 5, 12, 59, 68, 70, 107, 144
digital body 40, 57, 63, 75, 77, 98, 145
digital data 40–41, 55, 79
digital direct action 6–9, 37–38, 104–07, 126–27, 130, 138, 143
digital disturbance 87, 116, 129
digital performance 1, 99–100
digital protest 2–3, 10–14, 68, 87, 101–04, 125–26
digital resistance 40, 51, 63, 70, 75, 98, 141
digital sovereignty 13, 40, 45–46, 60, 145–46
digital technology 2, 5–6, 12–13, 20, 38, 40, 74
direct action 50, 66–68
discourse 2, 10–12, 26, 69, 103–06, 127, 137–43
disturbance: anonymity 111; performance 70, 116; politics 122
Dominguez, Ricardo 87–89, 94, 99, 100
Doyle, Michael William 81

Earl, Jennifer 5
Ejército Zapatista de Liberación Nacional (EZLN) *see* Zapatistas
Elahi, Hasan 57–58, 60
Electronic Civil Disobedience 9, 71, 89, 102
electronic civil disobedience cell 78
electrohippies 67–70
electronic data 40–41, 47, 53, 59; *see also* digital data
The Electronic Disturbance 11, 30, 34, 46
Electronic Disturbance Theater (EDT) 87–91, 98, 100–01, 106–07
electronic double *see* digital body
electronic frontier 18, 23–30, 38
electronic resistance 3, 40, 60, 104, 139
E911 document 71–72
Esche, Charles 79–80
Espiner, Tom 127
etoy.com 144–45

Fairclough, Norman 10
Falliere, Nicolas 140
FBI 57, 124, 138, 155
Feigenbaum, Anna 106
Felshin, Nina 79–80
file sharing 73–74
Finlayson, James G. 69
Flichy, Patrice 16, 19–20, 28
FloodNet 87–90, 98, 101, 123, 125
flow of information 43, 88, 112, 118
Foster, Susan L. 49
Foucault, Michel 56–57
Fusco, Coco 88, 99

Garcia, David 143
García Márquez, Gabriel 97
geeks 112–13
Geertz, Clifford 6
Gibson, William 21, 31, 54
Gladwell, Malcolm 108
Godwin, Mike 72
Goffman, Erving 6
Goldsmith, Jack 28
Goldstein, Emmanuel 71
Gould, Jonathan 59
Graeber, David 67, 135
Green, Joshua 105
The Guardian 109, 117
Guattari, Felix 34, 41
guerrilla theatre 80–83
Guevara, Alberto 51
Gunderson, Laura 41

Habermas, Jürgen 68
hackers 71–74, 78–79, 100, 112–16, 125, 128

hacking (computer) 47, 58, 60–61, 71–76, 103–04
hacktivism 5, 130
Halliday, Josh 129
Hammond, Jeremy 141–42
Hands, Joss 5
Hanson, Jeremy J. 52
Hart, Marjolein 'T 120
Hohle, Randolph 49–50
Holloway, John 93–94
humour 14, 97, 109, 119–20; *see also* lulz

I, Robot 54
IBTimes New York 137
identity theft 44
information politics 146
ITU 108
internet 5, 16–20, 27–28, 90–92
Internet Imaginaire *see* cyber-imaginaire

Jordan, Tim 21–22, 101, 130, 146
Joyce, Mary 5, 6
Juris, Jeffrey S. 82

Karatzogianni, Athina 5
Kemp, David 55–56
Kershaw, Baz 82
Kimport, Katrina 5
King, Martin L. Jr. 64, 65
Kirk, Jeremy 127
Klang, Mathias 5, 103
Kohn, Margaret 137
Kravets, David 74
Kroker, Arthur 26

Landow, George P. 36
Lane, Jill 101, 106
Lefebvre, Henri 36–37
Lennard, Natasha 142
Levy, Steven 73, 154
Li, Xiang 128
Licklider, J.C.R. 53–54
Lievrouw, Leah 5
Lippard, Lucy 79
Lister, Martin 20, 33
Lockard, Joe 29
Lovink, Geert 143
Low Orbit Ion Cannon (LOIC) 123–25
lulz 101, 112, 119, 124
Lyotard, Jean-François 145

Manner, Mikko 74
Marcos, Subcomandante 1, 95–97
The Matrix 39
McCarthy, John D. 4
McCaughey, Martha 5
McLaren, Margaret 48
McPhail, Clark 4
Meikle, Graham 4, 84
Mesch, Claudia 85
Metropolis 39
Miller, Laura 26
mobilisation 5, 13–14, 85, 130–36
Mondo 2000 26
Morozov, Evengy 108

National Infrastructure Protection Center (NIPC) 102–03
The Net 39, 59
Neuromancer 21–22, 31, 35
nomadic power 34–36
Norton, Quinn 116–18

Occupy movement 132–38
Occupy Wall Street (OWS) 135–42
Olson, Parmy 115, 119, 124
O'Neil, Lorraine 128
O'Neill, Gerard K. 25
Operation Averge Assange 109, 122
Operation Payback 109, 114, 116–18
Oppenheimer, Martin 50

Partnership For Civil Justice Fund (PCJF) 138
Pelaez, Eloina 93
performance 6–12; tactics 132
performative 6–12; utterances 7, 9, 13
performativity 8–9, 12–14, 37, 48–49, 61, 83, 134
Phelan, Peggy 98
Pilkington, Ed 142
The Pirate Bay 74, 138
Poulsen, Kevin 124
power-value 75–76
pranksters 110, 112, 120
prefigurative politics 134, 136
production of space 36–37
Project Chanology 113, 118
protest: digital 87; performance 93; symbolic 100
public space 68, 132–37
public sphere 58–69

Raley, Rita 143
Ramadan, Adam 135

Ramirez, Miguel G. 91, 92
Rapoport, Tamar 61
Rawls, John 64
Raymond, Eric 73
recombinant theatre 46–48, 98
Reed, T.V. 82
Reinelt G. Janelle 7, 8
repertoire performance 133, 145
resistance 8, 14, 15, 31, 35–38, 45–52
Rheingold, Howard 32
rhizome 35–36
Rid, Thomas 140, 141
Robocop 54
Ruffin, Oxblood 128–29

Salama, Hussam Hussein 132–34
Sande, Mathijs van de 134
Sassen, Saskia 136, 138
Sasson-Levy, Orna 61
Sauter, Molly 123, 125
Schechner, Richard 7
Scholette, Gregory 79
Seattle Municipal Archives 66
Seattle protests 66–68, 83–85
simulacra 101–02
simulation 87, 101–02
sit-in 4, 49–50,
Situationist International 120–22
The Six Million Dollar Man 54
social change 20, 68, 79, 99, 101, 132
social justice 131–32
social mobilisation 13–14, 131–32, 138
social movements 48, 50–51, 62, 65, 81–82, 92, 120
Solomon, Alisa 52
Solove, Daniel 42–43
Sterling, Bruce 71, 72
subversive body 51
surveillance 30–31, 55–61, 106, 145–46
SWARM Project 87–92, 98–107
symbolic protest 100

tactical media 143–45
tactical performance 131, 144–46
tactics 14, 34, 48, 58, 70, 77, 84, 114
Tahrir Square 131–35
Taylor, Paul A. 101, 130
The Terminator 39
terrorism 9, 103–07
Theatre of the Oppressed 99–100
theatrical performance 42, 77, 80, 101, 116
theatricality 7, 13–14, 51–52, 63, 100, 107
Thompson, Clive 59
Thoreau, Henry D. 62–64
Tilly, Charles 133
Tomas, David 21
Tracking-Transience.net 58
trolls *see* pranksters
Turner, Fred 18
Turner, Frederick J. 24–26
Turner, Victor 6

UK Home Office 44
United Kingdom Parliament 127
US Civil Rights movements 11, 49–53
US Computer Fraud and Abuse Act 71, 126, 139
US Department of Defense 27, 88, 109

Vegh, Sandor 104
virtual: body 39–40, 45, 48, 58, 60; condition 31–33, 38; performance 48, 87, 89; protest 75, 88–89, 107; public sphere 68–69; reality 20–22, 32; sit-in 84–88; theatre 47–48, 58, 61, 87
Vlavo, Fidèle 4, 98, 136

Wall Melissa A. 83
The War Of The Worlds 39
Wark, McKenzie 121, 128, 143
Weimann, Gabriel 105
Weinstein, Michael A. 26
Western frontier 11, 24–26
Wetherell, Margaret 10
WikiLeaks 109, 124
Wilbur, Shawn 26
Winston, Brian 33
WTO 66–67
Wray, Stefan 35, 90
Wu, Tim 28

Yang, Guobin 12
Yen, Alfred C. 24, 25

Zapatismo 95, 100
Zapatistas 2, 86, 93–95, 97–98
Zuccotti Park 135–38